THE OLD TESTAMENT WRITINGS
History, Literature, and Interpretation

THE
OLD TESTAMENT
WRITINGS

History, Literature, and Interpretation

JAMES M. EFIRD

John Knox Press
ATLANTA

Library of Congress Cataloging in Publication Data

Efird, James M.
    The Old Testament Writings.

    Bibliography: p.
    1. Bible. O.T.—Introductions. I. Title.
BS1140.2.E33   221'.61   81-82352
ISBN 0-8042-0145-5 (pbk.)   AACR2

©copyright John Knox Press 1982
10 9 8 7 6 5 4 3 2 1
Printed in the United States of America
John Knox Press
Atlanta, Georgia 30365

**For our son
TONY**

Hear, my son, your father's instruction,
and reject not your mother's teaching;
for they are a fair garland for your head,
and pendants for your neck.

(Proverbs 1:8–9)

Preface

It was a pleasant and gratifying surprise to have been invited by the good people at the John Knox Press, especially Dr. Richard A. Ray, Director, and Associate Editor Donald Hardy, Jr., to prepare a companion volume on the Old Testament to accompany our New Testament introduction. The occasion was tempered, however, by the realization of the complexity and magnitude of the task to be completed. The history of the period which is covered by the Old Testament writings is almost two thousand years. The difficulties involved in reconstructing that history with any degree of specificity and precision are staggering, not to mention all the attendant problems of literature, thought patterns, and sociological customs, many of which are known to us only through vague and sporadic references from the literature of the times, accompanied by some insights from the sphere of the archaeologists. To prepare a book examining only the historical setting of the Old Testament writings is a major task. In addition to the historical problems mentioned already, there is the further difficult and tedious task of sifting through the various and sundry methodological approaches to the Old Testament books proposed by centuries of learned scholarship and the attendant presuppositions and interpretative conclusions which are also part of these methodologies.

It is generally known that modern Old Testament study has developed from certain ideas and insights which began to appear as early as the Middle Ages and the period of the Reformation but which began in earnest about the end of the eighteenth century. The most famous name associated with the earlier years of study is Julius Wellhausen. It was he who took many of the suggestions and theories which were being argued and molded them into a kind of literary-critical synthesis which set the stage for the modern study of the Old Testament. While many contemporary scholars may not agree fully or at all with Wellhausen's conclusions and hypotheses, they still have to reckon with his influence, methodology, and especially, with regard to the first five books of the Old Testament, with his conclusions. With Wellhausen the broad impetus for the historical-critical approach to the study of the Old Testament books had been inaugurated with vigor.

The term "historical-critical" is quite frequently misunderstood, however, by many persons who interpret "critical" only with negative connotations. These people have been led to believe that "criticism" presupposes a negative interpretation of and approach to the biblical books; they think its purpose is to destroy any religious meaning found therein. The fact that some scholars have approached the biblical writings in a very negative manner has given impetus to this type of understanding. The historical-critical approach, however, has no such *a priori* negativism inherent within it. It simply wishes to study *how* the Old Testament books came into their present state, what source or sources were used in the writing of these documents, when they were written, in what setting, etc. It is an attempt to understand from a human point of view how these writings came into being and what the original writers intended by composing the material in a certain way and how the books were used and understood by the people for whom they were originally intended. To approach the writings in this way is to say nothing either positively or negatively about the religious teachings which are contained within them. The question of religious "truth" is a separate question which must be made from the perspective of each reader and interpreter.

After Wellhausen most of the work done on the Old Testament centered on study of "documents," written sources used in the composition of the various books. Much significant insight was gained from these researches, but it soon became evident that this was not the only avenue of approach to an appropriate understanding of the total situation. A highly influential scholar began a new approach to the Old Testament material. Hermann Gunkel began to apply to the Old Testament stories the type of research which had begun with "secular" study of older materials, namely the analysis of individual units or forms of tradition called *Gattungen*. This study focused on the materials before they had become incorporated into larger documents, i.e., while they still existed in oral form. The emphasis was naturally upon individual units of material. This pursuit led inevitably to a consideration of the "setting" in which any form and its content originated and the purpose served in that setting. The technical term for "setting" is a German phrase, *Sitz im Leben,* i.e., setting in life. Such research thus enters into the sociological spheres of a people's life, their religious cultus, wars, government, private lives, etc.

Out of that discipline, known as form-criticism, another evolved; it concentrated on the various individual traditions which became collections centered around certain themes. Usually these were considered to have been connected with certain cultic practices and with specific shrines (holy places) whose priests (holy people) used the materials, reinterpreted the material, and passed the traditions along from one generation to another. This type of research and approach is called "tradition-history." Some scholars have even suggested that a conflict existed between certain sets of traditions held by various groups at various places in Israel, such as the Moses-Sinai traditions in the north and the David-Zion traditions in the south.

Along with these approaches many other thought patterns were suggested as *the* theme around which all the religion and writings of the Old Testament revolved. Some thought that "salvation history," i.e., the interpretation of history through religious eyes, was the key to unlocking the fullest understanding of Old Testament religious development. Others suggested the concept of "covenant" as the key which was the common thread running through all the writings and which would unlock the mysteries of Old Testament faith. The plain truth is, however, that there is now no one hypothesis which can command consensus in being regarded as *the* pivotal element in Old Testament study. Therefore, the approach this book uses to present the Old Testament writings will be an eclectic one, for there are many positive elements and contributions to be found in each of the approaches and their secondary emphases. I will suggest various approaches at appropriate points in the study, but the primary aim of this introduction is to present as carefully as possible the religious emphases of the Old Testament writings.

It is, after all, in the area of religion that the Old Testament writings belong. These documents were not intended to be read primarily as history or science or psychology or sociology or any other discipline, but they were intended as faith documents evolving out of a people's experience of and relationship with their God. These understandings were treasured and passed along to succeeding generations to be applied to the life of God's people not just for one moment but for many moments. The writers or compilers intended these documents to serve religious purposes, to be documents evolving from the faith of the people, to sustain the faith of the people in the present, and to serve as a basis of faith for the future. To study these documents then from the perspective of history, criticism, etc., is only, however, to assist one in understanding the real purpose of the writings. That purpose was to present the revelation of the God of Israel and to present a religious proclamation of faith. To fail to see the religious dimension is to miss the entire point of the collection.

The purpose, therefore, of this presentation of the Old Testament writings is to introduce the beginning student to the complex yet marvelous world of the Old Testament, its history, literature, and the religious interpretation of the individual books. The procedure will follow the pattern of the title of this book, and the discussion will be divided into three major parts corresponding to the three divisions of the Hebrew canon, the order of which is different from that usually familiar to most persons today. These three divisions are called the *Torah* (Law, Instruction), the *Nebi'im* (Prophets), and the *Kethubim* (Writings). In each division there will be a brief history, insofar as one is able to reconstruct it, of the period covered by that portion of the Old Testament canon. The second section will present a discussion of the various literary questions *apropos* the books contained within that division. And finally there will be a discussion of each individual book in terms of critical problems and religious interpretation along with a tentative outline of the material included.

The student should read each biblical book in its entirety after reading the discussion in this introduction. This will provide a background and some direction as to what to look for and to emphasize in one's attempt to interpret that particular book. After having been introduced to the field of Old Testament studies, the student will then be able to view the wider range and broad spectrum of possibilities for further study and investigation. The area is large; the possibilities unlimited;

and the problems still to be solved are many. In spite of all this, however, the faith of Israel shines through.

There are far too many people to whom I owe large debts for their assistance to me through the years in the area of Old Testament study to name each one. I owe a great debt to my former teachers and my present teachers (my students) and to many colleagues who have encouraged me in this and other projects. To them I owe more than I can articulate. Several persons should be named specifically, however: my learned colleague, Dr. Lloyd Bailey, Sr., of the Divinity School for some helpful suggestions; my friend and adviser, Dr. Allan Page of Meredith College; the good people at the John Knox Press, Dr. Richard A. Ray, Director, and Mr. Donald Hardy, Jr., Associate Editor, along with many others; and my secretary, Mrs. Anne Kellam, who typed portions of the first draft. Most of all, however, I want to thank my wife, Vivian, for her encouragement in the completion of this project and for typing part of the first draft and all of the final copy, as well as for remaining a constant source of inspiration.

James M. Efird

Contents

THE OLD TESTAMENT WRITINGS
History, Literature, and Interpretation

Introduction

There is a popular misconception abroad that the Bible is an *easy* book to understand. Anyone, however, who has come to this collection of various pieces of literature with any degree of seriousness has discovered that this idea is totally unfounded! Far from being an easy book to understand, the Bible appears to many as an inscrutable and forbidding mountain, totally strange and foreign, the face of which simply cannot be scaled. This feeling is certainly understandable for the Bible is a collection of books from another time, place, culture, all of which are strange and unknown to most of us in the latter half of the twentieth century. In order to begin to understand and interpret these books, therefore, one must learn all one can about that time, place, and culture. This is especially true of those thirty-nine books known to many as the Old Testament. One can immediately recognize the truth of that by recalling that the books of the Old Testament contain within them traditions and teachings and history which cover almost two thousand years (but which are now four thousand years removed from us). Those two thousand years are not the easiest to reconstruct and understand since so much of our information is fragmentary and capable of being interpreted in various ways!

To illustrate the point one need only to be reminded that in the reconstruction of antiquity and ancient civilizations many historians are agreed on a broad outline of these times, dividing that historical period into different "Ages" such as the Stone Age, the Bronze Age, the Iron Age, etc. Within each of these "Ages" there are further breakdowns of history such as, for example, Bronze Age I, Bronze Age II, and similar divisions within other Ages with specific dates for each division. There are even divisions within the divisions! Broad agreement has been generally reached on these larger divisions, but there is no real agreement among researchers with regard to how to reconstruct the specific history within these Ages, and this is especially true when one examines the "lesser" peoples in a given period. It is difficult to reach uniform agreement on the larger nations, but the smaller and politically weaker peoples and nations are obviously quite difficult to investigate. The Hebrew people, from whom the Old Testament writings came, are politically and economically one of those "lesser" peoples of the ancient world.

Less than a generation ago there was some general consensus among scholars about certain historical and literary problems which relate directly to the interpretation of the Old Testament books. Because of continuing research in many areas, however, such as archaeology, sociology, literature, etc., there are now various and sundry approaches and theories which are hotly debated among Old Testament scholars; these theories relate directly to the interpretation of the documents. Some of these debated issues will be discussed at appropriate points, but the reader should be aware that there is presently no genuine consensus as to the historical and literary approaches to the Old Testament books, especially in the earlier portions of Israel's history.

At this point, however, it is of value to discuss several general ideas current in that culture so that when the student reads the Old Testament texts there will be better understanding of what was understood and intended by persons writing and living in that era. Some of these ideas may seem strange and unusual to us, but that is, of course, irrelevant. In order for us to understand their meaning and intention it is imperative that we place ourselves in their time, and think as much as we can as they did. Therefore it is appropriate to cite now certain presuppositions which will assist the reader in understanding many stories and aspects of that society included in the Old Testament documents.

First of all it is a given of the Old Testament era that God or gods exist. This fact is simply assumed and not debated. The question to be answered is, "What kind of god is this?" What the nature of the god was and what the god required were the primary considerations. It was further believed that there were different gods with different functions, and different gods had jurisdiction over different geographical areas and/or different specialties. Nomadic people could have a god whom they worshiped when wandering, but upon entering a settled land they may either voluntarily or as required by the laws of the land worship the god of that place.

In some instances it was thought that the god in a sense owed its existence to the people. If the people were destroyed, then that god would cease to exist. Further, it was often thought that the god (of a settled land) was tied in a quasi-physical way to the land itself. This meant that the actual dirt of the ground in some way was connected with the god: therefore to worship while away on a journey one had to have some of the actual dirt from home to accomplish this (cf. 2 Kings 5—6)!

Since there were so many gods, it was common for each one to have a name. This was especially significant because a name (whether of a god or a person) was supposed to reflect the inner nature or essence of that personality or being. This is the reason for so many name changes in the Old Testament traditions and why so much attention is given to the naming of people or things. It was further believed that to know someone's name gave a person a certain power over the person (or thing) whose name was known.

The God of the Hebrew people also had a name. In fact, in the various traditions which finally came together there were several names by which he (the Hebrews thought of God and addressed God as masculine; we shall do so in this book since that is "the way they did it!") was known. The name which finally triumphed over the others was *Yahweh*. When one reads in the RSV translation the words LORD or GOD in capital letters, one will know that the personal name Yahweh lies underneath in the Hebrew original. The meaning and the origin of this term will be discussed later.

Closely related to the idea of gods with certain powers, duties, people, etc., was the concept of Holy War. In those days it was believed that wars were fought in the name of and sometimes at the command of the god. In such a war everything conquered in a victory was considered to be *herem*, "under the ban," consecrated and dedicated to the god. In other words, when a military victory was won in the name of the god, all the conquered and their possessions were to be slaughtered and burned as an act of homage to the deity who had given the victory. Not all wars were considered to be "holy wars," but many were, and when a war was considered such, vows were often taken by those who fought, usually of abstinence from alcohol, cutting one's hair, and sexual activity; sometimes warriors even took vows not to eat until the battle was over.

Another idea firmly believed was that words (and certain types of actions) contained within themselves a degree of power which could or would set into motion forces that would bring the intent of the words to completion. This is why blessings and cursings were considered such serious matters to them, because once spoken the words could not be recalled. One ramification of this was the increasing reluctance of the Hebrew people to use the personal name of God, Yahweh. They began to substitute the word "Lord" or "my Lord" (Hebrew, *Adonai*) for "Yahweh" whenever it would occur so that they would not run the risk of saying or using *the* Name improperly, even unconsciously or inadvertently.

This type of thinking, in part, involved actions which also were thought to contain power. This is sometimes associated and identified with old ideas of sympathetic or mimetic magic (one performed an act on a small scale which was supposed to insure the completion of the act on a larger scale). Some of the most famous examples of this type of thinking and acting can be recalled from the old fertility cults so prominent (and perhaps popular!) in that time. Having intercourse with a sacred or cultic prostitute (called a *Kedashah,* in contrast to a common prostitute, a *zonah*) was supposed to simulate the union of the fertility god with his mate and to insure the fertility of the crops and the herds without which the people would literally perish. There are numerous instances of this mimetic type of action recorded in the books of the Old Testament, but there is a difference between these actions and the actions of many of the nations around Israel. To the worshipers of Yahweh any act done in such a manner was done at the command of Yahweh to illustrate God's will and purpose. These acts were in no way to be understood as a means by which Yahweh could be manipulated or used to serve the whims of the people.

There was in the ancient world an emphasis also upon covenants and the solemn duty involved in keeping the details of any covenant agreed upon by two or more parties. One ancient ceremony demonstrating the absolute sanctity and seriousness of such an agreement was observed by sacrificing an animal or animals, cutting the sacrifice in two, and having each person involved walk between the two pieces. The idea was that if one of them violated the covenant the same thing would happen to that person as happened to the slain animal! Another closely related tradition involved the practice of hospitality. One did not simply invite persons into one's home for shelter or food as a courtesy. This action involved the pledging of one's life to the person invited, who in turn by receiving the hospitality extended also pledged his/her life to the host or hostess. To violate this unwritten law of hospitality meant bringing a curse upon oneself (cf. Genesis 19:1ff.; Judges 4—5). Therefore every effort had to be made to insure that these agreements were kept. The understanding did not last indefinitely, however; it was generally agreed that the pledge to protect each other was to last until the food passed from the body, about three to four days. Violations of hospitality, then, were done at grave risk to one's own well-being, even one's very life, according to the thinking of that era and culture.

Survival has always been the chief goal of nature; this holds equally true for human beings who, while considered the crowning achievement in nature's order, nevertheless had to struggle fiercely to find food, shelter, and protection from enemies (both human and natural). Because life was extremely hard in that time (as it still is in many parts of the world), people grouped themselves together into families, clans, tribes, villages, cities or whatever for protection. Among these people the survival of the group was much more important than the survival of the individual. Therefore the most important element of life was the larger group to which an individual might belong. All society was directed toward the good and well-being of the group. Individuals were important but only as they contributed to or brought trouble upon the larger unit.

The Hebrew people also were directed in this manner. Among them, however, was the specific thought that all their people, past and future, were present in the group now living. Some have called this concept, "corporate personality." Not only was there a sense of unity toward the past and the future, there was also the idea that even in the present the group *was* the individual and the individual *was* the group. It is not enough to say that these entities symbolized the other; that would be our way of defining such a concept. To these people there was a more definite and specific relationship among the individual people who comprised the group and the group as a separate entity. Because of such thinking the duty and responsibility of each individual were heightened because one's solitary action could change the destiny of the group (cf. Joshua 7) or influence unborn generations (cf. Exodus 20:4–6). A covenant made with a person extended on toward that person's descendants (cf. 2 Samuel 7:4–17; 9:1–8).

This leads to a consideration of what type of concept of afterlife the Hebrews held. The idea here was that situated in the depths of the earth there was a gloomy shadowy place known as Sheol. It was here that all persons went upon death. Whether one was rich or poor, prince or pauper, good or bad, every person ultimately came to Sheol. This was a place of dim existence (there was no thought of annihilation in the Old Testament), the weakest kind of "life" one could imagine. They believed, however, that one's existence in Sheol could be made more bearable by having a "connection" with the land of the living through children and family. Exactly how this could be is not spelled out in detail.

That retaining this link was of paramount importance to those people is reflected in one of the early laws known as the "levirate" law. The term comes from the word *levir* which means "brother." If a man died childless, it was the duty of the next of kin, usually a brother, to "visit" the widow for the purpose of making her pregnant. This child was then considered to be the child of the deceased, thus assuring the link with the land of the living. At this point the levirate duty had been performed. Sometimes the two then married, sometimes not; even if they did marry, the child was still considered the child of the deceased husband.

There is a well-known concept among most modern persons which pertains to the ideas relating to the future. It is usually designated by the word *forever*. The understanding of this idea for most persons derives from the Greek concept of time, but there was a different understanding of the idea in the Hebrew background. The basic word in Hebrew, which is usually translated into English as "forever," is the word *'ôlam*. It basically means "age," and is most frequently found in the expression *l^e'olam* which literally means "to the age." This may have the connotation of "a long time" or "a certain set period of time" or something similar. It does not seem to carry anything like the connotation usually understood by present understandings of "forever," even though translators continue to render the term by that designation.

For example, in the book of Job, the main character, who is suffering intensely, says, "I would not live for ever" (7:16a). What is really meant is that Job does not want to live "to the age," meaning his full allotted period of time on earth. His suffering is so intense and his life so miserable that he does not wish to live out the remainder of his life.

The reader will need to keep in mind that when the term "forever" is found in the English translations, it does not necessarily carry the full weight of our understanding of that word. In fact there are some who argue that there was never any such understanding in Hebrew thought until the Greek period or perhaps even the turn of the era. The fuller implications of this will be pointed out at the appropriate places.

This leads to one final consideration with several subsidiary points. The people of the ancient world did not believe that the gods existed apart from communication with the created order. They believed further that the gods could and did intervene in the historical process. Whether this intervention had any kind of consistency, was for good or ill, or was predictable in any way was based on the character and nature of the god(s).

These people did not have a sophisticated understanding of the universe, atoms, germs, the make-up of the human personality or body, etc., and therefore when something occurred which could not be explained by their own understandings of the world that was labeled as the work of the gods, or what we might well call a "miracle." What happened in the physical order or in the process of history was a result of how human beings and the gods acted and/or reacted. There was to their way of thinking no such thing as a closed universe. And since there was no afterlife with rewards or punishments, they believed basically that people were rewarded or punished in this life according to whether they pleased the gods or not.

The gods, of course, were considered to have given the gift of life to the world, and life was considered sacred. Even though the ancient Hebrews did not know modern scientific understandings of the human (or other) physical make-up, there was one thing they did know by observation. One cannot live without blood. Thus their thinking held that the "life is in the blood." Blood, therefore, came to hold a place of high esteem and wonder, so much so that blood was considered by many cultures to be *taboo*. This idea took several directions, leading to the practice of sacrifice on the one hand (with various interpretations) and to the idea that blood could not be eaten or consumed along with the meat on the other. A person with an issue of blood was considered in Hebrew thought as religiously and ceremonially unclean (which meant that mature women were considered unclean for about two weeks of every month, the time of her menstrual period and the time required for "purification"!). Since life, and therefore blood, was of especial significance to both gods and people, various ideas and ceremonies connected with this precious substance arose.

To the culture of that time the gods had vital contact with the world of human history. Intervention into the *real* world by the gods was not an uncommon thought. This idea that God could and would enter the affairs of human history was one that became quite characteristic of Hebrew ideology. History became the sphere of Yahweh's activity and all human history has a purpose, Yahweh's purpose, and Yahweh will see to it that his purpose is finally realized. But Yahweh has to deal with people as and where they are. Human freedom is assumed, at least within general confines, but this freedom is not always exercised intelligently, wisely, or unselfishly. It is this kind of world that Yahweh encounters and deals with. But history is the arena where God meets the world; therefore the religious teachings of the Old Testament cannot be understood apart from some understanding of the history of the times and how the people of God understood God's revelation as coming to them in the midst of the historical process.

Many cultures of that era developed stories about the gods, usually called myths, to explain certain understandings and phenomena of the world as these were related to the realm of deity. The Hebrews, on the other hand, tended to look for such explanations in the historical process, resulting from the interaction of God with people and the world. This type of thinking led, naturally, to a process of concretizing ideas about God and his relationship to his people and the world in stories which were firmly rooted in history. And these stories were, of course, set against the background of their own historical traditions and understandings of the world in which they lived.

Another way in which this tendency manifested itself was to center sets or patterns of tradition in one individual as representative of the larger group (cf. the idea of corporate personality). For example, since Moses was a great lawgiver, they attributed all (or most) laws to Moses. Since Solomon was the epitome of a wise man, all wisdom in some way was attributed to Solomon. Since David was a writer of psalms, all (or most) psalms somehow were related to David. This tendency to concretize ideas or actions or understandings in certain people as representative of the larger group has caused some very real misunderstandings and misinterpretations of certain Old Testament passages!

To understand this fully, one must become acutely aware that these writings as they have come to us, the end product of hundreds of years of being passed along, interpreted, and even reinterpreted, are not to be judged by the standards of our own era. Their concept of "history" was much more flexible than some of our understandings. Their concepts of science were much more primitive or naive than some of ours. To understand their teachings, therefore, one has to immerse oneself as much as possible in their world. What they wrote primarily was *religion,* their understanding of God, his nature and purposes, his relationship with people, and how that relationship should affect people as they struggle with the world. To argue about the absolute specifics of the historical factuality of the stories, therefore, is to miss the point of the narratives. These books of the Old Testament are not books of history (though they certainly do contain some history), nor books of science (though they contain some "scientific" understandings as were understood in that time), nor a collection of "mythological" stories (though elements of some ancient myths are indeed still distinguishable in some of the stories). These books are products of a religious faith, a faith that had been hammered out on the anvil of their history (sometimes very harsh history). They spoke to the needs of the people through this faith which was still being understood and which had sustained the great heroes of the past. They were products of faith written to sustain and encourage that faith, and must be approached as such, if one is to understand their essential meaning.

Geography

No introduction to the traditions of the Old Testament would be complete apart from at least a cursory examination of the geography of the land. Palestine as it came to be called (from the Latin through the Greek for "Philistine") was known in the Old Testament as the Land of Canaan. This land, in contrast to some idealized and romantic nations, was not the best of all possible places! Basically it was a poor land whose value lay more in the fact that it was a buffer between the two great political areas of the ancient world, Egypt to the southwest and Assyria or Babylonia or Persia (and others) to the west and northwest. Because of the geographical makeup of the land any army or caravan from Egypt or Assyria had to pass through Palestine to get to the other destination. A large desert lay to the east of Palestine thereby necessitating one to travel in a "crescent" from Egypt to Mesopotamia (see map 1).

The geographical terrain of the area itself is very unusual. The land is only about 95 miles wide but about 500 miles long (only 150 ever really belonged to the people of Israel, however) and is divided into four distinct districts running from west to east. First, there is the coastal plain which gives access to the Mediterranean Sea and to the possibility of trade with the outside world. It was here that the Philistines settled about 1200 B.C. Next there arises a range of small mountains which helps to form the hill country of both Israel and Judah (as they came to be known). Thirdly there is a large geological fault or rift; the Jordan River runs through this and empties into the famous Dead Sea which has no outlet (except for evaporation and that is substantial) and lies about 1300 feet below sea level. As is well known, nothing can live in this body of water and it was known then as the Salt Sea. The fourth division is composed of another mountain range, and this area was usually called Transjordan. Some of the early tribes of Israel settled in Transjordan but the majority did not. There were some "kindred" (ethnically related) societies here in biblical times — namely the countries of Moab, Ammon, and Edom. This area then becomes a major desert (Arabian Desert) as one proceeds eastward.

Not only was the land divided along the east-west routes, it was also divided into sections by north-south phenomena as well. Mountains,

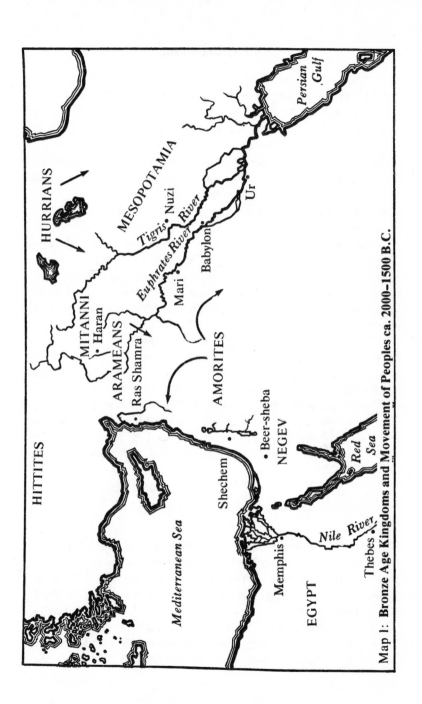

Map 1: Bronze Age Kingdoms and Movement of Peoples ca. 2000–1500 B.C.

plains, etc., cut across the land in both directions making real communication and consistency very difficult. As already noted, anyone wishing to come into Palestine from the northwest or the west had to come
into the land from the north. Because of the geographical nature of the
land, there was one major entrance in the north through the Valley of
Jezreel or the Plain of Esdraelon. It was here that invading armies were
often challenged, and some of the major battles of Old Testament times
(connected with the Israelite people) were fought in this valley. A city,
Megiddo, stood near the entrance to the pass, and this city is prominent
in several Old Testament incidents.

Far from appearing to us as a land overflowing with milk and honey,
a good land, it was a harsh and demanding land. The rainfall, so
important to the survival of any people, although sufficient to raise crops
is sometimes very fickle in its regularity. In years when rain does not
fall, there is famine. The rain along the coast (which the Hebrews did
not really occupy) is usually sufficient but as one travels from west to
east (and from north to south) the rainfall diminishes. Thus the northern
part of the land is much more suitable for raising crops, while the
southern area is more suited for the raising of sheep and goats which can
be moved from place to place in search of food.

As one studies the history of the Old Testament times and in particular the history of the Hebrew people, it will become much clearer how
the geography and climate of the land affected the process of history
which in turn helped to influence the religious understandings of the
Israelite traditions.

Types of Literary Material

The Old Testament writings as we have them were composed in final
form only after a long period of transmission. Some scholars have
argued that owing to the strong custom in this part of the world for
committing large amounts of material to memory that most of the material was remembered and passed along orally until finally written down.
Others argue that writing was not such a luxury as to keep a people from
committing certain important materials (such as laws, etc.) to written
form. The plain fact is, however, that we simply do not have enough

evidence to reach definitive agreement on how these writings originated, how they were preserved, transmitted, written down, and collected together emerging finally in the forms which we now have.

There are those who believe that the traditions of the Hebrew people were passed along by the popular storytellers; others argue for the priests and/or prophets; while still others argue for centers of tradition located at various shrines, the traditions being connected with the cultic practices of that particular area. Probably there is some truth in each of these theories.

The most important item is to attempt to understand the various units of the tradition and how one should interpret them. There are far too many to enumerate them all in a discussion such as this, but one should be aware of at least the following types of literary pieces which formed the basis for the later, more fully developed and larger traditions.

First, one must understand that the ancient peoples were just as curious about the world as we are. They did not, however, have access to the scientific explanations available to us (we cannot know what will be known three thousands years from now!). Therefore, a large number of stories in primitive societies revolved around explaining "why?" certain things are as they are. This type of story is called "aetiological" and answers questions such as, why is there a rainbow? What is this large rock doing at that place? Why does the snake crawl on its belly? Why do we have to work so hard for so little? Answers to these and hundreds of other questions were given in story form. One cannot but observe that in the traditions of the Hebrew people all of these are answered with respect to religious meaning and interpretation. This motif appears quite frequently in Old Testament stories but especially with regard to the more primitive traditions which attempt to explain the "misty recesses of the past."

Another important genre is poetry. Because poetry describes inner feelings and experiences in terminology far different from that of the merely pedantic historical narrative, one should not be surprised to find poetic compositions frequently in any religious literature. This is certainly true in the Old Testament writings. The characteristic of Hebrew poetry did not focus on rhythm or meter, even though these elements were quite frequently a part of the poetry of the Hebrews, but rather

Hebrew poetry had as its primary distinguishing feature a phenomenon known as parallelism.

This type of literary style was characterized usually by two lines, parallel to each other in *content of meaning*. The second line was related to the thought of the first line in one of three ways. First, the second line would simply repeat the meaning of the first line (though in different words). This is called *synonymous* parallelism. Several examples of this type are as follows:

> The heavens are telling the glory of God;
> and the firmament proclaims his handiwork. (Psalm 19:1)

> Whither shall I go from thy Spirit?
> Or whither shall I flee from thy presence? (Psalm 139:7)

The second type is characterized by the second line stating the antithesis of the first line. This is known as *antithetical* parallelism.

> A slack hand causes poverty,
> but the hand of the diligent makes rich. (Proverbs 10:4)

> A wise man hears his father's instruction,
> but a scoffer does not listen to rebuke. (Proverbs 13:1)

There is a third type usually cited, where the second line builds upon and expands the meaning of the first line. This is called *synthetic* parallelism. Some scholars do not agree that this is parallelism at all, but frequent use is made of this style and one should be aware that this too is poetic.

> Yet God my King is from of old,
> working salvation in the midst of the earth. (Psalm 74:12)

> You only have I known
> of all the families of the earth;
> therefore I will punish you
> for all your iniquities. (Amos 3:2)

These are the three most simple and basic types of Hebrew parallelism. It must be mentioned, however, that in some instances the forms became much more complex and complicated. The two line scheme still remained, however, at base and can be clearly discerned especially if the English translation has presented the poetry as poetry (as the RSV has).

To be alert to the poetry included in the Old Testament books is exceedingly important. Poetry and the poetic form comprise one of the most ancient means of remembering and transmitting the traditions of a people. Life itself in some ways revolves around poetry. This was especially true with the people of the Old Testament. Their daily lives were filled with poetry to the extent that in the Old Testament writings a multitude of various portions from the poetic traditions of the Hebrew people are preserved. Naturally there are *songs* — working songs, love songs (both for marriage and otherwise!), funeral dirges, songs denoting victory in battle, songs which exalted God, the king, the nation; there were practical proverbs, riddles, and the like; there were psalms used in worship, both public and private, which were of numerous types, the lament, the thanksgiving, the praise of Yahweh, and many others. It is also interesting to note at this point that most of the prophetic sayings are in poetic form!

Poetry does express the inner feelings and experience of individual persons, but it can also express the same feelings and experiences of a nation as well. This can be clearly seen as one studies the traditions and writings which comprise the books of the Old Testament.

In addition to poetic forms which can be incorporated into other types of literary style, and in many instances were, there are several other literary types which one needs to keep in mind before coming to grips with the text of the Old Testament.

First, there is the story that is known as *myth*. A myth is a story that usually relates the activities of the gods, especially as these activities are connected with creation and such matters over which the human race has no control. Almost all primitive societies had such stories, and many were prevalent in the ancient world and in cultures with which Israel had close relationship. The significant point for the student of the Old Testament is that there are no full-fledged myths present in these writings. There are overtones of such stories, especially in Genesis 1—11 where one would naturally expect to find them, but these have been so altered by the Israelite understandings of Yahweh that the usual characteristics of myths (i.e., two or more gods in a place apart from the known world) are completely gone or so historicized that they can really no longer be called myths *per se*. (There are some scholars who still use the term, *myth*, however, as a general term to denote any story felt to be basically non- or un-historical which has as its point some fundamental religious teaching. We shall not use the term myth here in this sense, however, since so many persons have preconceived ideas as to the content and meaning of the word.)

A second type of story that is found over and over in the early traditions of Israel is called *saga*. Some scholars call these stories *legends*, while others lump them together into one larger category, arguing that there are subtle differences between sagas and legends. We shall use the term *saga* only, because there is a very fine line of distinction between the two which is often difficult to determine. While Israel had no myths of her own and modified the ones she did use, those people responsible for the passing along of the traditions made extensive use of the saga. One of the foremost Old Testament scholars has said of this (i.e., the *saga*), " . . . Israel took particular pleasure in this type of material and cultivated it vigorously. It is thus precisely in this field that Israel made distinctive contributions." (Otto Eissfeldt, *The Old Testament: An Introduction,* trans. Peter R. Ackroyd [New York: Harper & Row, 1965], p. 38).

Different scholars again divide this type of literary story into various sub-groups. For example, some sagas tend to focus on an individual hero, others on tribes or nations, others on geographical areas or places, and the like. A saga is a story told to instruct the people about their heritage and to illustrate how the religious teachings of the present faith had their beginnings in the misty recesses of the past. These stories originally may have been told for entertainment, but within Israel's history they very soon became much more significant.

The question always arises, and perhaps rightly so, concerning the actual historical value of such stories. Did these events actually occur as depicted? Were these people about whom the story speaks real people, and did they do and say what the story says they did and said? Such questions should be secondary, however. It is not that these questions are illegitimate, but the point is that these are not the proper questions to be asking. They are our questions, but the historical validity of every item in each of the stories would not have made any difference to the people who told, transmitted, collected, edited, and finally wrote the stories down in final form. Likewise the absolute historical question would not have been a concern of the people who heard the stories because historical accuracy was not as important to them as religious understanding and teaching. It is probable there may well be quite a substantial amount of accurate historical data still contained in the sagas (though many Old Testament scholars would not agree with that assessment). The stories have been handed down through so many generations that whatever kernel of history there may have been probably lies obscured from our ability to distinguish.

Finally, there are the legal "codes" or collections of laws which were preserved and which were extraordinarily important. To exist and to survive any commuity of people has to have certain regulations by which their lives are ordered and structured. One of the most famous of these collections from the ancient world is that known as the "Code of Hammurabi" which dates back into the patriarchal times (ca. 1850 B.C.). These collections of laws illustrate how important such legislation was for society in that era as well as shed some light on the practices and customs of the peoples in this area. It is interesting to note that certain practices mentioned in the sagas of the Old Testament writings reflect some of the same customs as seen in some of these old collections of laws.

It is also interesting to note that very early laws were written down. This means that in all probability Israel also had written collections of laws (some of which are reflected in the biblical writings) over and above those famous "Ten Words" or Ten Commandments written upon tablets of stone.

There were, of course, different types of laws. Some were direct commands or prohibitions, "you shall ...," "you shall not ...." Certain legal customs were also included, i.e., what to do in particular instances, e.g., if a certain circumstance occurs, you shall do thus and so. There were also a large number of casuistic laws which regulated and gave direction to certain actions, depending upon the circumstances of the case. If a person is killed and another person is responsible, what happens to the person responsible? It would depend on whether the killing was deliberate, premeditated, caused by carelessness or by some possession (perhaps an animal), or some other means.

The literary background for the material contained in the Old Testament is varied and complex. If one, however, is aware of these literary types and their meaning and purpose, one is greatly assisted in understanding the stories which comprise a large part of the Old Testament, especially the earlier books.

Canon

The word "canon" is derived from a Greek word which means a reed, a standard of measure. Thence it came to imply an authoritative standard by which certain ideas, practices, etc., were judged and came to be used of the collection of religious books which were accepted as authoritative for a certain group of people professing a common faith. The Old Testament writings never use this term of themselves. In older Jewish traditions these books are called "Sacred Writings" (or Scripture), or they are designated as books that "defile the hands." This expression indicates that the books are holy and sacred and touching such a book demands that the hands be "desanctified."

There are a large number of questions being debated at the present time among Old Testament scholars revolving around the problems associated with the establishment of the canon. When did these books become accepted as authoritative? Who accepted them? Were the writers (or editors) of these books consciously aware that what they were doing was compiling and transmitting authoritative religious works? These and many other questions are being discussed presently, but no real consensus has been agreed upon in relation to these matters.

The older view of the canonization process, and one which still holds some merit, basically understood the process as centering at three points. After the exile in Babylonia (587–538 B.C.) and the restoration in the land of Judah, Ezra came from Babylonia bringing with him a "book of the law of Moses" (cf. Ezra 7:7–10; Nehemiah 8:1ff.) which he read to the people. Many are convinced that this "book of the law of Moses" was in all probability the first five books of the Old Testament (Genesis, Exodus, Leviticus, Numbers, and Deuteronomy). These are known in Hebrew as *Torah,* frequently translated as "Law" but more appropriately as "Instruction" or "Teaching." They also are known as the Pentateuch (the five rolls). It is believed that by ca. 400 B.C. these books existed in the form in which we now have them and were considered authoritative by the Jewish community. Other books had been

written, and still others were being composed. The question then became: which of these (if any) should be accepted as authoritative for the
Jewish people?

There is a writing which was not included in the canon of the Old
Testament which sheds some light on this problem. The "Wisdom of
Ben Sirach," sometimes called Ecclesiasticus, was written ca. 190 B.C.
and seems to know a second division of prophetic literature (cf.
48:22—49:12) in the order in which we know it. And the translator of
the work into Greek (Ben Sirach's grandson, ca. 117 B.C.) indicated in
the prologue that there was a three-fold division of the most sacred
books: the law, the prophets, and the "other books" which have come
down from the fathers. It was indicated that Ben Sirach himself had
studied these carefully.

If this tradition is correct, it indicates that by about 200 B.C. a second
collection of books had also been compiled and was considered to a
certain degree authoritative. This would be the collection known as the
Nebi'im (the Prophets). Books included in this were: Joshua, Judges,
Samuel, Kings; and Isaiah, Jeremiah, Ezekiel, and the Book
of the Twelve (the twelve shorter prophetic books). This first group
later became known as the Former Prophets and the second group the
Latter Prophets.

The third grouping of books did not become finalized until sometime
late in the first century A.D. but had already begun to be collected as
early as 200 B.C. The older understanding was that a council of rabbis
meeting at Jamnia ca. A.D. 90 finally decided which books belonged in
the last collection. This collection was called the *Kethubim* (the Writings) and included all the other books of the Old Testament not included
in the earlier two groupings. There was no set order for these books but
Psalms usually was placed first. The total collection of books contained
in the Hebrew canon is placed at twenty-two by the Jewish historian of
the first century A.D., Josephus. The book of IV Ezra (also known as II
Esdras) refers to a collection of twenty-four. These numbers initially are
puzzling to us but can be explained fairly simply. In our English translations there are thirty-nine books of the Old Testament, but the Hebrews counted as one book certain books which are now divided into two
or more. For example, the number twenty-four can be arrived at by
considering Samuel, Kings, the Book of the Twelve, Chronicles, and

Ezra-Nehemiah as one book. Josephus' accounting of twenty-two books
can perhaps be understood using the same method but in addition he
considered Ruth as part of Judges and Lamentations as part of Jeremiah.

However one wishes to count the books, those considered canonical
by the Jewish people are as follows:

Torah		Prophets	Writings
Genesis		Joshua	Psalms
Exodus	Former	Judges	Job
Leviticus		Samuel	Proverbs
Numbers		Kings	Song of Songs
Deuteronomy			Ruth
		Isaiah	Lamentations
	Latter	Jeremiah	Ecclesiastes
		Ezekiel	Esther
		Book of the Twelve	Daniel
			Chronicles
			Ezra-Nehemiah

The question may well be in the mind of the student: how did the
order we now are familiar with come into being? The answer to that is
fairly simple. As one is aware the books of the Old Testament were
originally written in Hebrew (a few chapters and passages in Aramaic).
After the return from exile in Babylonia, there was a long period of
exceedingly hard times for the Jewish people. As a result many of them
spread to various parts of the Mediterranean world. Some refer to this
as the *Diaspora*. When this occurred these people began to speak Greek
and could no longer understand the Hebrew text. Therefore, a translation
was made of the Old Testament books, beginning of course with the
Torah, in ca. 300—200 B.C. This Greek translation is known as the
Septuagint, frequently designated by the symbol LXX, referring to the
tradition that seventy (or seventy-two) elders of the Jewish people had
translated the books. When the Greek translation had been completed,
the translators attempted to place the books in what appeared to them to
be chronological order. This arrangement was taken over by the Latin
versions of the Old Testament and came ultimately to the English versions via this route.

In pursuing the study of the books of the Old Testament in this
volume, we shall follow the divisions of the Hebrew canon. There seems
to be good cause for so doing since this is the order in which the books

were accepted as canonical and also, in all probability, closer to the original order of composition.

The Apocrypha and Pseudepigrapha

If certain books were finally accepted as authoritative, this would mean that other books were rejected and not included in the canonical collection. What happened to these others? Some obviously have disappeared; but many were quite popular with the people and also with certain religious leaders. These did not go away, therefore, and are still preserved. To simplify matters they may be divided into two groupings: the Apocrypha and the Pseudepigrapha.

The term *Apocrypha* basically means "hidden" but this does not indicate that somehow they were hidden away because they contained certain esoteric teaching. It means that while they were popular works and widely read they were not deemed worthy to be incorporated into the authoritative collection. Because they were so popular, however, they had been translated into Greek or had been written in Greek originally and were incorporated into the Greek versions of the Old Testament writings. The term Apocrypha, therefore, is in reality a technical name for those books which are found in the Greek versions of the Old Testament but failed to find acceptance into the official Hebrew canon. Many Bibles today have the books of the Apocrypha included along with the "authentic" writings.

The second term *Pseudepigrapha* basically indicates a writing composed under a pseudonym. Most of these works belonged under a literary genre known as apocalyptic which flourished from ca. 200 B.C. to A.D. 100. These books are characterized by wild imagery and symbolism and led to some very serious problems for the Jewish people when certain zealots used the literature, with disastrous consequences, to fan rebellion against Rome. It is therefore understandable that these books were excluded as well. Many other writings have been discovered from this general period, and since they do not belong to the Apocrypha the tendency is to place them under the general rubric of Pseudepigrapha.

In the late 1940s a large library was discovered near the Dead Sea at a place called Qumran. This place seems to have been the home for a religious sect group known as the Essenes, an ascetic type community which believed that all other people were corrupt and that the true religion had been corrupted and diluted. These people were looking for a dramatic reversal of fortunes for the "true" people of God (whom they considered themselves to be), attempted to keep their religion pure, and had very strict rules for participation in this community. Portions of many Old Testament books were found in this library along with numerous writings peculiar to this group. These are known as the Dead Sea Scrolls and shed additional light on the religious thinking which was prevalent during the so-called "intertestamental period" (ca. 150 B.C.–A.D. 50).

The official books of the Old Testament are our concern in this study, however, and to these books we shall now turn.

CHAPTER I

Torah

History (2000–1200 B.C.)

It is exceedingly difficult to reconstruct the history of the Hebrew people in the Ancient Near East during the period of time reflected in the first five books of the Bible. This is the case because one cannot with any degree of accuracy date the stories about the patriarchs to determine an upper date and, further, because of the complexities involved in reconstructing the general history and culture into an agreed upon chronological scheme. The evidence is somewhat sketchy and subject to varying interpretations. But before one can understand as fully as possible the stories contained within the biblical books, one must know something about the general history and culture of that era.

The patriarchal period is most probably to be dated somewhere during the Middle Bronze Age. The Bronze Age, as it is known, began ca. 3100 B.C. and continued until the beginning of the Iron Age which is usually dated ca. 1200 B.C. This long period of history is generally broken down into three subdivisions, Early Bronze, Middle Bronze, and Late Bronze which are in turn further subdivided into shorter periods which are designated Early Bronze I, Middle Bronze II, etc. The Early Bronze Age is dated ca. 3100–2200 B.C., the Middle Bronze ca. 2200–1550 B.C., and the Late Bronze ca. 1550–1200 B.C.

Almost no one presently dates the patriarchal stories in the Early Bronze Age. Quite a few scholars find that the stories reflect the period usually designated as the Middle Bronze period. Some date the stories even more precisely ca. 1800–1550 B.C., or Middle Bronze II. Others, however, argue for sometime in the Late Bronze Age anywhere between 1550 and 1200, usually in the earlier part of that period. The reasons for this variation depend on numerous factors ranging from the scholar's view of the history of the times, to the interpretation of the stories as they have been preserved, to the historical value placed upon the stories.

What can be learned in brief about this long period of time, both in terms of movement of history as it can be reconstructed and in terms of culture? Scholars do agree on certain general points though none escapes some sort of debate.

In terms of the history of the period one can designate this era as a time characterized by constant movement of peoples, causing new nations to be formed and altering the shape and history of some of the nations that remained. One of the best ways to understand this flow of people and culture is to follow the discussion on the maps provided and to read further in biblical atlases and resource books (cf. bibliography at the conclusion of this chapter).

To understand the political geography of this area of the world at that time one is reminded of the older characterization of this segment of the earth as the ''Fertile Crescent.'' This designation is somewhat misleading but it is generally speaking a true picture of the times. This crescent began in the eastern portion where the two great rivers, the Tigris and the Euphrates, come together at the northern portion of the Persian Gulf, the land known as Mesopotamia. Along these two rivers great civilizations were established, overrun, re-established in the course of time. The crescent proceeded northwest until it touched the mountains of Asia Minor (Anatolia), then turned to the west and southwest along the coast of Palestine and thence into Egypt along the Nile River. The most powerful settled civilizations were anchored in the east along the two rivers and in Egypt along the Nile because of the possibility of raising crops from year to year. Naturally there were periods of great power and weakness in various areas, sometimes even changes of people and leadership, over such an extended period of time.

At the beginning of the second millenium B.C. there appears to have been a wave or waves of Semitic-type peoples which spread into much of the area (except Egypt), disrupting the civilizations already there and establishing new centers and culture. These people are known as *MAR.TU* or more commonly as Amorites. Some of these groups obviously settled in Palestine as well as in the land to the east and established civilizations although they seem to have been at first rather uncivilized nomads. These movements of people seem to have begun ca. 1900 B.C.

Another group of people, non-Semitic, appeared shortly after the beginning of the second millennium also, namely the Hurrians. They came from the mountains to the northeast of Upper Mesopotamia and established a very powerful nation known as Mitanni ca. 1500 B.C. Yet another group, the Hittites, came and established a great nation in the midst of Asia Minor. Their empire lasted for about 500 years (ca. 1700–1200 B.C.).

About this same time, the Egyptian historian Manetho tells us, a group of people whom he called "Hyksos" invaded Egypt from the east (via Palestine). The scholars are divided as to where these people originated, etc., but it is clear that they at least nominally ruled over at least Lower Egypt (i.e., northern Egypt). These people began to come in ca. 1720 (1800–1700) B.C. and many think that these were in fact Semitic peoples. They were finally driven out ca. 1550 B.C. by the native Egyptians.

There was yet another "wave" of Semitic people which began to move into the area of northwestern Mesopotamia, some into the area of Palestine as well. These people were called Arameans. The exact time of their appearing is a matter of some debate, certain scholars arguing for ca. 1400 B.C., while others think that 1100 B.C. is the most likely date.

One other segment of people which appears in many ancient texts is a group known as the *SA. GAZ*. They are identified with others known as *Habiru* (or *Hapiru*). As one can readily see there is a great similarity between the term *Habiru* and the Old Testament word, Hebrew. Where these people came from or what their basic characteristics were is not exactly certain. Some have theorized that they were groups of foreign mercenaries, roving groups of marauders from the desert, groups of outcasts, or people who had separated themselves from association with kings and city-states. One notes that all of these are social descriptions, but there are a few who argue that these people ought to be understood as an ethnic group. Wherever they came from and whatever they were, many persons have tried to associate these people with the Hebrews of the Old Testament. Whether this is legitimate is yet an open question.

This period of history was therefore one of almost constant movement of different groups and types of peoples who originated in different places but who were drawn to the more settled and prosperous areas of the land. This caused much disruption, especially among the more settled cultures, because the new peoples quite often overthrew the older settlements and established new ones, only later to become victims themselves of new movements. Constant movement is, therefore, one of the chief characteristics of the history of this period in this area of the world. One must be cautious, however, and recall that events and movements in that time took place much more slowly than they often do today.

What is seen as one attempts to gather a bird's eye view of the period is, therefore, a succession of different people from different places and of different ethnic origins working, wandering, settling, growing, being overthrown, in an almost endless cycle.

As for the social and cultural practices of this long era of history, we know from certain ancient tablets something about those times. For example we have the ancient law code of Hammurabi, as well as other collections. From Mari, an Amorite city in Upper Mesopotamia ca. 1700 B.C., we have documents which contain names that reflect the names given in the stories about Abraham and Isaac. From Nuzi, a Hurrian city east of the Tigris River ca. 1500 B.C., we have some legal regulations which seem to reflect the kinds of customs depicted within the patriarchal stories, such as customs dealing with adoption, inheritance and the like. Some have used these seeming parallels to advocate that the patriarchal stories are therefore absolutely true, but such preoccupation with literal history often obscures the religious point of the stories.

The land in which the Hebrew people finally settled was the land of Canaan. It seems wise to look more closely at this land for clues in understanding certain accounts given to us in the stories from the Old Testament about the political and religious problems encountered in the confrontation between the people already living there and these new intruders who had appeared.

From the time reflected in the biblical traditions the land of Canaan seemed to be a mixture of various and sundry peoples (cf. Exodus 3:8, 17). Beginning in 1929 some very old texts were discovered at a place on the coast of northern Palestine called Ugarit (or Ras Shamrah). These texts along with some Egyptian texts called the Amarna letters tell us something about the religious, social, and political makeup and beliefs in this general area around 1400 B.C.

The life there was sedentary (settled) with the economic system based upon the raising of crops and trading. Politically the structure was that of a city-state system, each ruled over by a king who exercised almost absolute power. The king usually was surrounded by "advisers" who functioned as instruments of the king and who received land and privilege from these services. The king levied taxes of various types and exercised the right of conscription for military service and also forced labor!

There were numerous city-states in Canaan, some more isolated, others closer together forming almost a "chain" of cities stretching from west to east. Most of the life of the people here centered around the cities. Because of the sociological structure and the geographical arrangement, the land was heavily populated at some points, sparsely at others. This allowed for wanderers to come in and settle in certain areas without opposition.

As for the religion of the Canaanites too little is known to present a simple, unified picture. Basically it was polytheistic (i.e., they believed in many or various gods and goddesses), but the stories about the gods seem to reflect a belief in one supreme god known as *El*. This personage was the creator, the father of the gods. But this god seems to have been pushed into the background and the stories primarily focus upon Baal and his sister/lover, Anat. Baal (whose name in Hebrew means Lord, Master) was the god of fertility who gave rain for the crops. Anat was the goddess of war and love.

Baal was opposed by two other gods, Mot (which means death), god of the underworld, and Yam (which means sea), god of waters. There was bitter enmity between Baal and Mot (along with Yam), and the stories told seem to revolve around the idea of creation and order vs. chaos, viewed as the covering of the earth with the primeval waters, and the cycle of the seasons, Baal being "dead" or imprisoned for a portion of the year and released to give life to the earth for the other portion. Upon his release from and/or triumph over Mot, Baal and Anat reunite in acts of sexual passion which thereby ensures the fertility of the land.

Part of Baal worship, therefore, was the practice of ritual prostitution, simulating the union of Baal and Anat to assist in the process of making certain that the rains would come and the crops would be good. This was not for these people a license for promiscuity but a very real and serious attempt to help promote the fertility of the land without which many would die. This type of activity was repulsive to Yahwism, and the fight against Canaanite religious ideas and practices continued for centuries.

Having examined some of the background material for the history of that era, let us now determine, if possible, how the biblical narratives could be fitted into the history, as it is now perceived, of these peoples. About 1900 B.C. a movement of peoples began which occupied Babylonia, the land along the two rivers, and probably the land of Palestine as well. These people are known as Amorites (or "westerners," west-Semitic people). These people became settled (or "sedentized") in certain areas, while others roved about as semi-nomadic people. The names of these people and certain practices (cf. Mari) are reflected in some of the patriarchal stories, especially those connected with Abraham.

Later, another movement of Semitic peoples took place, these being known as Arameans. The date for this migration is disputed but probably somewhere ca. 1500–1400 B.C. would not be far from wrong. The Hurrian movement into northern Mesopotamia also took place in this period. The Hurrian practices are described somewhat in the Nuzi tablets. Many of the stories connected with Jacob (Israel) reflect these characteristics.

There are some scholars who would argue that these similarities between the culture and customs of the period from 1900–1300 B.C. demonstrate beyond all doubt that the stories about the patriarchs are absolutely, historically authentic. Others argue that in spite of these similarities there are too many discrepancies, anachronisms, and definite signs of later editing to allow for any consideration of historical validity in these stories. The truth probably lies somewhere in between. The fact that there are so many early customs and ideas retained in these stories seems to substantiate at least the recognition that they originated in very early times. For example, the patriarchs worshiped at stone pillars and trees; this was strictly forbidden later! But the purpose of the stories was basically religious, not historical; and these stories were told and retold for centuries and then set within later religious contexts to serve the purpose of the later collectors and writers. That these were altered in the course of the passing along of the tradition and that they were used in different ways from the purposes of the first recitations of the stories seem to be without question.

What the stories seem to tell us about the ancient history of the Hebrew people probably is something like this. Abraham (or the Abrahamic tribes) belonged to the Amorites, migrating from Mesopotamia, being connected in some way with Haran, and finally settling in the southern part of the land of Canaan, centering around Hebron. While the stories about Isaac are of much less importance historically, they are important in that the tradition has made Isaac the link between the Abrahamic peoples and the Jacob peoples.

Jacob (or the Jacob tribes) seems to have been a part of the Aramean migrations, having connections in the section of northern Mesopotamia known as Padan-aram. These people settled in the central and northern part of Canaan and had special ties to the religious centers at Shechem and Bethel. It was the descendants of some of these people who went into Egypt and later escaped.

Another puzzle directly relating to this aspect of the story revolves around exactly when the Hebrew people came into Egypt. If the Exodus is dated ca. 1300–1250 B.C. as most scholars agree, and if the 430 or 400 years in Egypt is correct, then the Hebrew people came into Egypt ca. 1700 B.C. There are numerous scholars who have argued for such a date since this would coincide with the Semitic Hyksos ruling in the delta region where the Hebrews settled. It would also account for how a Hebrew lad such as Joseph could have been elevated to such a high position in the land of Egypt.

The major question to be raised at this point is whether the Joseph story as it now stands really reflects the period of the "descent into Egypt" or whether it presupposes a remembrance of such an event which has undergone a literary metamorphosis which in reality allows for no concrete historical date to be reconstructed from it. This is really what appears to have happened (cf. below, pp. 51f).

What begins to appear from a careful study of the archaeological data, the history of the times, and the conflicting accounts in the biblical traditions is a large number of different traditions from various backgrounds and viewpoints. Through the years these were welded together, not always smoothly, to construct a unified background for the people of Israel which had been founded from the Exodus and subsequent events.

In the course of time the southern groups, the group which came from Egypt, and the people left in the central and northern areas gradually came together into a loosely knit confederation based primarily upon a common religion. This type of confederation is commonly known as an *amphictyony*. This came to be acknowledged as a "union" of twelve tribes. It is interesting that the lists of the tribes do not always coincide, reflecting the varied and differing backgrounds for the traditions which were joined together to form an "all Israel" background for the people of Israel.

Is it possible to postulate any dates for these occurrences? Only by conjecture and with great caution can this be done. Abraham can be dated ca. 1700–1600 B.C.; Jacob (Israel) ca. 1500–1350 B.C.; the beginning of the sojourn in Egypt has been variously set at ca. 1700 B.C., 1500 B.C., and there are those who argue that there were numerous Semitic peoples who came to Egypt and settled in the delta area perhaps over several centuries. It was a common practice in times of famine for people from Palestine to come to Egypt. If true, the settlement of Semitic peoples in Egypt may have been a cumulative matter over a longer period of time. It is interesting to note that the later chronology given in the biblical texts states that the sojourn in Egypt was to last for 430 years (cf. Exodus 12:40). Genesis 15:13, likewise, says that Abraham's descendants would be slaves for 400 years. But in Genesis 15:16 the reader is told that Abraham's descendants would return in the fourth generation, a much shorter stay! Some of the genealogies also seem to reflect this idea (cf. Numbers 32:40; Joshua 7:1). The discrepancy here may well reflect a truth, namely that some of the people had come into Egypt and remained there for a long period, and some had been there only a short time. There are very many of these instances which point directly to a splicing together of various traditions from various peoples who ultimately became "Israel."

It is a bit easier to date the Exodus, however, even though that date as well is debated. The biblical text states that the Hebrew people were forced to assist in the building of the Egyptian cities of Ramses and

Pithom. These were under construction about 1300 B.C. Therefore the Exodus probably took place ca. 1300–1225 B.C. Several other problems are related to the Exodus. One concerns how many people there were who left Egypt. Numbers 2:32 (which originates from a later source strata, cf. below, p. 40) lists the count of males eligible for service in the military upon leaving Egypt at 603,550. If this were supplemented by women, old people, and children, one would get a figure into the millions! It is interesting to note two bits of information in thinking about these figures. Exodus 14:6–7 indicates that only a small Egyptian police force pursued these people, and further Exodus 1:15 states that only two midwives were needed to assist in delivering all the children born to the Hebrew women. The late figure given in Numbers may be a subsequent census read back into the enslavement period, not really surprising given the idea of corporate personality held by these people.

Another problem has to do with the marvelous and famous event at the "Red" Sea. It is interesting to note that the Hebrew text does not read "Red Sea" but *yam suph* which means "Sea of Reeds" or a marshy swampland, just the kind of place a group of fleeing fugitives may find suitable. Such places are located along the eastern frontier of Egypt. The earliest source strata indicates that the Egyptian chariots bogged down in the mire (Exodus 14:20). It may be that there was a skirmish and that the Hebrews used the Egyptians' own weapons against them (cf. Exodus 14:30–31)! The later source strata is the one which depicts the more dramatic telling of the story with the walls of water on either side of the Israelites but returning to normal as the Egyptians were in the midst of the sea, thereby drowning many (Exodus 14:22, 28). Interestingly enough the tradition linking these events with the Red Sea did not arise until almost a thousand years later.

After the escape at the Sea of Reeds, there is some question as to which direction the fugitives proceeded. The traditional view has it that the Hebrews turned south along the coast of the Sinaitic Peninsula until they reached what is now known as *Jebel Musa,* the Mountain of Moses. For those who have seen this site either in person or through photographs it is not surprising that such a place would have become attached to the tradition of the Mountain of God. Numerous persons have commented that if this is not where Moses was called and received the commandments, it ought to be!

But again the biblical traditions give "mixed" signals. With the exception of the events surrounding Sinai all the history as we have it is directly related to the region surrounding and near Kadesh (see map 2). There is a mountain in this area (and there are also mountains further east in the land of Midian) which may have been the original site. Further, Exodus 3:18 (cf. 5:3 and 8:27) indicates that these people were to go from Goshen into the wilderness to worship at the mountain, which was about a three day journey. From Goshen to the region of Kadesh is about a three day journey, but the Sinai site takes longer to reach. The larger group, when it finally left, however, did not make the trip in three days, and this caused some consternation among the people (cf. Exodus 15:24).

Another indication that the place may have been near Kadesh can be detected from Numbers 10:29–32 where Moses' father-in-law is urged to remain with the group for a while longer (his home was in Midian). Had he been with the people in southern Sinai, he would have been obliged to continue with them for a while until they came closer to his homeland.

The people under the leadership of Moses wandered about in the region for a long period of time, forty years being a typical designation for a long period or a generation. Finally they came to the area of Transjordan across from central Canaan, ready to enter the land promised to them. The history of the Hebrew people as it is concluded in the Torah depicts the group looking forward to settlement in the new land.

The Name of God: Yahweh

One other matter of importance quite appropriately catches one's interest at this point. This relates to the name of God as it was known in the period before the Exodus event. It is clear in the various traditions dealing with the patriarchs in Genesis that they worshiped deities which were directly related to the clan and whose "priesthood" centered in the patriarchal leader. To these different groups God was known by various names, e.g., the god of Abraham, the shield of Abraham, the fear (or kinsman) of Isaac, the mighty one of Jacob. In fact Exodus 6:3 specifically says that Yahweh was revealed to Abraham, Isaac, and Jacob as El-Shaddai.

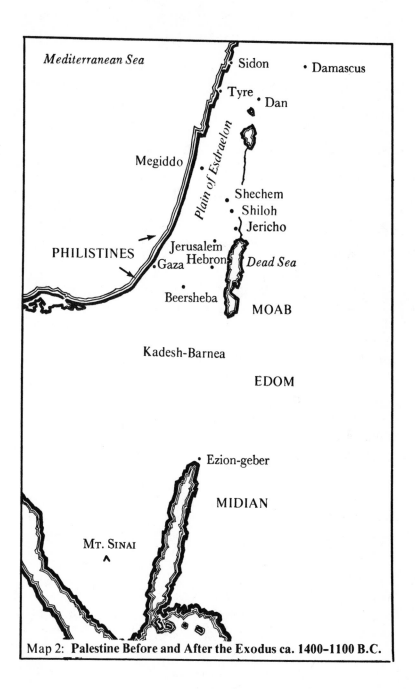

Map 2: **Palestine Before and After the Exodus ca. 1400–1100 B.C.**

This will suffice to illustrate how complicated any detailed analysis of this problem is. What is generally agreed is that the patriarchal religion was tied basically to the god of the patriarch. This god was considered to be related to the clan and traveled with the nomadic group wherever it wandered. It also appears that the patriarchs could worship and sacrifice to their god in many different places, even in sanctuaries already established and dedicated to other gods! It appears that many of these places were connected with stones or stone foundations and large trees. (It is interesting to note again that those practices were condemned later!)

Where, then, did the name Yahweh originate? How exactly did it become known to the Hebrew people? Absolute certainty is simply not available in answering this question. One of the early source-strata traditions has it that the name Yahweh was known to people from about the very beginning, but two other source-strata traditions clearly indicate that it was not until the time of Moses that the name Yahweh was known for this God. One could argue that the source-strata which placed the name of Yahweh early was simply reading back the familiar name used later into the earlier stories. This would not be unusual given the way traditions were sometimes passed along then. But it is also possible that this discrepancy points to a historical kernel of truth. For example, one notes that the traditions linking the name Yahweh to the oldest times are all southern traditions, and it appears that the older traditions link Yahweh to the southern area (cf. Judges 5:4–5). It may be that these southern peoples had known the name of Yahweh for a long period and this is reflected in their traditions.

But the traditions which argue for a later learning of that name for God are also very strong. These traditions are connected, however, with Moses and the people who participated in the Exodus. These people became the nucleus of the northern people, and the northern traditions indeed are the ones which reflect this idea.

Where did Moses, then, learn the name? The usual explanation is that he heard it from his father-in-law who was a priest of Yahweh. Many scholars hold to this theory, emphasizing Jethro's Kenite background. The Kenites were a group of people in the southern area friendly to the Hebrews. In reading the old traditions there is some close connection of the early Hebrew people with those known as Kenites. It has been a matter of curiosity for some time as to what part the Kenites played in the development of Old Testament religion. In spite of the numerous references made to Kenites in the traditions, however, there are not enough to give us any strong clues upon which to base a solid theory.

Exactly what does the name Yahweh mean? One is reminded of the importance of names in that culture in that the name was reflective of the inner essence of the person or thing. Once again there is no absolute answer which can be given, for the origins of the name are lost in the recesses of the past and scholars differ in their assessment of its meaning. Some have attempted to detect a link between the root *hwh* which means "to blow," giving the idea of a storm god. In all probability, however, the word came from the Hebrew root *hyh* which means "to become" or "to happen." The form of the word results from a Hebrew verb stem which indicates causation, thus yielding the meaning, "he will cause to happen." It is interesting that in the only place where the origin of the name is mentioned (cf. Exodus 3:14) there is really no attempt given to explain the meaning within circumscribed limits.

This seems to be quite in accord with the understanding of Yahweh which one finds in the Old Testament writings. Yahweh is a God active in the historical process, who can and does reveal himself to human beings, but who is also above and beyond human comprehension and who can in no way be limited by human knowledge, not even the "knowledge" of knowing his name. Yahweh then is the God who causes things to happen, who is open to the future, who has goals and purposes for the created order, and who wishes to share his power for good with human beings. He cannot be manipulated or bound by human actions, thoughts, or words, however. Yahweh is the One who causes things to happen; he is the One who really controls all the created order.

Literature and Sources

The first five books of the Hebrew Scriptures were first recognized as "authoritative" by ca. 400-350 B.C. and obviously existed as a unity even at that time. The tradition calls this collection "the books of

Moses,'' but in those times this title would not necessarily indicate Mosaic authorship, only that Moses was the central figure in the story. It was only later, probably around the turn of the eras (first century B.C., first century A.D.), that the strong emphasis on Mosaic authorship of the Pentateuch began.

It is interesting to note what clues the Old Testament writings themselves give toward understanding this problem. There is no claim that Moses was the author; the pre-exilic prophets do not seem to be acquainted with the "Mosaic law"; there are numerous references in the books themselves which indicate a later date for the writing down of the traditions. For example, the term, "unto this day," is found in Genesis (32:33), Deuteronomy (3:14; 34:6); there is a reference to "no prophet since like Moses" (Deuteronomy 34:10); there is a reference to a "king" in Genesis (36:3) even though a king did not arise in Israel until centuries after Moses. Add to these observations the high number of "doublets" (i.e., two versions of what is essentially the same story) and the varied names used for God and one can see why Mosaic authorship began to be questioned (after it had been uncritically accepted).

By the eighteenth century several persons studying these books began to be intrigued by the alternation in the names of God. One of these, Jean Astruc (ca. A.D. 1753), argued that sources had been used in the writing of the Torah. Other researchers began to examine and analyze the material and four "sources" finally were determined to have been used in the writing or editing process. There was one source that used the name, Yahweh, for God from the very beginning. This source was labeled J (from the German spelling of Yahweh, *Jahweh*). A second source which used the general word for God *(Elohim)* up until the time of the Exodus (and even afterward to some degree) was called E. A third source which was characterized by an emphasis on covenant, genealogy, and cultic matters was designated P (for Priestly). The last source was called D (for Deuteronomy) which was different from the other three in that it basically stood apart in a book by itself. (It was an outgrowth of the Deuteronomic code which was discovered in the Temple in 626 B.C. and probably included at least what is now Deuteronomy 12—26 and 28.)

For some time it was recognized that the P source, assumed to be the oldest source, formed the basic structure and outline for the larger work.

But subsequent study seemed to indicate that this was erroneous. The oldest source was J (from the ninth century, ca. 850 B.C.); next was E (from the eighth century, ca. 750 B.C.); this had been followed by D (from the seventh century, ca. 650 B.C.); and the most recent was P (compiled in the fifth century, ca. 450 B.C.). The name of the scholar associated with this scheme, even though he was not the first to discover these items, is Julius Wellhausen, and the theory about the construction of the Pentateuch from these four sources is called the "Documentary Hypothesis." This hypothesis has served as the basis for study of the Torah since the mid-nineteenth century.

Much controversy has surrounded the debate about this theory. Many felt that such an analysis of the material was in fact a denial of the authority and inspiration of God's revelation. Others did not hold that viewpoint but wanted rather to continue to refine and analyze further the gains which they believed had been made in studying these books. Refinement and further analysis indeed did take place. For example, the dating of the sources was (and still is) questioned. Most moved the sources back in time—J to ca. 950 B.C., E to 850 B.C., the beginnings of D and P into the ninth century. More speculation was suggested as to how, when, where, and why the sources came together. Most argued that J and E were combined early into JE and later combined with D and P to form the Pentateuch as it now exists. (For a good discussion from this perspective, cf. C. R. North, "Pentateuchal Criticism," in H. H. Rowley, ed., *The Old Testament and Modern Study* [Oxford: The Clarendon Press, 1951; paper edition 1961], pp. 48–83.)

Some other scholars thought that the Pentateuchal sources could be traced not only through the first five books but beyond these into others, especially Joshua. The idea that Joshua may have been part of the original work led to speculation about a Hexateuch; and some have even argued for the sources continuing through Kings thus yielding an "enneateuch" (i.e., nine books). Other sources lying within the primary sources were thought also to have been discovered, some being labeled S, L, N, K, J^1, J^2, etc.! This should indicate the analytical pressure which was being applied to the texts. The development of other possible approaches to the material, however, has caused some very real modifications in the "documentary" theories.

In the early part of the twentieth century, Hermann Gunkel began to study the individual stories contained in the ancient sources against the background of "literary types" (called *Gattung*, plural *Gattungen*) which led to an emphasis on the study of the material in its *oral* stage. This type of methodology is called (in English translation) *form-criticism* (German *Formgeschichte*, literally "history of the form"). The nature of this study then led to an emphasis on what is called the *Sitz im Leben*, the "setting in life." This kind of analysis could and did lead in various directions, e.g., what was the *Sitz im Leben* of the story as it was *originally* told, or what was the *Sitz im Leben* of the story as it was remembered and passed along in the tradition of that people. This latter approach which has as its basic purpose the analysis of "threads" of tradition centering around certain motifs to show how and why and where the tradition was passed along, came to be known as "tradition history." Several prominent names connected with this type of study are Gerhard von Rad and Martin Noth. Quite frequently the traditio-historical approach assumes that there were specific "schools" of persons who handled and passed along the traditions in specific places.

Scholarly debate is even now questioning and analyzing, theorizing and postulating about the specifics of these matters; and scholars now use an eclectic approach to the problems. For the purposes of this study there is no real need to go further, having pointed out the "unstable" situation at this time. One should not, however, feel that there is as much confusion in this area as it may first appear! Most scholars still basically speak in terms of J, E, D, P, even though there are those now who would think of these as source-strata rather than specific written documents. Some even doubt that there were any written sources, but most still believe, however, that at least J was a written source as was D. The jury is still out on E and P, but even so it is clear that written or not, E and P represent strands of tradition with certain peculiar characteristics and emphases.

What exactly are some of the characteristics of the sources or source-strata? (The term "source-strata" is used in this book as a designation for the older sources and the later recognition that included within these sources are numerous levels of traditions which come from various and sundry places in the background of the history of the religious traditions of the Hebrew people. The term "source-strata," then, while a grammatical paradox is used to emphasize the complex nature of the make up of the sources. See the listing of the sources at the conclusion of the present chapter.) The oldest is probably J which found its final form in southern Judah ca. 950 B.C. perhaps during the reign of Solomon when that ruler encouraged the pursuit of "wisdom." This writer (or editor) is usually referred to as the Yahwist. One of his chief interests is in aetiology, i.e., stories which attempt to give answers to various questions concerning the world in general and certain specific interests in particular. There are many "name etymologies " in J, for example. And most of the traditions seem to be related to southern Judah.

Certain distinctive style and vocabulary also are indicators of this source. The Canaanites are called Canaanites; Ruel (or Hobab) is the father-in-law of Moses; Israel is the third of the great patriarchs; the verb "to know" is used frequently to indicate sexual intercourse; Sinai is the mountain of God; and, of course, Yahweh is the name for God throughout the source. There are many others, but these will suffice for illustration.

The style of this writer is rather vivid but it lacks polish. Further, he does not attempt to hide the sins of the old patriarchs but paints them "warts and all." He is extremely interested in the connection between the patriarchs and the land, including its sacred sites. His presentation of Yahweh is filled with anthropomorphisms (i.e., the attributing to God of human form) and anthropopathisms (i.e., the attributing to God of human feelings). He depicts Yahweh as a person who has a purpose for history and who wishes to relate positively to the human race.

The E source or source-strata (called the Elohist) also has certain distinctive characteristics. These traditions are more closely related and concerned with northern sites and places, thus causing many to date the source ca. 850 B.C. from the Northern Kingdom of Israel after the division into northern Israel and southern Judah. Some have even seen E as the northern counterpart of J.

This source does not view God as relating as directly to people as did J. Angels or messengers of God, as well as dreams, take the place of direct contact. There is a marked interest in the ethical demands of these religious understandings, witnessed to by the fact that there are attempts to ignore or to explain away the sins of the patriarchs (e.g., Sarah was really Abraham's half-sister) and also to the fact that the Decalogue (i.e., the Ten Commandments) is included in this source-strata.

E also differs from J in style and vocabulary. Amorite is the term used for the people dwelling in Canaan; Jethro is the father-in-law of Moses; Jacob is the third patriarch; Horeb is the mountain of God; and the name Yahweh is not known until the time of Moses. Also there is the tendency to repeat names, e.g., "Moses, Moses." And there is an added emphasis upon offerings and sacrifices.

The third source is called "P" because of its interest in "priestly" matters, proper ritual, sacrifice, and the like. This was the first source to be exposed more fully and for a period of time was felt to be the oldest of the sources. There is really very little narrative contained in this source, and the emphasis seems to have been on the covenants and on connecting the ancient traditions with the Mosaic traditions especially by means of elaborate genealogies. There is great emphasis on ritual purity, the proper methods of cultic worship, some even finding its closest parallels in Ezekiel (especially chapters 40—48). The "P" traditions emphasize monotheism and the transcendance of God. Although some scholars now question whether this source was actually a written document, there is no denying that there are certain characteristics and concerns which distinguish this collection of traditions as a kind of unity. The date for the drawing together of these materials is generally argued to be sometime in the post-exilic period from ca. 500–450 B.C. It probably goes without saying but should be noted, however, not only with reference to this "source" but to all, that the date of the "final source form" does not mean that much older material has not been incorporated into it.

These three sources supply the basic material for Genesis, Exodus, Leviticus, and Numbers. Deuteronomy, however, seems to stand apart from this grouping not reflecting any discernible evidence of the use of material from these three source-strata. It is also interesting to note again that many scholars do feel that the three sources continue into the book of Joshua, thus causing some to argue for an original Hexateuch (six scrolls) rather than simply a Pentateuch. Many believe that Genesis through Joshua was the original work.

The German scholar, Martin Noth, in examining these data and problems finally concluded that Deuteronomy was different from the other four books of the Torah and that it seemed to reflect the style, thought patterns, and religious teaching of the books of Joshua, Judges, Samuel, and Kings. He argued for a continuous "historical" work from Deuteronomy through Kings which he designated the "Deuteronomistic History" and the person(s) who collected these books together the Deuteronomistic Historian(s). He argued that in reality these books constituted a complete work beginning with Moses and continuing through the end of the kingdom of Judah. Since the book of Deuteronomy was structured around Moses and the Exodus, that work was later detached from its original setting and placed with the other four books (the Tetrateuch) to form the Pentateuch as we now know it. This theory has found many advocates in scholarly circles, though some do not accept the theory and others have, of course, modified the original arguments at certain points. It seems best, upon examination of the material, to accept Noth's basic idea, that Deuteronomy was originally the first book or segment of a larger work which concluded with 2 Kings.

The problem with the book of Joshua remains. This books seems to contain a continuation of the sources utilized in the Tetrateuch (i.e., J, E, and P) and appears to be the logical conclusion to the story as it is left at the end of the book of Numbers. Also there is the problem of how this book became then a part of the Deuteronomistic History, which with Joshua included contains two accounts (and very different accounts) of the settlement in the land of Canaan.

The answer to certain of these questions may be resolved in the following way. The original work done by the "Priestly" school which seems to have been the entity responsible for at least compiling the Tetrateuch consisted of Genesis, Exodus, Leviticus, Numbers, *and Joshua*. This work was later connected with the Deuteronomistic History which consisted of Deuteronomy, Judges, Samuel, and Kings. When the final decision was made concerning the books which at that time were to be considered as standard for the Jewish community, the books dealing with Moses and the law were selected. This meant that Deuteronomy was broken away from its position as the introduction to the Deuteronomistic History and Joshua from its position as the conclusion to the Priestly history which emphasized the promise to the patriarchs of the land and concluded with the division of the land among the tribes. This would explain why the Tetrateuchal sources continue into Joshua but are not in the Deuteronomistic History. When Joshua was broken off, it then became the lead book in the Deuteronomistic work, and it is clear from careful analysis of the text that the book has received more than one Deuteronomistic revision. This explains its Deuteronomic flavor and also explains the two accounts of the taking of the land which are so very different since each originated from different traditions and were part of two originally separate "historical" works.

It must be emphasized that all these possibilities are only working hypotheses. Unless some marvelous discovery is made, which is possible but not probable, the exact manner of the composition of the Pentateuch will remain a mystery. What we do know is that by ca. 400-350 B.C. these five books were viewed as a unity and considered authoritative for the post-exilic Jewish community.

One must also bear in mind that in each of the source-strata lies some very old material, but this material has been passed along from generation to generation, from century to century, from certain peoples to other peoples, from one nation to another nation! In the course of time certain alterations could be made and the stories could be used and understood in ways different from what was originally intended! The task of the interpreter of the Old Testament writings is to understand these traditions as they have been placed together in the form and within the context where they found their final resting place.

Genesis

The first of the books of the Torah is called "Genesis." This writing is a collection of various types of literature which seems to have been structured to form an introduction to the Exodus and Moses traditions. Great care was taken to insure that the stories about the ancient past would form a link between the ancient traditions and the later nation. This was done by editing the stories in such a way that the links between them were concretized in certain significant personalities who were then interpreted as direct descendants of one another. The book of Genesis directly connects the people of God with the world and creation, reflecting a rather broad understanding of God's purpose for his people and for the world. This writing is then an introduction to the history of God's dealing with the world in general and his chosen people in particular.

Genesis: Outline

Genesis begins with an account of creation usually assigned to the P source-strata. This story while reflecting certain ideas from other creation accounts (such as the *Enuma Elish,* a Babylonian account) has been thoroughly accommodated into the faith of the Hebrew people. There are no other gods, no struggles with persons or elements, no debate in the mind of God about how or what to create. The story is straightforward. "In the beginning" there was chaos, usually described as it is here as the covering over of the earth by water which prevents order and growth. Out of this setting God creates a structure which leads to an orderly creation. The work is done simply by the "word" of God. God speaks—and it is done.

As one might expect from the priestly tradition the story is structured around the seven day week centering on the sabbath as God's special day. Creation was completed in six days, and God himself "rested" on the seventh. One further point to be made here is that the acount as it literally stands does view a "day" as the same as our twenty-four hour day. Otherwise the sabbatical structure of the account loses its meaning. Arguments have raged for many years now about the biblical story of creation and scientific theories of how the universe and the world came into being. If one remembers that these stories were told against the background and knowledge of their own times basically to present *religious* understandings not scientific data, one is more likely to understand the creation account as it was intended. The fact that a second creation account immediately follows this one and is entirely different in its "objective facts" should at least raise the question as to whether even the ancients accepted these types of stories as literally as some more recent interpreters have done.

The meaning of the first creation account appears to be to establish the God of the Hebrew people as the one God of creation (this idea probably did not come to full flower until the exilic period ca. 550 B.C.). It asserted that God created order from chaos, that all things were originally created "good," i.e., they functioned as God intended and created them to function, and that the crowning point of all creation was the creation of the human race. There are two items here which need emphasis. The first is that people were created in the "image" of God (both male and female, no distinction being made here). Many attempts to explain the exact meaning of the "image" have been attempted, but in the context here it appears that this idea reflects that motif of the ancient world where a king or person in authority would send out a representative to perform a task for the king. This representative was known as the "image" and acted with the delegated authority of the superior. Here the human race, and this is the second point of emphasis, is depicted as God's crowning achievement in the creation process and is given authority to "have dominion" over all the living things in creation (quite a high designation!).

The first account quite probably concludes with 2:3 even though many feel that 2:4a should be viewed as the last comment in that story. It seems to be more likely that 2:4a is an introductory statement rather than a concluding statement. Wherever that clause should go, the next verses contain what most scholars believe to be the J account of creation. The term Yahweh is used for God; the story seems to be very old, and it is filled with less sophisticated narrative than the later account of P. God is depicted in quite anthropomorphic and anthropopathic terms.

In this account the description of creation is depicted differently. The first created being is a man, Adam. The account of the man's creation describes quite pointedly the idea of the human makeup held by the Hebrew people. Most of us usually think of people as being dualistic, i.e., having a physical dimension and a spiritual (or psychological) dimension. Quite frequently many view these as separate and distinct, but this is the result of the influence of Greek thought on our culture rather than of Hebrew thought. To the old Hebrews human beings were composed of a physical dimension and a spiritual dimension which *united* together to form a "living being." Hebrew anthropology viewed people as "psycho-physical totalities" (a term commonly used to designate this understanding). What one is results from the combination of the two elements. There is, therefore, no spirit-flesh dualism or dichotomy in Hebrew thought, at least insofar as humans are concerned.

The J creation account proceeds with Yahweh attempting to find a suitable mate for the man which finally culminates in the famous episode of the woman being taken from one of the man's ribs. Human sexuality is here acknowledged and encouraged as one of God's gifts to the human race. The act of sexual intercourse does not become something potentially sinful until after the fall.

That story is told with the serpent as the villain of the piece. There is no idea here of a devil; that concept did not develop until much later in the progress of Israelite religion. Why the serpent was chosen has been a debated point for some time. Was it because the serpent was one of the symbols for the Baal cult so hated by the Yahwists? Or was it a result of the fact that people in general have an almost inborn fear and loathing of these creatures? Whatever the reason, the serpent tells the woman that if she and her man eat of the forbidden fruit, they will become ". . . like God. . . ." According to the story the great sin of the human race is its attempt to usurp the place of God! Because human beings cannot be content with their place in creation but attempt to exercise the authority belonging only to God, the highest created beings fall from the pinnacle upon which God has set them.

At this point in the story a number of aetiological motifs come to the fore (cf. especially 3:14–21). Why is there pain in child-bearing? Why do people have to work so hard to exist? Why does the snake crawl on its belly? These questions and more are answered in this account. The story concludes with God placing the people outside the garden which makes it clear that the rebellious sinfulness has caused a severe rupture in the relationship between God and the human race. And further, it is possible that death in some way was regarded as a punishment for rebellion against God, even though physical death was an accepted and normal part of the created order.

The next chapters, 4—11, are structured so that they bring out clearly the increasing wickedness of the human race. The murder of Abel by Cain sets the tone for these stories. The genealogy in chapter 5 probably serves two purposes: to exalt the "good old days" when people were more sturdy than they came to be (the idea that "they don't make 'em like they used to!''); the clear teaching that increasing sinfulness brings shorter lives; and the attempt to form a link between God's people and the beginning of creation.

The flood story told in chapters 6—9 reflects to some degree an old Babylonian story contained within a larger work known as the *Gilgamesh Epic*. Such stories were common in the ancient world especially among people living by great rivers. The flood in Genesis is caused as a direct result of human sin and depicts God's attempt to deal with that sin. There are basically two accounts (J and P) woven together to form the story as it now appears. By means of the story God is presented as a covenant-making God who is also a God of promise to those who respond positively to his directive call. The story also reflects the Hebrew use of aetiology by explaining the origins of the nations of the world (as they knew them) and again tracing the lineage of God's people to the very beginning.

This story is followed by another which again depicts humans as trying to substitute themselves for God (chapter 11). This results in and explains why there are different languages in the world. But toward the end of chapter 11 there comes a definite shift in the way God deals with the world. Up to this point God has basically dealt with the world as a whole, but now the scene begins to narrow considerably. There is a new tactic introduced in God's relationship with the world and his dealing with human sin. A small group of people is selected to be the "chosen" people. The genealogy at the end of chapter 11 demonstrates the connection between this smaller group and the larger setting of human life.

With chapter 12 there begins a very basic biblical theme, the idea of "election." God "elects" Abraham and Abraham's descendants to be a people special to him. This election does not take place because Abraham is better than others or more deserving, but simply because of God's call to service. Election is basically that, a call to service. The task to which Abraham is called is that of making God's *name* (i.e., his person, himself) known to all people. "And I will make of you a great nation, and I will bless you, and make your name great, so that you will be a blessing . . . by you all the families of the earth shall be blessed" (12:12–3). This concept is one of the key themes which constantly recurs in the biblical writings. To be "elected" is not so much a privilege as it is a tremendous responsibility. And the task is always that of witnessing to the nature and purposes of God.

Abraham began his journey toward and into the land of Canaan and there are many interesting tales related to demonstrate the problems and trials which beset the ancient patriarch. Most have, however, a religious dimension which directly shows how Yahweh worked through the historical process to accomplish his purposes. There are several stories which illustrate certain ideas and motifs which should be noted.

The first story concerns the covenant made between God and Abraham as told in Genesis 15. Here there is an account of an ancient covenant-making ceremony (verses 10–18) where animals are sacrificed and then split in half. One half is placed opposite the other half with enough room for a path between. The two parties to the agreement then walk between the two halves to "finalize" the covenant. The idea was that if one or the other violated the agreement, what had happened to the sacrificed animals would happen to the culprit who had broken the promise!

A second point to be noted from this episode is the idea of the "theophany." The word theophany literally means, "the appearance of God," and there are many biblical stories which make use of this motif. In the biblical writings a story incorporating the theophany element usually contains a reference to fire. This fire represents the presence of God in a particular time at a particular place to accomplish a particular purpose. One finds such stories at crucial points in the history of the Hebrew people (e.g., the burning bush and Moses). Here the emphasis is upon God as a covenant-making God who has entered into a special relationship with Abraham for the purpose of granting to his descendants a land in which to live and from which they could continue their "elected" calling.

The second account which needs special consideration is the story in Genesis 17 which explains the rite of circumcision. The ancient ritual of covenant-making contained in chapter 15 (J and E) is here described in much more aetiological and cultic detail by P. Much is made of the name change of both Abraham and Sarah, and new "personalities" are the result of the name changes according to the religious interpretation. Originally, however, the name changes were probably only linguistic changes which reflected simply the change of locale from Mesopotamia to Canaan.

It is also significant that the covenant described here is called an "everlasting" covenant, probably meaning a covenant which was to last for a long time. This covenant demanded from Abraham and his descendants certain ethical considerations (cf. 17:1), clearly implying that there were conditions attached. The promise of the giving of the land of Canaan is repeated in this setting, and there is added the ritual of circumcision as the outward sign of the covenant. There are several stories in the Old Testament writings which attempt to explain the origin of this rite from a religious perspective. Circumcision as such was practiced by various peoples from ancient times for various reasons. The Canaanites practiced this rite at about this time in history, and the Hebrews could have taken the practice over from them. The meaning of the act has been totally altered so as to become a sign and seal of the covenant which required of Abraham and his descendants trust in God, commitment of their life to the manner of living God required, and the practice of circumcision as the outward proclamation that these people were different and were committed to being God's people.

The third story of major import is that recounted in Genesis 22, the famous account of Abraham's offering of his promised son, Isaac. The theme of the promise of God to Abraham for descendants to inhabit the land is put to a severe test in this episode. The child who was to be the hope for a host of descendants is to be sacrificed at the command of God. This idea was not unusual for the ancient world where child sacrifice was fairly common. One of the most frequent points where evidence of such activity is to be found today is in the archeological discoveries of young skeletons buried beneath the thresholds of houses or in the cornerstones of buildings or walls of cities. This type of sacrifice was supposed to insure the well-being and safety of the people who dwelt within. It is also probable that some human sacrifice was done to atone for sins. Thus the "command" to Abraham to sacrifice his son to God was quite in keeping with the sociology of the times.

The story as it was utilized by the writers or editors of Genesis does not emphasize the sacrifice, however, but rather the command which was interpreted as a testing of Abraham's faith. Some interpreters have argued that while the story in its present setting does have that import, the original story was one which reflected the understanding that this God did not require nor did he wish for human sacrifice to be made to him. The providential finding of the ram with its horns caught in the thicket originally stood for the approved substitute for human sacrifice. The practice of sacrifice was quite widespread in the ancient world, and while it is difficult to determine exactly why or where or how sacrificial ideas developed, it is not difficult for us to follow their thinking that some life had to be poured out so that other life could continue.

Abraham believed that God had commanded the sacrifice of Isaac, his hope for the future, but without questioning and without hesitation, he took his son up to a sacrificial site to perform his duty. His faith, i.e., his commitment to God, having been found strong, Abraham was rewarded by having the promises reiterated and his son returned.

The Abraham and Isaac stories also were told to illustrate the kinship between the people of Israel and the neighboring nations. From Abraham came the Arabs (the descendants of Ishmael); Ammon and Moab were sons of Lot (by his daughters, cf. Genesis 19:30ff.); the Edomites were children of Esau, Isaac's son. The point is that the traditions recognized that the people of Israel understood themselves to be a part of the history of their predecessors and that these predecessors and kinsmen were quite numerous.

The Isaac stories do not seem to have been of any great consequence by themselves, being in reality the link between the Abraham cycle and the Jacob-Israel cycle. Isaac is the son of Abraham and the father of Jacob. The Jacob-Israel stories transfer the reader from southern Palestine and its sites and traditions to central Palestine with its sites and traditions. The theme of God's promise is still prominent, as is the idea of God's electing purpose. Isaac was chosen as the one to carry through God's promise to Abraham and to continue the work which God commissioned him to do. Abraham had many other children, but Isaac was the "special" one. With Isaac's children the elder does not automatically become the one through whom the promises are continued even though both Esau and Jacob are children of the same woman conceived at the same time! God's purpose is now to be continued through Jacob.

The stories about Jacob depict him as a cunning and scheming, even devious, person. He bargains his brother Esau out of his legitimate birthright; he tricks and deceives his father so he can obtain the blessing; he makes bargains with God; and he finally is deceived himself by his father-in-law, Laban, who seems to be as good at this type of behavior as Jacob. Jacob marries two wives and has children by them and by their handmaids. Aetiologically the children of Jacob are the ones from whom the twelve tribes are descended. (It is interesting to note that there are several listings of the tribes, no two of which are exactly alike.)

Having fled from the land for fear of his life at the hand of his brother Esau, Jacob settled in the region of northwestern Mesopotamia where there was a settlement of kindred peoples in Paddan-aram. He became prosperous and finally decided to return to the land of his youth. Along the way an incident occurred which is one of the most peculiar of all the stories in Genesis and one of the most difficult to interpret.

This story is told in Genesis 32. It is the account of Jacob sending everyone on ahead at the brook Jabbok while he remains behind. During the night he wrestled with a "man," and when day was about to break, the man wanted to leave. Jacob wanted the man to bless him first, but instead of receiving a blessing Jacob was given a new name, "Israel," which is interpreted as the "one who strives with God," or perhaps "God strives." As one remembers, in those times the name is significant of the personality of the individual or entity named. Jacob no longer is the "Supplanter" but the one committed to the "God who strives." He has asked for the "name" of his adversary but receives no name! What Jacob does is to name the place Penuel or Peniel which means the "face of God." Jacob, therefore according to the story, interpreted his night opponent as having been God.

As can be determined by a reading of the account (32:22–32) there are a number of aetiological motifs in this old tradition. One of these is so old that there is no other reference to it in the biblical writings. This is the reference to not eating the "sinew of the hip on the hollow of the thigh," (i.e., the sciatic muscle on the hip). Interestingly enough this prohibition is not found among the dietary proscriptions of the later laws.

The basic importance of this episode, however, seems to center in the change which takes place in Jacob and the linking of the Jacob traditions with the Israel traditions. This transformation is specifically emphasized by the change of the name. Jacob is now more sensitive to the commands of God, to the preservation of descendants and the settlement in the land, and to the idea of the God of the covenant who makes certain claims upon his people.

The final sequence of stories is placed at this point and this leads up to the events of the Exodus. The transition will now be complete. The tracing of the genealogies from the Hebrew people in Egypt back to the very beginning, the weaving together of many ancient traditions into a unified story so as to present a picture of Israel the nation as one with a common history from common ancestors, and the link now between the old patriarchs and the people in Egypt form the background for the most significant event or sequence of events in the history of the Hebrew people. This last segment of the history is told in Genesis 37—50 and centers on the person of Joseph, one of Jacob-Israel's favorite sons.

There are many problems related to the study of these chapters. In the older documentary analysis this story was thought to be a product of the blending of the J and E sources. While one can discern two separate strands in the story as it is presented, the tale is one which seems much more likely to have been composed separately and to have existed independently of the other sources. There is very little in the story which could have been told "by itself," but rather the developing plot seems to indicate a larger self-contained unity which was reworked so that it would fit into the narrative at this point.

Many recent interpreters have argued that the Joseph cycle originated from ancient traditions but was worked into this longer and more detailed story by persons who were connected with the Wisdom movement. (For a fuller explication of the movement and its characteristics, see below pp. 225 ff.). Note that there are numerous differences between the Abraham-Isaac and Jacob-Israel traditions and the Joseph cycle. The stories in the former seem to have been originally self-contained while these in the Joseph cycle cannot really stand alone. There are many aetiological motifs in the former while there are very few (and these may have been included by the final editor) in the latter. God is very active in his dealings with Abraham, Isaac, and Jacob, but there is little said about God in the Joseph stories until the conclusion. The motifs of the hated brother, the rags-to-riches rise of a hard working person, the youth tempted by an older woman who is rejected and turns her wrath upon the young man, and others are all found within this sequence of narrative. All of these motifs are characteristic of wisdom traditions in the ancient world. Given these differences and the story's own characteristics it is quite probable that the Joseph cycle came from the wisdom tradition and was originally separate from the sagas of the old patriarchs, but placed in this setting the story explained how the Hebrews came to be in Egypt and the stage is set for the Exodus events.

Religiously speaking there seems to be one basic religious thesis for the story which is revealed near its conclusion: "As for you [the brothers of Joseph], you meant evil against me; but God meant it for good, to bring it about that many people should be kept alive, as they are today" (Genesis 50:20). The teaching is that the hand and purpose of God can be seen even in tragic events working to accomplish his purposes, a theme which the people for whom these works were compiled would find quite meaningful.

There are several other intriguing episodes contained within this cycle. The story of Judah and Tamar in chapter 38 has intrigued scholars for a long time: why is the story placed where it is? What does it mean? Also the so-called "Blessing of Jacob" in Genesis 49:2–28 is a puzzle. What about the order of the sons in the blessing? Why are some dismissed so quickly? And some so negatively? Is the poem a much later composition or does it contain some very ancient tradition? For a fuller discussion of the entire book the student is referred to the better commentaries (which may be found listed at the conclusion of this chapter).

The book of Genesis is an intriguing, fascinating, and sometimes amusing book which tells about the "beginnings"—of God and the world, of God and human sin, of God and the "elect" people whose duty it is to make the name of God known in all the world.

Exodus

As one turns to the traditions contained within the book of Exodus, one finds more positive commentary on the historical data among scholars than one has discovered in relation to the traditions of Genesis. This does not mean, however, that the majority feels that all the material in Exodus is historically accurate as it is presented. It does mean that many believe with the events surrounding Moses and the Exodus one is much closer to historical actuality, but this material is still the product of centuries of having been passed along both orally and in written form. Religious interpretation has altered the traditions and in some instances their original meaning. The sources used here are J and E but with a strong element of P towards the latter half of the book as it deals with cultic matters.

There are those who have argued that the Exodus tradition was originally separate from the Sinai tradition. The supporting base for this idea can be found in several "old" credal formulae which have no reference to the Sinai events (cf. Deuteronomy 6:20ff. and 26:5ff.). The argument is that these traditions, i.e., the Exodus story and the Sinai events, were originally separate and were basically related to certain cult festivals which enacted and perpetuated these motifs. Scholars argue that the Exodus tradition was located at the old shrine at Gilgal while the Sinai tradition was centered at Shechem. The resolution to the question of how these two were placed together is explained by postulating that the Yahwist was the first to do that.

An additional problem has arisen with reference to the sources found in the book of Exodus. According to the older documentary hypothesis all the legal codes found in the book could be located within one of the three major source-strata, J, E, and P. More recent study has shown that such a simple explanation does not appear to stand hard examination. Therefore, many now believe that most of the law codes are to be derived from sources *other* than the three major source-strata. One can readily see that a consensus of scholarly opinion is difficult to find in this discussion.

What one finds when one comes to the book of Exodus, as it now stands, is the story of how the Hebrew faith really began and what obligations were involved in being a member of that religious community. The Exodus is the key event above all others which undergirds the religion of Israel. And Moses is looked upon as *the* great leader who gave impetus to the movement. Some have through the years questioned whether Moses was actually a historical figure. As some have said in response to that idea, "If he was not, we would have to invent him to explain the movement!" Such a movement is not usually the result of group action but of a group's response to a gifted, strong, and charismatic leader. Moses probably was very real!

Exodus: Outline

I. The Events of the Exodus 1—15
   A. Background and Call of Moses 1—4
   B. Moses and Pharaoh 5—15
     1. The Plagues 5—11
     2. The Institution of the Passover 12
     3. Leaving Egypt 13
     4. Pursuit by the Egyptians 14
     5. Songs of Praise to Celebrate Yahweh's Victory 15
II. Wanderings in the Wilderness 16—18
III. Sinai and the Making of the Covenant 19:1—20:21
IV. The Covenant Code 20:22—23:33
V. Ratifying the Covenant 24
VI. The Cultic Articles 25—31
VII. The Golden Bull Episode 32—34
   A. The "Cultic" Decalogue 34:14–26
VIII. More Cultic Regulations 35—40

While there are not nearly as many aetiological stories as in Genesis, the Exodus traditions nevertheless have a strong interest in aetiological matters, and the reader must be alert to these instances even though more genuine history *may* be included in these traditions. The early verses of Exodus were obviously written as a transition from the Genesis stories of the patriarchs to the account of the Exodus events. The problems of the date of the Exodus and the exact identification of the pharaohs of the oppression and the Exodus have been debated quite extensively in past Old Testament study. The evidence from the biblical texts themselves leads to very different conclusions. For example, 1 Kings 6:1 states that the Hebrews came out of Egypt 480 years before the building of Solomon's Temple, ca. 1450 B.C. If this is true then the figure of Ah-mose I is to be identified as the pharaoh of the oppression and Thut-mose III would be the pharaoh of the Exodus. But Exodus 1:11 depicts the Hebrew people as building the store houses of Pithom and Ramses, which would make the date ca. 1250 B.C., and the two pharaohs involved would be Ramses II and Merneptah (or perhaps Seti I and Ramses II) as the pharaohs of the oppression and Exodus respectively. The archaeological evidence is not interpreted uniformly by the various scholars, thus causing even more uncertainty in the attempt to date this event. The exact identification can be at best, therefore, only a guess. It is interesting that those who preserved the traditions of the Israelite people did not really seem to be concerned about the exact identity of these persons!

The story itself relates in vivid terms the harsh treatment of the Hebrews by the Egyptians, not at all surprising in the light of the cultural and social conditions of the time. The hero of the story is named Moses, probably an Egyptian name which means "son of" (cf. the Egyptian names Ah-mose, Thut-mose, Rameses, etc.). In all likelihood Moses had a full Egyptian name which was shortened to Moses, but it is interesting that in the course of the passing along of the tradition the name is given a (strained) Hebrew etymology.

The basic points of the story of Moses are usually well-known even to those who know little else about the history of Judaism. The infant child was hidden, found by the pharaoh's daughter, reared in the court of pharaoh, learned his true identity, made an ill-advised attempt to help one of the Hebrew people, and was forced to flee. He went to the land of Midian, met the seven daughters of a priest [of Yahweh (?)], married one of the daughters, and lived there with them as a keeper of the flocks. This was his occupation when he experienced the events recorded in the story of the burning bush (cf. the theophany).

At the burning bush on the "mountain of God" Moses received his call or election—to lead the people out of the land of Egypt—which he was very reluctant to undertake. He argued quite vigorously and finally said simply, "Oh, my Lord, send, I pray, some other person" (4:13).

In the course of the discussion Moses inquired who this God might be. It is here that the tradition made it explicit that the God (or gods) of the old patriarchs was the same as the God who was now being revealed. God gave his name as "I am (or shall be) who I am." As discussed previously, there is great speculation as to the exact meaning and origin of this term. Some interpret the phrase as simply the one who exists or perhaps the self-existent one.

The Hebrew verb root appears to be causative, however, and the meaning of the word should probably contain the idea of "causing to be" or "causing to happen." Yahweh is the One who "causes." Whatever the exact meaning, it is also clear from the story that knowing God's name did not give Moses (or the people) any power or control over God. This God wished to be known and wished to be served, but anyone who chose to know and to serve him did so on Yahweh's terms or not at all! From this point on in the narrative of the biblical text God is known as Yahweh to the Hebrew people.

Moses did then go to the pharaoh, but naturally the pharaoh refused to allow the people to leave. At this point the plagues began, even though the total number of ten was the result of merging all three accounts (J, E, P) into one. Many have attempted to explain these occurrences as natural phenomena which it is quite possible to do, but for the people for whom these "signs and wonders" occurred, they were miraculous in that God was seen as acting on behalf of his people. Whether these happenings can be explained rationalistically or not does not detract from the interpretation placed upon them by the Hebrew people—God had acted mightily on their behalf.

The last plague, the death of the first born, completed the list. Most interpreters view this catastrophe differently from the other nine, for this one is directly linked to the explanation of the origin of the Passover and the feast of Unleavened Bread. It was *the* event which finally accomplished the release from bondage. The plague in the narrative, however, assumed a secondary role to that of linking the Passover sacrifice and the feast of unleavened bread with the events of the Exodus. Much discussion has occurred concerning the origin of the Passover ritual. Most scholars believe that the Passover rite derived from the time when the nomadic or semi-nomadic peoples sacrificed in order to insure the safety

of the people and the herds from evil powers. The eating of the unleavened bread may also have originated from this same background but
many think this celebration is more appropriately located within a settled
agricultural community. If it is true that these ritual observances originated in the nomadic period, then they very easily may be part of the
Exodus experience. Some scholars, however, feel that they were later
developments which were read back into the events surrounding the
leaving of Egypt. The celebration of the Passover seems to have been a
family type event in its earliest times; later it was celebrated in the
Jerusalem Temple.

The Hebrew people left Egypt (with many Egyptian possessions!)
but were pursued by a small "police force." They came to the Sea of
Reeds, passed through, and the Egyptians could not follow. There may
have been a battle in which the fleeing slaves emerged victorious. Which
version (J or P) one accepts is again irrelevant, for the religious interpretation is that whatever happened the people were delivered and that
by the hand of Yahweh. A very old piece of poetic thanksgiving com-
memorating the escape at the sea is preserved in 15:21, known as the
Song of Miriam.

> And Miriam sang to them:
> "Sing to the LORD, for he has triumphed gloriously;
> the horse and his rider he has thrown into the sea."

Almost immediately the group which had now been led out and set
free began to complain. They obviously had not expected hardships as
part of this new religious teaching! They complained of having no food
or water, ". . . you have brought us out into this wilderness to kill this
whole assembly with hunger" (16:3b). Before the deliverance at the sea
they charged, "Is it because there are no graves in Egypt that you have
taken us away to die in the wilderness?" (14:11a). This seems to set the
stage for further trying of Moses' (and Yahweh's) patience.

After having wandered for a short while (about three months), the
group arrived at the mountain of God. Where this mountain was actually
located is not definitely known, but the traditional site is in the southern
part of the Sinai peninsula. The thunder and the fire and smoke described
in the accounts have suggested to some that a volcanic mountain was the
original place. Since there are no volcanic mountains in the Sinai pen-

insula, some have suggested a site further east in the area of Midian (see map 2). Whether these descriptive elements are to be taken literally or simply as a literary means of emphasizing the significance of this momentous theophany cannot be stated with certainty. But what transpired between God and the people at Sinai was of tremendous significance in the life of the people of Israel. It was here that a "formal" covenant was established and here that the basic regulations and directions for this new community were made.

The Decalogue, or the Ten Commandments as they are more popularly known, is obviously an ancient code. An older, shorter form may have existed earlier known as the "Ten Words." It is recognized that this code does not reflect a settled society as do the other codes of law found in the traditions, and it seems to be certain that the early prophets presupposed such a collection (cf. Hosea 4:2). In all probability the original code was much shorter than the versions which were finally incorporated into the traditions as we have them. Some have even argued that the reason for the fact that there are ten originally resulted from the idea that this was an easy memory device since, of course, each person has ten fingers!

The law itself was directly rooted in the act of God on behalf of his people. The covenant and the law were grounded in an act of deliverance, "I am Yahweh your God, who brought you out of the land of Egypt, out of the house of bondage" (20:2). In the Jewish heritage, this is considered as the first commandment! Because of this act of redemption the covenant which would set down guidelines and directions for God's relationship with his people and the people's relationship with God and with each other could be established.

It is well known that the God of Israel was a "jealous" God, accepting or allowing no rivals. There was to be for Israel, therefore, no other gods "before" Yahweh. Many have argued as to whether this early religious teaching was indeed monotheistic, i.e., denied explicitly the existence of any other gods. The question has been debated, but it appears that this statement cannot be used as a denial of the existence of other gods, only that Israel is not to worship any other god but Yahweh. This idea is called *henotheism,* worshiping only one God but not necessarily denying the existence of others. Mosaic religion was probably henotheistic.

A second feature of Israelite religion which was very unique and unusual was in the prohibition against making any image or likeness of Yahweh (20:4–6). Why this prohibition was made is not exactly known, but it may well have been the result of the idea in the ancient world that to have an image of the god was therefore to have in some way a certain power over that god. It has already been noted in the episode of Moses at the burning bush that Yahweh refused to give human beings any power over him at all. The prohibition of the image could probably relate to that same idea. Yahweh was not a God who could be manipulated or controlled by human beings.

In the second commandment one also notes the ancient belief in "corporate personality" where one's sin and guilt are passed along to one's descendants, but there is, in addition, the promise that keeping God's covenant law would insure blessings to many more to come.

Using Yahweh's name "in vain" has puzzled persons for some time. The term "in vain" literally means in Hebrew "to nothingness" or "to vanity." The reference is probably to the use of the name of God in oaths or for magical purposes. Thus one is prohibited from using Yahweh's name wrongly in oaths or for some evil purpose. This idea probably originated in the concept prevalent in the ancient world that the person or thing itself was somehow part of the name. So seriously was this prohibition relating to the name of Yahweh taken in ancient Israel that very soon thereafter the name was not spoken at all, the term *Adonai* (my Lord) being substituted for it. In the Hebrew text where the divine name is found, it was pointed with the vowels of the word for "lord, master," so that one would not somehow inadvertently or accidentally say that powerful and awesome word!

The command to observe the Sabbath is clearly an early part of the Hebrew faith even though where the tradition began remains a mystery. The Exodus account has it that since God created in six days and rested on the seventh, this was the reason for the observance. Another account states, however, that the reason for the resting results from the stay in Egypt where they were slaves until Yahweh brought them out and established a covenant with them (cf. Deuteronomy 5:15). The Sabbath then was to be a constant reminder to the Hebrew people of Yahweh's act of deliverance from Egypt, according to this explanation. In either case the Sabbath was to be observed and dedicated to Yahweh.

At this juncture in the sequence of the commandments the emphasis shifts from one's relationship with God to one's relationship with one's society. The first of these requirements was to honor one's father and mother. This admonition was probably not directed so much at the young in obeying their parents; this was a "given" of that society, but rather it seems to be directed at taking care of parents after they have become old.

The prohibition against killing often has been misunderstood in terms of the meaning of the command in the culture of those times. The idea here was of not committing "illegal murder," not a prohibition against any killing. To those people killing in war, or in revenge for someone's taking the life of a relative, or in a capital offense was quite acceptable, but they were very strict when the taking of life was arbitrary, cruel, vicious, or vindictive and usually premeditated.

Of all the commandments the seventh is probably the most well-known (and the most abused!). In the society of that time adultery could not be committed against a wife, only against a husband. If, for example, a married woman had intercourse with another man, she and he had committed adultery against her husband. If a married man had intercourse with a married woman, they had committed adultery against her husband but not against his wife. If a married man had sexual relations with an unmarried woman, no adultery was involved. It is not difficult to perceive the one-sidedness of this law which reflects that women in that culture were looked upon more or less as property. It was basically a male-dominated society. There may have been another factor in this thinking, however, and that may have been related to the ideas connected with the afterlife. Since it was considered such a tragedy for a person to die without descendants (which led to the old levirate law), the husband needed to be assured that the child born to his wife was really his! This commandment included not only wives *per se* but any woman after she was betrothed since she was considered the wife of the man even before the actual and final legal ceremonies.

There has been some concern over the exact meaning of the next stipulation, against the stealing. The question appears to be what difference was intended between this commandment and the final one. Since there is no object stipulated here, some have argued for a prohibition originally against the stealing of people for the purpose of making them slaves. Later, it is argued, the command was expanded into a more general prohibition against stealing. In any event, the background here is not as clear as it could be for finding a precise meaning for the command.

"Bearing false witness" is definitely related to the courts of law. Evidence in the "court" (which in settled times met at the gate of the city) had to be substantiated by two witnesses. That violations of this took place, there can be no doubt (cf. 1 Kings 21). That there was a concentrated effort to keep this from happening and that the ancients recognized the importance of "truth" in trials are reflected in this stipulation.

Finally, there is the prohibition against "coveting." Here the commandment has objects specifically designated, not a general prohibition as in the eighth commandment. Some have argued for an interpretation here emphasizing the "emotion" of coveteousness, but there are others who feel that the intent of the command was directed more specifically toward the actual scheming and subsequent actions to insure the taking of what was "coveted." In fact, some argue for an interpretation which sees in this a prohibition against illegal action to take what was not rightfully owned. Probably both the attitude and the overt act were in mind at this point.

These, then, were the basic fundamental requirements for the new covenant community. It is interesting to note that they are all *apodictic* in nature, i.e., they are in the form of a direct command. There are no *casuistic* laws included here even though there are many included elsewhere in the collected legal codes. A casuistic law is one that stipulates specifics in certain cases, if this happens, then that is to be done, etc. A further note of interest is that there are very few, if any, overtones of a religious cultus (i.e., specific and designated religious ceremonies) connected with the Decalogue.

Almost immediately following this basic set of guidelines there is another collection of laws called the "Book of the Covenant" (20:22—23:33). Here one does find casuistic directives, some of which are similar to the formal law codes of the ancient world, namely the Code of Hammurabi and the Laws of Eshnunna as well as laws from other societies. This collection of laws seems to have come from a settled community and was probably later than the time of Moses. Some scholars argue for a very early date, however, locating the code shortly after the settlement in the land of Canaan (ca. 1100 B.C.). The collection appears to be a kind of legal guidebook which would insure fairness and equity in the interpretation and the application of the legal system.

There are two problems which the beginning student should address at this point. The first arises from the tradition that all of the Israelite laws originated with Moses, but upon closer examination this assumption appears to be wrong. How does one explain such discrepancies? We have already discussed (cf. above, pp. 8 f.) the ancient and Hebrew tendency to telescope history and data and the tendency to concretize certain trends or movements in one person. Moses was the first and greatest law-giver; therefore in Hebrew thought patterns all laws would go back to Moses. The fact that laws (and all customs) develop and change through the years was irrelevant to them. Though disturbing to some modern people, the attributing of all laws to Moses held no problems for the ancient mind, even if Moses did not set forth each and every one. This same tendency, i.e., to attribute to the inauguration of a movement all subsequent development of the movement, will be observed at several significant points as the remainder of the Old Testament writings is examined.

The second problem emerges from a study of why this later code was placed at this specific point in the redaction work done by the final editors of this "history" of the Hebrew people and their religion. The most probable answer is that they wished by placing this code directly following the Decalogue to emphasize some of the specific manifestations and relationships of human life as that life was now to be lived in the new covenant relationship with God. The teaching is clear: a new relationship with God means a new way of life!

At this point in the account the reader is introduced to some of the cultic operations and requirements of the new faith. This account is interrupted by the story of the "golden calf" (32—34) but really continues through the entire book of Leviticus. The first item of note is the ratification of the covenant by means of a sacrifice, the sprinkling of blood on behalf of the twelve tribes, and a communal meal.

Then there are the regulations concerning cultic items, the major ones being the ark and the "tabernacle." The ark was portrayed as a wooden box or chest which was supposed to be the "throne" of the invisible God. In the chest were to be kept certain cultic items such as the two tablets of the law (later it was believed to have contained also some manna from the wilderness and the rod of Aaron). The ark was not very large being two and one-half cubits long (a cubit is about eighteen inches), but it appears to have been a very ancient cultic item in Israel's religious history.

The second cultic piece in the wilderness period was the "tabernacle" (chapter 26). This was an important item because it was here that the ark resided in a special place (the Holy of Holies) when not being carried around, and it was in the tabernacle that the official worship of Yahweh was to be performed. This portable building, as it is described here, may have been originally a tent and the precise dimensions of the tabernacle could very well be a later description drawn from the plans of the Jerusalem temple built by Solomon.

As one would expect, so much of the material which deals with cultic items and matters comes from the source-strata P. Into this material, however, there is inserted the narrative about the "golden calf" episode, and this material (32—34) seems to come from the older source J, although this is questioned by some scholars. To insert the story at this point in the narrative, the editors must have felt that its significance was of some importance.

The episode begins with the people wishing to have some concrete manifestation of God and Aaron's willingness to make for them the golden calf. Actually the figure was intended to be that of a bull, and it is interesting to note that the bull was the symbol for Baal, the god most revered by the Canaanites whose land was to be the ultimate home of these people. The emphasis upon the bull and the fact that it is called "your gods" also reflect a later time when Jeroboam I set up bull images at Dan and Bethel when the kingdom of Solomon was divided into northern Israel and southern Judah.

When Moses came down from the mountain with the two tablets of the covenant, he threw them down and broke them into pieces indicating that this was exactly what the people had already done, broken their covenant with God. The gold of the image was taken, ground up, and scattered on the water. The people were then made to drink the water, indicating thereby whether they were guilty or innocent of participating in such forbidden activities. It is the old idea of trial by ordeal.

After this Moses then returned to the mountain and received (or made) another set of tablets. These regulations are given in chapter 34 which is often referred to as the "ritual decalogue." Many interpreters believe that this chapter contains the J account of the Ten Commandments (that in 20:2ff. belonging to the E source), and one notes very clearly that the wording, order, and number of the commandments are different from chapter 20. The question arises as to why this second account of the giving of the law was included and why it was attached to the story of apostasy in the wilderness.

The answer seems to be found in the religious interpretation of the final editors. They wanted to demonstrate that the people could become apostate, thus breaking the covenant between themselves and God. The religious teaching here implies that the covenant was not to be taken for granted simply because the people believed in God's mercy and long-suffering nature. Breaking the covenant was a serious matter which brought serious consequences, but God was merciful and after a period of suffering because of their apostasy the people could be restored and the covenant remade. This in fact happened quite frequently in the course of the history of God's dealing with the Israelite people, and this later understanding may well have influenced the editors as they made the final redaction of the traditions here. The story of the apostasy in the wilderness, which probably did take place, served as a good example of how God had had to relate to the people for many generations. God was always ready, however, to restore the covenant—but only on his terms!

The last chapters (35—40) reflect the fulfilling of the instructions which had already been formulated in chapters 25—31. Naturally most of this material derives from P. At the conclusion of the book of Exodus the people had come out of Egypt, a covenant had been established between themselves and Yahweh their God, the cultic apparatus had been enumerated and now completed. One would think that the movement on to the land of Canaan would be the next step. Instead there was inserted at this point a long collection of instructions for the people basically in the area of cultic laws and regulations for those who were to constitute the community of God's people.

Leviticus

The book of Leviticus continues with the cultic regulations which had begun to be enumerated at the conclusion of the book of Exodus. These regulations were to be followed and observed by the people in their covenant relationship with God. Earlier scholarship attributed all the material here to P, since it deals with cultic matters, but this has been questioned of late. Only chapters 8—10 seem to be part of a narrative, and the remainder of the book is composed of a series of longer and shorter collections of cultic rules and regulations which may have come from various sources. The purpose of the collecting and editing of this set of regulations here seems to be to emphasize the idea that certain guidelines had to be followed if a group truly wanted to be the community of God's people. Edited as it was in the post-exilic times, this book places the emphasis on the sin and guilt of the people as the cause of tragedy in the past history of the nation. And further, it seems to challenge the new community to adhere to the proper rules in order to be truly the proper people of God.

Quite a large amount of space is given over in this book to the proper manner and mode for sacrifices. This area of practice constitutes a large puzzle to many Old Testament interpreters since there is some evidence which leads to the conclusion that sacrifices were not required in the early days. Several of the prophets refer to the wilderness period as a time when sacrifices were not carried out (cf. Amos 5:25; Jeremiah 7:22). This would not necessarily mean that sacrifices were not performed in early Israelite history, but that they were not *required.* The debate over this matter is very complex, but it seems certain that sacrifice goes back to the earliest days of the Hebrew religion. Whether it was understood as being required is still open to debate, however.

The basic teaching of the book of Leviticus seems to be that found in the Holiness Code (17—26). "You shall be holy; for I the LORD your God am holy." Although ritual purification is a concept that seems strange to our culture and tradition, the people of the ancient world took ceremonial cleanness and uncleanness very seriously. There were, they believed, certain things in the material world which could cause one to be unclean if one came into contact with them, and in some way uncleanness was a violation of the covenant rules for a religious community. There had to be available, therefore, means whereby the unclean person could be restored to a state of cleanness. The fact that we do not understand things in this way should not detract from understanding their perspective. The underlying religious principle is completely clear: the people of God are to be different from the world.

Leviticus: Outline

    I. What Is Required in Sacrifice, How to Conduct Sacrifice 1—7
        A. From the Devotee's Perspective 1:1—6:7
        B. From the Priest's Perspective 6:8—7:38
   II. Regulations for the Priests 8—10
  III. Regulations for Ritual Cleanness 11—16
  IV. The Holiness Code 17—26
   V. Gifts and Vows 27

The idea of concretizing a movement or set of ideas in one single event and/or one single person is probably nowhere more manifest than in the book of Leviticus. This book sets all these varied laws and regulations from many different backgrounds and time periods directly against the Sinai experience and the figure of Moses. Sacrifice and atonement were considered part and parcel of the religion of Israel from its inception at the holy mountain.

It is interesting to note that chapters 8—10 are in reality the logical sequence of the chapters in Exodus which have to do with the cultic regulations (cf. Exodus 25—31; 35—40). These passages set out regulations for the priests and the guidelines for their installation.

The segment dealing with specific regulations for determining what is clean and unclean is for most moderns either fascinating or boring. Most, however, find the material fascinating partly because there are numerous theories as to why some animals, diseases, etc., were considered to make one "unclean." It is interesting to note that a large part of this section deals with sexual matters indicating that numerous problems were connected with that popular but troublesome area of human relationships and activity (cf. also chapter 20:9–21).

In the Holiness Code there are again numerous regulations. One of the more interesting areas concerns the regulations covering some of the ancient festival celebrations such as Passover, etc. (cf. chapter 23). One should not conclude, however, since these regulations are so cultic in nature that there was no social concern among the Hebrew people. There are included in this book numbers of references of concern for one's neighbor (cf. 19:18), and for the land itself (cf. 25:1ff.), and, of course, for the poor and helpless (cf. 25:35ff.). Even at the point of highest cultic interest the religion of Israel (at its best) was concerned for others. It is true that the concern for others was not a universal one, the "neighbor" being a fellow Israelite or resident alien, but such references demonstrate to a certain degree an understanding of the nature of Yahweh which looked with favor upon the helpless and powerless.

There is perhaps one other point which should be mentioned about this book. This concerns the oft-quoted phrase, "An eye for an eye, and a tooth for a tooth" (24:20). Most persons today understand this saying as vengeful and cruel, but that kind of understanding really misses the meaning of the regulation as it was meant in that time. In ancient times there was the concept of just and proper retribution for a crime against society. In fact, in some cultures and in Israel there was the ancient concept of the *Go'el*, the avenger (usually a kinsman), whose duty it was to exact penalty on behalf of someone who had been hurt or wronged or malaciously slandered. Needless to say, the carrying out of vengeance quite frequently got out of hand!

The regulations concerning the eye for eye, tooth for tooth, therefore, reflected two basic points. First, there is the idea which was prevalent in Old Testament times that the punishment for a crime should fit the crime. Closely related is the understanding of those laws that limited the "vengeance" which could be exacted on behalf of society or some person who had been wronged. One was not to exact "interest" on the debt owed! Restitution should be made as equally as possible to the wrong done. To them this was justice.

Numbers

Numbers is the fourth book of the Torah. If one accepts the theory that the Pentateuch was composed of five books at one time, this book is simply one of those. For those who believe that there was originally only a Tetrateuch, Numbers becomes the last book in that sequence. It is also possible that this material was followed by other material which depicted a triumph of the Hebrew people by showing the people settled in the land of Canaan. If so, this later material was separated from the book of Numbers probably when the book of Deuteronomy was added at this point in the story. That this may be correct can be seen in the fact that the material near the conclusion of the book of Numbers appears to have undergone some editorial revision to make the transition to the book of Deuteronomy more fluid.

As for the arrangement of Numbers, interpreters have noted that there is less formal structure in this writing than in any of the others of the Pentateuch. It is therefore very difficult to outline the book. This is partly because there is much question as to the sources used in the composition. There is P material; and the older traditions (JE) also seem to have been utilized, but there is additional material which does not seem to fit into the J, E, P source patterns. Therefore some scholars argue that this material comes from sources or traditions other than these three.

Whatever the final disposition of the source problem, the book picks up the Exodus narrative again with the people of Israel at Sinai. Interspersed in the narrative are traditions which give more rules and regulations about religious and social matters as well as two census reports (from which the book takes its name). The picture which is portrayed is that of a group of people who are rebellious and doubt the promises of their God. Because of this they are required to wander for a generation (forty years is a typical expression indicating approximately one generation) before being allowed to enter the promised land. The story of their wandering does not really seem to follow a pattern either chronologically or geographically even though some scholars argue for one or the other approach. Rather the account gives what appears to be "typical" stories about what happened during that time of wandering. It is possible that the lack of structure and order to the account of this wandering may have been deliberate on the part of the final editors to illustrate the confusion of the people and the subsequent meanderings caused by their lack of faith.

When the book concludes, the people are located east of the Jordan waiting for their opportunity to enter the promised land. As the text now stands the ending does not appear to have been in the form in which the work originally concluded. Some have argued that Deuteronomy 34 was the original ending to this segment of the narrative. This conjecture may be correct, as far as it goes, but it is also true that the story lacks something else as well. The entire work, beginning with Genesis, up to this point has been directed toward the possession of the land promised "from of old" to the people. It would be odd if something about the entrance into the land were not at least mentioned if not described to complete this long story. This is the reason some scholars have argued that there was some additional narrative which originally concluded the larger work, a narrative depicting the settlement in the land.

Since Deuteronomy did not really belong to the literary composition which began with Genesis (cf. below, pp. 71ff.) but was placed after Numbers probably because it contained material and traditions which dealt with the figure of Moses, and since the book of Deuteronomy did not contain any reference to the specific taking of the land, the reader of the biblical books must look elsewhere for the conclusion to the account which through the editing process now culminated in Numbers. Scholars have long felt that the traditional sources of the Tetrateuch (J, E, P) can be traced into the book of Joshua. (Some even think these sources extend into Judges through Kings, but most reject that view.) Since Joshua is an account of the taking of the land, the division of the land into tribal territories, and the renewal of the covenant, it seems logical to postulate that the book of Joshua was the original conclusion of the larger work which began with Genesis, basically put together by those connected with the Priestly traditions. (Deuteronomy was, of course, not a part of that work originally but itself was the initial book of a long work which culminated with the exile.) More will be said about Joshua and its relation to other literary traditions at the appropriate point (cf. below, pp. 107f.).

The book of Numbers is indeed a curious mixture of sources, materials, and teachings. But the main thrust of the book is clear. The people who were supposed to trust God doubted, and the result was that they would be unable to enter the promised land.

Numbers: Outline

    I. Israel at Sinai 1:1—10:10
        A. Census (for military purposes) 1—2
        B. Census and Duties of Levites 3—4
        C. More Regulations and Instructions 5:1—10:10
   II. Journey to Southern Canaan 10:11—12:16
 III. Spies, Doubt, Defeat 13—14
 IV. Miscellaneous Regulations and Stories 15—36
        A. Rebellion Against Moses 16
        B. The Balaam Episode 22—24
        C. The Second Census 26
        D. Joshua Selected as Moses' Successor 27:12–23

As already noted the book of Numbers is a curious collection of narrative incidents along with rules and regulations. It is interesting to note that the two accounts of census differ in several points. The first, in chapter 1, is supposedly for the purpose of military service and lists 603,550 fighting personnel which would presuppose a huge number of people (probably more than two million) living in and off the Sinai peninsula! Some have argued that the figures given here have simply been exaggerated, or reflect a later counting, perhaps from the time of David, or that the word for "thousand" referred to a troop originally, or that the numbers are simply fictitious. The second census was supposed to number all the people as they were preparing to enter the promised land (chapter 26). It is of interest to note that the *total* number of people here in chapter 26 is less than the young men of military age in chapter 1! This probably means that there is some discrepancy in the figures in chapter 1, but it also reflects the religious idea that because of their unfaithfulness and sin the number of the people had decreased. Several accounts of the people and their sin are recorded in this book.

Numbers also clarifies the question as to why Moses and Aaron did not make it into the promised land. In chapter 20 Moses was told to speak to the rock so that water would be available. Instead he struck the rock twice; this action angered God and was interpreted as a lack of faith. Even the leaders were not immune from God's judgment if their faith faltered. Therefore Moses and Aaron were told that they would not enter the new land. One recognizes that this is another one of many aetiological stories contained within the traditions of these early times.

Another very curious story is told in chapters 22—24 and concerns the relationship of Israel with Moab and centers in the figure of a special religious person called Balaam. This man was supposed to have special powers and was unusually adept at "cursing." (One recalls the ancient idea about "power" in words.) He was hired by the king of Moab, Balak, to curse Israel, but instead Balaam was prevented by God from doing that and instead blessed Israel not once but several times. This episode was firmly fixed in the traditions of the Hebrew people so much so that it was quite frequently referred to in other writings as a marvelous deliverance by God on behalf of his people (cf. Deuteronomy 23:4; Joshua 24:9f.; Micah 6:5; Nehemiah 13:2). Whatever happened must have been of some important and lasting significance to have made such an impresson.

Since Moses was not to be allowed to enter the land of Canaan, a successor to him had to be selected. The man chosen, Joshua, was identified as one of the early spies to the land of Canaan who had not been afraid and had recommended immediate entry into the land (cf. Numbers 13—14). He was known originally as Hoshea. Even though more regulations and traditions are added at this point in the narrative, the stage was set for the entrance into the land promised to the people.

Deuteronomy

As it stands now, the book of Deuteronomy constitutes the conclusion of the Torah. The setting has Israel waiting to go into Canaan, and Moses summons the people together to deliver to them what may be called his farewell address. The structure of the book is set in the style of a long sermon (or perhaps a series of three shorter sermons), and it concludes with a narrative which includes an account of Moses' death.

Having read Deuteronomy along with the other four books of the Pentateuch, the student is struck with the different style, tone, and at times theology of Deuteronomy from the others. In addition, there is no sign of any of the old sources having been used in the composition of

Deuteronomy. It is the "odd man out" of the Pentateuchal books!

Critical study of the book really began with a discovery by W. M. L. de Wette (ca. 1805) who connected the reform movement of the Judean king, Josiah, with the book of Deuteronomy (cf. 2 Kings 22—23). That reform had certain characteristics, most notably the centralization of all worship in one sanctuary. The reform itself had either begun or was continued with the finding of a "book of the law" in the Jerusalem Temple. This "law book" then became the foundation for the reform. If one reads the book of Deuteronomy carefully, one becomes aware of the remarkable similarity between the demands made in that book when compared with the actual components of the reform under Josiah. De Wette argued that this law book was the book of Deuteronomy as it now exists. Others, however, were not convinced of that and argued that only part of what later came to be the book of Deuteronomy was involved (especially chapters 12—26, 28). There is still no unanimity of opinion on this subject, but there is general agreement that the traditions incorporated into the book of Deuteronomy are the same as those utilized by King Josiah.

A later development came with the thesis argued by Martin Noth that Deuteronomy was in fact only the first part of a much larger work extending through the book of Kings. This larger work was designated as the Deuteronomistic History Work. It was pointed out that the writer or compiler of this material had a particular style and very definite theological ideas which could be traced through the entire work. One of these religious motifs which is found even in the structure of some of the books basically taught that if one was loyal to Yahweh, one was rewarded; but if one disobeyed Yahweh, catastrophe would surely follow. Quite often the reader finds the schematic outline in the material of: apostasy (the people go astray), judgment (the people experience bad times), repentance (the people cry to God for help), deliverance (God delivers the people from their trouble).

Noth's theory has been accepted by a large number of Old Testament scholars, even though numerous alterations have been argued and modifications made to the original thesis. There are some, however, who still view the various books as separate entities which were finally put together by some later editor thus rejecting Noth's basic idea. Noth's theory seems rather strong, however, when one examines the work carefully. The books—Deuteronomy, Joshua, Judges, Samuel, and Kings—do seem to constitute a continuous and sequential unfolding of the history of the Hebrew people from Moses to the exile, and it appears that the entire work holds together as a unity whether completed by one editor or author or a "school" of persons holding to this general theological viewpoint, as some have argued.

The major difficulty in accepting that theory lies in the book of Joshua. The chief question is: why would someone have composed two entirely different accounts of the same event, i.e., the settlement in the land, and placed them side by side? One is not surprised with "doublet" stories from two sources (this is a common occurrence in the other Pentateuchal collections), but why would the same group or person go to such lengths to compile two separate lengthy books? The answer may well be found in the argument that Joshua was originally the conclusion of the historical work done basically by the Priestly writers which included Genesis, Exodus, Leviticus, Numbers, and Joshua. The other history, done by the Deuteronomic school, began with Deuteronomy and continued with Judges, Samuel, and Kings.

In the course of accepting certain books as authoritative for the religious community, it was obviously agreed that anything dealing with Moses and the law should be considered as a standard for the people. Deuteronomy, therefore, was removed from its place at the beginning of the Deuteronomistic History and attached to the Priestly History in place of its original conclusion (basically what we have as Joshua). To do this some editorial revision was necessary. The story of the death of Moses(which probably stood at the end of Numbers) was moved to the end of Deuteronomy. And the book of Joshua was placed at the beginning of the Deuteronomistic History but obviously was reworked from the standpoint of the Deuteronomistic theology. This explanation would also account for the fact that most scholars find the older source-strata traditions in Joshua but not definitely in the remainder of the Deuteronomistic History.

Another problem connected with Deuteronomy centers around where the traditions in that book originated. Much speculation has arisen but most agree that they came from northern Israel shortly before or after the fall of that nation to the Assyrians in 721 B.C. Exactly who brought them to the south, probably to Jerusalem, is not known, however. The most frequently recurring idea is that a group of Levites was responsible for bringing the material and preserving it. Many have recognized in the Deuteronomistic History a definite tendency toward the prophetic ideology and a high regard for the prophetic movement. It is quite possible, therefore, that the persons responsible for this work had close connections with the prophets and their circles of tradition. In fact, certain prophets seem to have been quite close to the Deuteronomic style and teaching (cf. especially Hosea and Jeremiah). The truth is, however, that all conjectures are essentially that —conjecture.

Whatever the exact history which lies behind the formation and editing of the book of Deuteronomy, it is a fact that the book stands as the last in the authoritative collection known as the Torah. The name Deuteronomy means "second law," perhaps indicating a second "giving of the law." This title came from the Greek version.

As already noted the book is structured around a sermon (or sermons) given by Moses to the people as they were ready to enter the land of Canaan. It contains a stirring challenge to them to commit their lives to the service of this God who has made a covenant with them and, in fact, loves them. To fail to do so carries with it serious consequences. The message for the people who heard this was: forewarned is forearmed!

Deuteronomy: Outline
  I. Introductory Speeches 1—11
 II. The Central Challenge 12—26
III. Promises for Obedience and Consequences of Disobedience 27—30
 IV. Historical Appendix 31—34

The book of Deuteronomy begins with Moses recounting briefly how God has taken the people of Israel from Horeb (another indication that the D material may be from the North) and has finally brought them to the place where they are about to enter the promised land. As one reads the text it is difficult not to remember that the place and time of origin of the Deuteronomic work in its final form were Babylonia during the exile, in all probability toward the end of that period. (Many scholars date D from ca. 550 B.C.) In a sense then this exhortatory sermon of

Moses is not only intended to reflect what Moses would have said to the people then, but what Moses would say to the people now!

With the typical Deuteronomic understanding of theology then, one finds clearly in these early chapters (1—4) the historical evidence that when the people are faithful, all is well; but when they are disobedient, judgment comes. It is interesting also to note that the speech contains a specific reference to the fact that if Israel is unfaithful after having come into the land, God will scatter them among the nations (4:25–31). This was painfully clear to the people in exile, but there was hope, for if the covenant was renewed God would be merciful again and reestablish a relationship between himself and the people.

There is another interesting point to note in this section. Until the exile (ca. 586–538 B.C.), the ancient traditions of the Hebrew people seemed to reflect the henotheistic concept of God, i.e., that Yahweh only was to be the God of the Hebrews, but they did not explicitly deny the existence of other gods. This viewpoint is basically reflected in Deuteronomy as well, but there is one passage which obviously has been influenced by the great prophet of the exile whose work is found in Isaiah 40—55. The clear teaching of this prophet was that Yahweh *alone* is God. In Deuteronomy 4:35–39 the same teaching, in fact in quite similar wording, is found. This may be simply coincidence, but it is more likely the result of both passages having originated about the same time in the same place.

The second part of the introductory section (chapters 5—11) contains the stipulations of the covenant. For example, another version of the Decalogue is found here (5:6–21), but one of the most significant parts of the book is found in 6:4–5. These verses are even today considered to be part of the very heart of the Jewish faith and are known as the *Shema* (the Hebrew word for "hear"). The usual translation of this important passage is: Hear, O Israel: The LORD our God is one LORD; and you shall love the LORD your God with all your heart, and with all your soul, and with all your might.

Many persons have understood this command as the foundation stone for a monotheistic faith, and it has been interpreted in this way for many centuries. But the first part of the verse can be translated in any one of several ways. For example: (1) Yahweh our God, Yahweh is one; (2) Yahweh is our God, Yahweh is one; (3) Yahweh is our God, Yahweh alone. While exact agreement is not to be expected among scholars in the interpretation of this great theological proclamation, it seems that in the light of the Old Testament understandings (and this seems to make the most logical sense) the third option is the best. Yahweh was to be their God, and Yahweh *alone* was to be served! This is obviously an ancient call to obedience, reflecting the henotheistic nature of the ancient beliefs.

There is really no logical break between chapters 11 and 12, as they stand in the text of Deuteronomy, but most interpreters feel that chapter 12 begins a new section which sets out specific regulations which will cause the people of God to be distinguished from all others. The purpose of these regulations was to ensure the continuation of the covenant and the blessings of God for his people.

The chapters 12—26 (and some scholars add 28) form the core of the regulations which many believe lay at the foundation for Josiah's reform in 621 B.C. The basic element in this reform was the regulation which centered all legitimate worship in the Jerusalem Temple. Since most scholars strongly believe that these Deuteronomic traditions originated in northern Israel, it is argued that the tradition originally did not designate Jerusalem as *the* place of worship (cf. 12:1–7). Rather, the original teaching probably designated a northern site as the proper place to worship, perhaps Shechem. It was only when these traditions came to Judah that the reinterpretation was made, naturally selecting Jerusalem as the place to worship Yahweh. A change closely associated with this new emphasis on worship in one central place involved the command to celebrate the Passover in the Temple at Jerusalem; until this time it obviously had been celebrated (when it was) in the home (cf. 16:1–8).

Other elements of the Deuteronomic Code designated that all astral worship, sacred poles and pillars, and any practice of magic and divination be forbidden (cf. 17:3; 12:3; 16:21–22; 18:11). The sacrifice of children was also proscribed (cf. 18:10), a practice which obviously reoccurred through the history of Israel and had been practiced just before Josiah's reign under the kingship of Manasseh (cf. 2 Kings 21:6; 2 Chronicles 33:6, perhaps also 2 Kings 21:16) who had offered his own child (or children) as a human sacrifice.

Since the centralization of worship in one place would naturally have displeased many priests at the outlying shrines, it was ordered that all the rural priests (who were Levites) be admitted to officiate in the services in Jerusalem (Deuteronomy 18:6–8), but interestingly enough this was not deemed practical at the time of Josiah (cf. 2 Kings 23:8–9).

Some interpreters argue that chapter 28 was the original conclusion of 12—26 and that chapter 27 was inserted later and is therefore out of place. This may be true but in the final redaction of the work chapters 27—30 seem to hold together around the themes of obedience and disobedience which are the twin avenues of life under the Deuteronomic theology. This section (27—30) concludes with a challenge to the people to follow the way of life and good and to shun the way of death and evil (30:15–20).

The final portion of Deuteronomy contains a final charge to the people and a challenge to Joshua to lead the people into the land under the power of Yahweh. Moses himself then was allowed to see the land from a mountain east of the Jordan (whether Mt. Nebo or Mt. Pisgah is not clear) before he died. Joshua was now the leader of this group which was about to embark on a new adventure.

Summary

When the Pentateuch is studied with some intensity, one begins to understand better something about the literary makeup and religious purposes of the final editors of this collection of books. The Torah then is not a single literary product composed by one person, but rather it is the final product of a long and complicated history in which many ancient traditions from many ancient groups have been remembered, used, reused, interpreted, reinterpreted, and finally codified in these writings. The writing down in this "final" form of these traditions, after a long and complex history of having been transmitted orally and by written sources, preserved these religious truths for all succeeding generations and demonstrated how the ancient traditions could still speak to the people of God in a new age and in new circumstances. The most important point of the composition and final editing of these writings is perhaps the understanding of those ancient people that the truths of the past were still relevant and could yet be applied to the present crises of life. These five books were the first to be accepted and understood to be authoritative for the Hebrew people in their understanding of God and God's relationship to the people and the subsequent responsibilities of the people to God and to each other.

Here is a rough listing of the passages which are associated with the three source-strata found within the Tetrateuch (and Joshua). Not all scholars agree on the specifics of any listing and certain passages do not seem to fit into any one of the three sources. The listing given here, it is hoped, will be of some usefulness to the beginning student. Some have found it helpful to go through these biblical books and mark off the passages belonging to the different sources by the use of "color-coding," one color for each source. One must also keep in mind that in some passages it is extremely difficult to separate the materials neatly, especially J and E.

The J Material

Genesis 2:4—4:26; 6:1–8; 7:1–10, 12, 22–23; 8:2b–3a, 6–12, 13b, 20–22; 9:18–27; 10:8–19, 21, 24–30; 11:1–9; 12:1–4a, 10–20; 13:1–18; 16:1–2, 4–14; 18:1—19:28, 30–38; 21:1a, 2a, 7; 22:15–18, 20–24; 24:1—25:6; 25:21–34; 26:1–33; 27:1–45; 28:13–16; 29:2–14; 29:31–35; 30:4–5, 9–16, 24–43; 31:1, 3, 46, 48–50; 32:3–12, 22, 24–32; 33:1–17; 34:3, 5, 7, 11–12, 18, 25–26, 30; 37:12–18, 21, 25–27, 28b, 31–35; 38:1—39:23; 42:38—44:34; 46:28—47:4; 47:13–26; 49:1–28a; 50:1–11, 14.

Exodus 1:6, 8–12; 2:15–23a; 3:2–3, 5, 7–8, 16–18; 4:1–16, 19–20a, 22, 24–26, 30–31; 5:3, 5—6:1; 7:14–18, 21, 23–25; 8:1–4, 8–15, 20–32; 9:1–7, 13–21, 23b, 25b–34; 10:1–11, 13b, 15–19, 24–26, 28–29; 11:4–8; 12:21–27, 29–30, 13:3–16, 21–22; 14:5–7, 10–14, 19b–20, 21b, 24–25, 27b, 30–31; 15:22–27; 16:4, 5, 25–30; 17:1b–2, 7; 19:3b–9; 24:1–2, 9–11; 32:9–14, 25–34; 33:1–4, 12–23; 34:1–28.

Numbers 10:29–36; 11:4–35; 13:17—14:45; 16:12–15, 25–34; 20:14–21; 21:21–35; 22:2—24:25; 25:1–6; 32:1—42.

The E Material

Genesis 15 (mixed with J); 20; 21:6–21, 22–34; 22:1–19; 28:10–12, 17–18, 20–22; 29:1–14; 29:31—30:24 (with J and P); 31:2, 4–45, 47, 51; 32:1–23; 33:19–20; 35:1–8, 16–20; 37:1–11, 19–20, 22–24, 28a, 29–30, 36; 40:1—42:37; 45:1—46:5; 48:8–22; 50:15–22, 23–26.

Exodus 1:15—2:14; 3:1, 4, 6, 9–15, 19–22; 4:17–18, 21, 27–28; 5:1–2, 4; 7:15b, 17, 20b; 9:22–25, 35; 10:12–13a, 14a, 20, 21–23, 27; 11:1–3; 12:31–39, 42a; 13:17—14:31 (combined with J); 15:1–18, 20–21; 17:3–16; 18; 19:2–20 (with J); 20:1—23:19; 24:3–8, 12–14, 18b; 31:18b; 32:1—33:11.

Numbers 11:4–35; 12; 13:17—14:25; 20:14–21; 21:4–20; 21:21–35; 22:2—24:25 (with J); 32:1–38.

One must recall that in certain passages, especially in Numbers, it is difficult to separate neatly the J and E materials since these have been blended together so well by the redactors.

The P Material

Genesis 1:1—2:3; 5; 6:9–22; 7:6, 11, 13–16a, 18–21; 8:1—2a, 3b–5, 13a, 14–19; 9:1–17, 28–29; 10:1–7, 20, 22–23, 31–32; 11:10–27, 31–32; 12:4b–5; 13:6, 11b, 12a; 16:1a, 3, 15–16; 17; 19:29; 21:2b–5; 23; 25:7–10, 12–17, 19–20; 26:34–35; 27:46—28:9; 31:18b; 33:18a; 34; 35:9–13, 15, 22b–29; 36; 37:1–2a; 46:8–27; 47:5b–6a, 7–11, 27b–28; 48:3–7; 49:29–33; 50:12–13.

Exodus 1:1–5, 7, 13–14; 2:23b–25; 6:2—7:13; 7:19–20a, 21b–22, 8:5–7, 16–19; 9:8–12; 11:9–10; 12:1–20, 28, 40–51; 13:1–2; 14:8–9, 15–18, 21–23, 26–27a, 28–29; 16; 24:15–18a; 25:1—31:17; 35—40.

Leviticus All.

Numbers 1:1—10:10; 13:1—14:45; 15; 16—19; 20:1–13, 22–29; 22:1; 25:6–18; 26—31; 33—36.

The materials have been combined in the book of Joshua so as to make separation of the sources almost impossible. Here is an accounting to demonstrate the idea, however.

The Combination of J and E: Joshua 2; 3:1—5:1; 6—7; 8:1–29; 9:1—10:15; 11:1–9; 18:2–10.
J material left separate: 5:2–9, 13–15; 19:51b; 21:43–45.
E material left separate: 14:6–15; 24 (but with Deuteronomic editing).
P material left separate: 12; 13:15–33; 14—19; 21:1–42; 22:9–34.

For further and more detailed analysis and listings see Ernest Sellin, *Introduction to the Old Testament*, Revised and rewritten by George Fohrer. Trans. by David E. Green. (Nashville: Abingdon Press, 1968), pp. 147–58, 179–86, 201–5.

Also Norman Gottwald. *A Light to the Nations* (New York: Harper & Row, 1959), pp. 214–24, 246–54, 448–55.

Suggestions for Further Study

Walter Brueggemann and H. W. Wolff. *The Vitality of Old Testament Traditions*. Atlanta: John Knox Press, 1975.

Norman Habel. *Literary Criticism of the Old Testament*. Philadelphia: Fortress Press, 1971.

Martin Noth. *A History of Pentateuchal Traditions*. Translated by B. W. Anderson. Englewood Cliffs, N.J.: Prentice-Hall, Inc., 1972.

Gerhard von Rad. *The Problem of the Hexateuch and Other Essays*. Translated by E. W. T. Dicken. New York: McGraw-Hill, 1966.

Julius Wellhausen. *Prolegomena to the History of Israel*. Translated by J. S. Black and A. Menzies. Edinburgh: A. & C. Black, 1885. Paperback ed., 1958. A classic, though now dated in many ways.

The following commentaries and discussions are recommended for a study of the individual books.

Genesis
Robert Davidson. *Genesis 1—11*. Cambridge: Cambridge University Press, 1973.

_____. *Genesis 12—50*. Cambridge: Cambridge University Press, 1979.

Hermann Gunkel. *The Legends of Genesis: The Biblical Saga and History*. Translated by W. H. Carruth. New York: Schocken Books, 1964. Original ed., 1901.

Nahum Sarna. *Understanding Genesis*. New York: Schocken Books, 1970.

Gerhard von Rad. *Genesis: A Commentary*. Rev. ed. Translated by John H. Marks. Philadelphia: Westminster Press, 1972.

Bruce Vawter. *On Genesis: A New Reading*. Garden City, N.Y.: Doubleday & Co., 1977.

Exodus
Brevard S. Childs. T*he Book of Exodus*. Philadelphia: Westminster Press, 1974.

Ronald E. Clements. *Exodus*. Cambridge: Cambridge University Press, 1972.

J. Philip Hyatt. *Exodus*. Greenwood, S.C.: The Attic Press, 1971.

Martin Noth. *Exodus*. Translated by J. S. Bowden. Philadelphia: Westminster Press, 1962.

Leviticus
Martin Noth. *Leviticus*. Rev. ed. Translated by J. S. Anderson. Philadelphia: Westminster Press, 1977.

J. R. Porter. *Leviticus*. Cambridge: Cambridge University Press, 1976.

N. H. Snaith. *Leviticus and Numbers*. London: Thomas Nelson & Sons, 1967.

Numbers
Martin Noth. *Numbers*. Translated by James D. Martin. Philadelphia: Westminster Press, 1968.

John Sturdy. *Numbers*. Cambridge: Cambridge University Press, 1976.

Deuteronomy

Ronald E. Clements. *God's Chosen People: A Theological Interpretation of the Book of Deuteronomy.* London: SCM Press, 1968.

E. W. Nicholson. *Deuteronomy and Tradition.* Philadelphia: Fortress Press, 1967.

Anthony Phillips. *Deuteronomy.* Cambridge: Cambridge University Press, 1973.

Gerhard von Rad. *Deuteronomy.* Translated by Dorothea Barton. Philadelphia: Westminster Press, 1966.

Moshe Weinfeld. *Deuteronomy and the Deuteronomic School.* Oxford: Clarendon Press, 1972.

CHAPTER II

Nebi'im

History

Before discussing in some detail the history of the Israelite people during the period included within the time span of this collection of writings, it would be wise to explore the overall historical picture of that era. After all, no people exist in a vacuum, especially such a small and politically insignificant group as the early Hebrews. The story of their history is integrally bound up with the story of the peoples and nations around them. And the fortunes of the Hebrew people were directly geared to the fortunes, strengths, and weaknesses of their neighbors both near and far.

When some of the Hebrew people left Egypt under the leadership of Moses ca. 1300–1250 B.C., Egypt was a fairly strong nation though not as powerful as it had been in earlier times. During the latter part of that same century (ca. 1220 B.C.) the Egyptians encountered a movement of potential invaders known in the Egyptian texts as the "Peoples of the Sea." These invaders were allied with Libya against Egypt and were composed of various groups of peoples. Who they were and where they originated are still matters of debate. But the Egyptians, first under Merneptah (ca. 1220 B.C.) and later under Ramses III (ca. 1180 B.C.), repelled their attacks, driving them away. Some of these "Sea Peoples" then settled along the coast of Palestine, and these people were of great significance in the development of the history of Israel. This group was known as the *Prst* in the Egyptian documents, as *palastu* in the Akkadian language. They came to be known to the Hebrew people as the Philistines, and from their name the entire land has become known as Palestine. It is believed that they came originally from Crete or Cyprus or perhaps even southern Asia Minor. Whatever their origin, they came down the coastal plain of Palestine and fought the Egyptians. Having been repelled there, they settled along the coast and established a loose network of five strong cities (Gaza, Ashkelon, Ashdod, Ekron, Gath). The Philistines were of obviously superior cultural achievement (they possessed the ability to make iron weapons), and they exercised a great deal of control in the area which they occupied and over other parts of Canaan as well. The Philistine presence and power was a source of some genuine concern to the people of Israel after they had settled in Canaan.

The second nation which affected the people of Israel through many centuries continued to be Egypt. Though Egypt never really regained the power and importance it had enjoyed in earlier times, it nevertheless was a major power, if only a major second-rate power. During the years of Israel's existence Egypt was weak, but periodically would feel strong enough to make military incursions into Palestine. For the most part, however, Egypt was usually too busy attempting to keep whatever super-power there was (usually in the east) away from her. She did this by encouraging the smaller nations of Palestine and the surrounding areas to ally themselves together to throw off the yoke of the nation in control of the area. On numerous occasions Egypt would encourage the revolt, pledge its support, and then withdraw when it would become obvious that the rebellion was going to be crushed. On one occasion the leader of the rebellion fled for asylum to Egypt, and Egypt promptly turned him over to the nation seeking him (in this case, Assyria). It is not really difficult to understand why the prophets had so little respect for Egypt.

The primary group which affected Israel's history during this lengthy period, however, was the nation known as Assyria. This power-ful and brutal nation began to rise slowly, but it developed surely. The first king who began it on its way to "super-power" status was Tiglath-Pileser I (1112–1074 B.C.). From this time on the succeeding kings gradually developed a system wherein the idea of conquest was under-taken not simply for the short term view (i.e., the gathering of slaves, booty, etc.) but for the long term. The idea was to conquer lands and incorporate them permanently into their own empire. The practical reasons for this type of action are obvious.

For a number of centuries Assyria ruled over its own area in the Mesopotamian region and to the west along the mountains of Asia Minor. Ultimately, however, the nation began to move into Palestine toward Egypt. For various reasons the movement was temporarily blocked or delayed, but it was not long before the power of this nation was to be felt in Israel. For example, in 802 B.C. Adad-nirari III dealt Syria (Israel's northern neighbor and sometimes enemy) a death blow, but was unable to follow up this victory immediately by subduing Israel. Therefore, Israel enjoyed a long resurgence of past glory. With the ascent to the throne of Tiglath-Pileser III (ca. 747 B.C.), however, that situation changed. Pul, as he is known in the biblical texts, revised the relationship of Assyria with the smaller states and designed the strategy of occupying these countries permanently. It was, of course, under Tiglath-Pileser III that northern Israel was taken into the Assyrian sphere, and later under Sargon II totally destroyed.

The peak of Assyria's power came about this time (750–650 B.C.), but the student of history can aleady see that her days were numbered. Assyria had never really been able to control Babylonia as it would have liked, and since it had begun a rather ambitious period of expansion of the empire, it had, in spite of all appearances to the contrary, spread itself too thin. Even though Assyria defeated Egypt, that nation successfully rebelled in ca. 655 B.C. Babylonia had begun to grow stronger. With the death of the king Asshurbanipal in 627 B.C. the end was not far off. Nineveh fell to the Babylonians in 612 B.C. Final destruction came at Haran in 609 B.C., and by 605 B.C. (the battle of Carchemish) the Babylonians were in rather complete control of the situation, having also defeated the Egyptians.

For a number of years Egypt continued to encourage the smaller states of Palestine to continue resistance to Babylonia ruled by the well-known king, Nebuchadrezzar. Each time the revolt was crushed. It was during this period that Judah was destroyed and carried into exile in Babylon. Babylonia was the most important nation in world politics for a short time, but none of the succeeding rulers matched Nebuchadrezzar in ability with the result that by ca. 539 B.C. Cyrus, the leader of Media-Persia, had overthrown the Babylonian Empire and established another power center further east in what is today basically Iran. The great Persian Empire grew out of this kingdom.

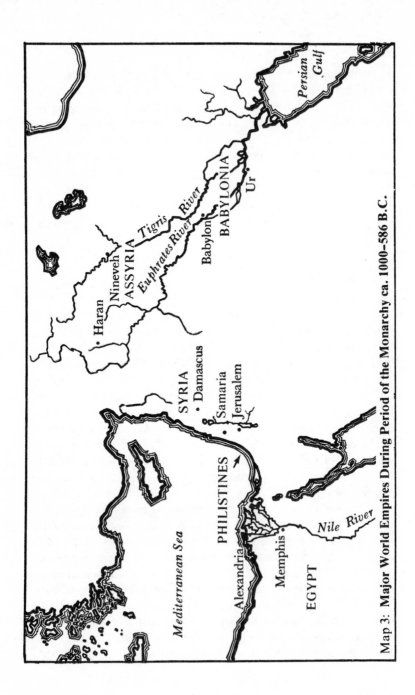

Map 3: Major World Empires During Period of the Monarchy ca. 1000–586 B.C.

The Persians ruled for several hundred years (until they were defeated by the Macedonian, Alexander the Great, ca. 331 B.C.). Their rule was rather enlightened, and the organization of the Empire under their leadership was efficiently done. The areas of their territory were divided into *satrapies,* i.e., administrative units, and the people of Judah were part of one of these units. Each of these units was headed by a governor called a *satrap.* Thus the history of the larger world directly influenced the development of the Hebrew people.

The events of the "dim, misty past" in Isarel's history begin to give way to more concrete and historically reliable data in the period now under consideration. The patriarchs and the time of the Exodus wanderings all appeared on the historical scene in the Bronze Age, but beginning ca. 1200 B.C. when the Israelite people were beginning to settle in the land of Canaan human history moved into what is known as the Iron Age. More accurate data is available for these times.

Problems relating to the first entry of the Hebrew people into Egypt, how long they stayed, the route of the Exodus have already been discussed. One resumes the history with the Israelite people in the "wilderness" wandering about as a nomadic or semi-nomadic group, but encamped on the eastern side of the Jordan River looking toward entrance into Canaan. There are two basic theories among scholars as to exactly how the Hebrew people finally took over the land. One group of scholars argues that the land was taken by a series of military conquests and that certain archaeological findings (i.e., evidence of the destruction of certain cities in the thirteenth century B.C.) support this theory. Another group argues that there was no such military campaign, that people moved into the sparsely settled areas of the land gradually and ultimately merged with the people there while retaining certain distinguishing features, most especially their religious beliefs. This proved to be, therefore, a gradual and non-militaristic settlement in the land. These scholars point out that only some of the cities mentioned in the Old Testament books were victims of military destruction and that it is impossible to know who it was that caused the devastation of the others, arguing that it could have been people other than the Hebrews. Further, there are certain cities, such as Jericho for example, which were destroyed but in an entirely different time, in fact two centuries earlier!

Another group understands the situation to have developed in a somewhat different manner. People came into Canaan and settled in areas which no one was occupying. These people then merged with certain "natives" who were disgruntled with the city-state governance of the area, forming a socio-religious group claiming the authority of the God, Yahweh. Later this group emerged into what became known as Israel.

What actually occurred will probably never be fully known. The truth usually lies somewhere between the extremes. In studying the evidence there appears to be a telescoping of traditions and events into a unified picture, when in reality there were various ideas and occurrences from many differing backgrounds and sources which made up the pieces of the whole.

What can be known has to be derived, however, from the narratives and traditions found in the books of Joshua and Judges and part of 1 Samuel. The picture one receives from these sources seems to be something like this. After the Hebrew people had come into the land either by conquest or infiltration or a combination of both, it appears that they evolved into basically a loosely-knit group of separate peoples. One quite popular theory holds that the tribes were bound together into an *amphictyony,* i.e., a loosely-knit group of tribes bound together by a common religious belief and centered at a religious shrine. Supposedly when one of the groups needed some type of assistance the others were to come to its aid.

The administration of the groups appears to have been rather loosely attended, however, since most of the people refused to assent to a king or strong leader to govern over all the groups. Each group was led by charismatic persons called "judges"; some judges seem to have arisen because of military necessity, while others appear to have been local leaders who dispensed justice and were overseers of the life of the group. Since the Israelite people had settled in areas where the Canaanite city-states exercised little authority, they were basically left alone except for periodic intrusions upon them by outside marauders.

With the establishment of the Philistines solidly along the coast, however, that situation changed. The tribe of Dan seems to have been dislodged from its territory along the sea and was forced to migrate to the extreme northern area of what later became Israel. Since the Philistines had iron implements and were culturally and militarily superior, they denied the use of iron to the people of Canaan and exercised a solid hold over the area, though they were not powerful enough to subdue all the people in the land. This Philistine threat caused the Hebrew peoples to think carefully about their future. The natural question was: should there not be some form of central government which would enable them to resist such tyranny as the Philistines had imposed? The thinking of the people, however, was definitely divided. Some advocated the appointment of a king, but others argued that to have a king would be an act of idolatry; Yahweh was their king. The pro and anti-monarchial factions seem to have existed side by side for a long period of time. Ultimately the people had to yield to the harsh practicalities of the moment. Someone was needed to lead them in some organized and unified way against the enemy.

A member of the tribe of Benjamin was, therefore, selected to be the first "king." His name was Saul, and he was a tragic character from the start. Identified with the ecstatic rovers known as the "sons of the prophets," he did the best he could in very trying circumstances. He attempted to be an ardent Yahwist, but he angered the man who had anointed him to be king, Samuel, who was a priest-prophet-judge all rolled into one. When Samuel became disgusted with Saul, he anointed David, a young man from the south, to be king in Saul's place. This angered Saul, and he pursued the young man rather diligently but was unable to catch him.

This set of circumstances caused David to become an outlaw, the leader of a band of motley brigands, who finally hired himself and his group out to the Philistines as mercenaries! When the great battle between Saul and the Philistines was about to take place, however, the Philistines sent David back to Judah. At the battle at Gilboa Saul was killed along with most of his sons. His body was horribly displayed and hanged on the wall at Beth-shan. Not all, however, disliked Saul, and when the people at Jabesh-gilead heard what had happened, they went to retrieve the bodies to give them proper disposition. Most scholars place Saul's reign ca. 1020–1000 B.C.

In the meantime David was attempting to ingratiate himself with the people of (southern) Judah. In time they proclaimed him to be king at Hebron. Since he was on relatively good terms with the Philistines, there was no real threat to his kingship. Then a series of happy "coincidences" occurred which caused David to become king over all Israel, a United Kingdom at last. First of all Saul and most of his sons had died fighting the Philistines, an event about which David made great public display of mourning. Saul's remaining son, Ishbosheth (or Ishbaal), had fled to the Transjordan area and was made king, being supported by Abner, the surviving general of Saul's army who also happened to be a kinsman; but Joab, David's general of the army, killed Abner (presumably as the result of a blood feud), while David disavowed any association with the deed. Before Abner's death, however, David had sent word to Ishbosheth that he wanted to have his first wife delivered back to him. This woman, Michal, was Saul's daughter, but David had not seen her for years and she was now married to someone else. David did not want her for love because he had several wives and many concubines by now, but her presence in his house as his wife gave him a legitimate claim to the throne.

Then when Ishbosheth was murdered by some of his officers and his head brought to David, the way was cleared for the northern peoples to request that David become king over them as well. Displaying again the "proper" response, David had the murderers of Ishbosheth killed, supposedly to demonstrate that he had not been responsible for this dastardly deed. After about six years as king at Hebron over the south, David became king of the United Monarchy (as it is known) ca. 994/3 B.C.

One of the first moves which he made was to capture the old Jebusite fortress of Jerusalem and make that the new capital of the nation. This was a very shrewd action, for this city was closer to the northern territory and had no connections with either group from past history. In addition David brought the ark to Jerusalem and made plans to have a Temple built to house this sacred object, which had basically been asssociated with the northern peoples.

Because this was a time of relative weakness for both Assyria and Egypt, David had a free hand in expanding his borders, making treaties with certain nations, and fighting against the enemies of the people, especially the Philistines. He was greatly successful in almost everything he did initially, and the nation was established on solid ground.

Toward the end of his reign, however, there were rumblings which portended things to come. The northern peoples were beginning to feel neglected in the administration of justice and exploited at the point of taxation, conscription, and such matters. There were two rebellions, one led by David's own son, Absalom, both of which were crushed by David's loyal troops under the command of Joab. When the king was near death, intrigue began as to who was going to succeed him. Adonijah, the eldest surviving son, laid claim to the throne with the support of Joab and Abiathar, the priest; but Bathsheba wanted her son, Solomon, to become king. Therefore she and Nathan the prophet and Benaiah, the new leader of the military, championed the cause of Solomon who ultimately became king. Later Adonijah was killed at the order of Solomon, as was Joab. The priest, Abiathar, was deported to the city of Anathoth, a city not far from Jerusalem to the northeast.

Almost everyone, religious or not, has heard of the great wealth, wisdom, and many wives of Solomon! During his reign both Egypt and Assyria were still weak and preoccupied with other matters. He inherited a rather large area from his father over which to rule, and he increased the economic wealth of the country by shrewdly using the trade routes through the land as a source of income. But his grandiose schemes and building programs were more expensive than the revenue which was coming in. He, therefore, rearranged the nation into a series of twelve districts for the purpose of taxation, conscription for the military, and for forced labor. (Interestingly enough these districts did not follow the older tribal boundaries.) Solomon's economic policies were so bad that he ultimately had to give away territory and cities in order to pay his debts (cf. 1 Kings 9:10ff.). Most of the burden for all of this fell upon the people of the northern area, causing unrest among them. There was a revolt of minor consequence among some people from the north under the leadershp of a man named Jeroboam. The revolt came to nought and to save his life Jeroboam fled to Egypt where he was given asylum. Egypt, being very weak, was probably quite glad to give assistance to anyone who could undo the rather powerful state ruled over by Solomon—and to whom, in fact, the Egyptian king had given one of his daughters! But the seeds of rebellion had begun to grow.

Solomon died about 922 B.C. and was succeeded by his son, Rehoboam. Having been crowned and acclaimed king in the south, he traveled to the northern shrine at Shechem to receive similar recognition there. Much to his surprise and chagrin he was greeted by a delegation from the northern people with certain "demands." Having heard advice from two directions ("ease up" or "crack down"), Rehoboam chose to flex his muscle. Whereupon the people of the north under the leadership of Jeroboam, now returned from Egypt, seceded from the United Monarchy.

Jeroboam moved quickly to establish a new government for the northern peoples. He named the old amphictyonic center at Shechem as the new capital and established two major religious shrines at Dan and Bethel. At each of these shrines he had erected a large image of a bull which was supposed to be reminiscent of the cherubim on the ark at Jerusalem. They were not really intended to be "idols" even though the religious leaders of the south and some of the prophets interpreted them as such. These images were to represent the throne of Yahweh above which God was seated. (According to some observers of the time the erection of these images was *the* sin of Jeroboam and of the entire Northern Kingdom ultimately causing its demise.) But Israel had been given both political and religious centers of its own.

After the division of the Kingdom ca. 922/1 B.C. the northern nation was known as Israel, the southern as Judah. Rehoboam may possibly have been able to cement things back together had it not been for the invasion about that time by a new Egyptian pharaoh, Shishak (Sheshonq), into Palestine. Even though both sections of the land were affected by this incident, the preoccupation of Judah with the problem allowed the northern peoples to become established as a separate nation.

For approximately fifty years the two nations existed about equally. But because of the geography and size of Israel that nation gradually became more powerful and, by necessity, more involved in international politics. Because Judah was off the beaten track it had less involvement in larger political matters. Further, in Judah there was a certain stability in the government because of the Davidic dynasty, but there was no such stability in Israel. Kings and dynasties came and went with some frequency.

Perhaps it would be simpler to sketch briefly the history of Israel and the history of Judah separately. In this manner one can see the full sweep of the life of each nation until the time of the destruction of each. There are points, naturally, where these will be related to each other, but for the most part each had a separate existence.

The Kingdom of Israel to the north was stronger and richer than its southern neighbor. Located along the trade routes between east and west, and north and south, Israel had more contact with the people of the world than Judah. It also had a large Canaanite population within it which caused problems for the "pure" worship of Yahweh.

Jeroboam ruled until 901 B.C. He had established the capital at Shechem but moved it to Tirzah. After his death a period of internal problems developed over succession to the throne, and several different people (and families) ruled or attempted to rule. Their times were short, however, and it was not until a general of the army, Omri, took control that any stability was established. The Deuteronomic writers did not like Omri, and little is said about him in the biblical texts. Omri (876–869 B.C.) was a superior leader, however, and established Israel as a strong (though small) state. Even after the house of Omri no longer sat upon the throne of Israel, foreign nations still thought of the rulers of Israel as belonging to the house of Omri. The capital was moved to a new location, a location which had not been occupied recently, and a new city was built. This city, Samaria, became the seat of government and remained such until the fall of Israel in 722/1 B.C. Omri also attempted to establish good relations with Judah.

On the international scene Egypt's attempted resurgence had fizzled out, but in the east the relative quiet in Assyria's history was coming to an end. A succession of more ambitious and sometimes ruthless kings had caused Assyria to become more powerful and to begin to move to the west for the purpose of conquest. The king Asshur-nasir-pal II (883–859) took his armies to the Mediterranean Sea so that they could wash their weapons in it! In the light of such activity Omri tried to establish peaceful relations with most of the smaller neighboring states.

Upon Omri's death his son, Ahab (869–850 B.C.), came to the throne of Israel. Ahab had problems with his immediate northern neighbor, Syria, but the menace of Assyria sometimes caused them to have to become allies. Such an occurrence developed in 853 B.C. when several of the smaller states banded together to fight the Assyrians, desiring to stop their westward progress. In that year these allies fought the Assyrians in a famous battle, the battle of Qarqar, and while a victory was not won, the Assyrians under Shalmaneser III did not move toward this area again for some time. During the interim Syria and Israel began fighting again and in one of the battles Ahab was killed.

He was succeeded by two of his sons in rather quick succession. But internal matters were not right in Israel. During the reign of Omri and Ahab there had been a resurgence of religious interest in the worship of Baal. The famous queen Jezebel from Tyre, wife of Ahab, had aggressively pursued the worship of the Tyrian Baal, and since many of the Canaanite people now residing in Israel had never really given up the old beliefs, there was a ready and receptive audience to embrace the new emphasis.

The prophets Elijah and Elisha were both actively involved in the struggle against the worship of Baal. Finally, Elisha anointed a general of the army, Jehu, to be king, and the overthrow of the house of Omri had begun. Jehu behaved as if this were a holy war, which in some sense it was, against his own people. Many were brutally slaughtered, and the *coup de grace* came when he assembled all the Baal worshipers in a temple of Baal under the guise of showing great honor to Baal. When the people were assembled, he ordered his troops to slaughter the group. These events took place in 842 B.C. and the years immediately following.

Since the blood-letting had been so extensive the new government of Israel was very weak. Most of the experienced personnel had been killed and many of the treaty alliances had been broken. In 841 B.C. Jehu is depicted on an inscription as paying homage to the great king of the Assyrians, Shalmaneser, who again was making his way into this region. After Shalmaneser, however, there was a period of some internal weakness in Assyria. This gave Syria the opportunity to harrass its southern neighbor, Israel. During this time Israel was almost helpless against Syrian domination.

A new era, short as it was, dawned ca. 802 B.C., for Israel. Assyria was again flexing its muscles and in that year destroyed Syria. Israel may have been subject to Assyria also had it not been for the fact that Assyria had problems with the growing nation of Urartu, a people and land just to the northwest of Assyria. With Syria weakened and Assyria otherwise occupied, Israel experienced a great rejuvenation. Prosperity and expansion of territory was the order of the day. All this happened under the kings Joash (801–786 B.C.) and Jeroboam II (786–746 B.C.).

These were good times, politically speaking, for Israel. Along with this prosperity, however, came social injustices and internal decay. It was during this period that the classical prophetic movement began.

After the death of Jeroboam, there was considerable chaos and confusion as to who was going to exercise power. In the course of a few years there were no less than six rulers. Couple this with the fact that at this moment Tiglath-Pileser III had inaugurated a new policy of empire-wide expansion in Assyria, and one can see rather clearly that the end of Israel was in sight. In 735/4 B.C. the states of Israel and Syria, weak as they were, attempted to put together a new coalition of smaller states similar to that of Ahab a century earlier with which to fight the Assyrians. But this time Assyria was too strong and the smaller nations too weak or afraid. The alliance failed, and in 733 B.C. Assyria crushed it. The last king of Israel, Hoshea, presided over only a small part of what had been the nation Israel. The remainder had been taken and incorporated into the Assyrian Empire.

When Tiglath-Pileser III died (727 B.C.), Hoshea revolted. This time the Assyrians under Shalmaneser V came into the land and laid seige to Samaria. Shalmaneser died, and Sargon II finally captured Samaria in 722 B.C. Many, if not most, of the people were deported to other lands, and Israel was no more. Other peoples were brought in by the Assyrians to populate the area. The exiled people of Israel gradually blended into their new surroundings and were heard of no more, while those who were left in the land intermingled with the new groups settled in the area by the Assyrians. This caused the people of Judah to look with even more disdain upon those people to the north.

The southern nation of Judah was shocked by the withdrawal of the northern peoples in 921 B.C. and then almost immediately was further beset with problems when Shishak of Egypt invaded in 918 B.C. The nation lost territory and was forced to pay tribute to Egypt. Judah during the next half century was busy trying to protect itself both from Egypt and from fighting along the border with Israel. Internally, while the line of David was continued, there was a struggle going on between those who like Solomon encouraged or at least tolerated foreign cults and those who opposed them. Under the reign of Asa (913–873 B.C.) there was a reaction to the toleration of such cults and a reform was carried out.

There had been enmity between Israel and Judah for some time immediately following the division of the kingdom. In fact, during Asa's reign Judah had appealed to Syria for assistance in turning back an attempted invasion by the northern people. When Omri came to the throne in Israel, however, he thought it best to make allies of Judah as well as the other nations in the area. To cement the ties of friendship Ahab's daughter, Athaliah, was married to the son of the king of Judah, Jehoshaphat.

When the revolution in the north under Jehu occurred, certain members of the royal family from Judah were in Israel, particularly the king Ahaziah, son of Athaliah and Jehoram of Judah. Jehu killed Ahaziah, and when Athaliah heard of this she moved to kill all the members of the Davidic line so that she could control the government in Judah. Only one infant son of Ahaziah was saved; Joash was hidden in the Temple and was proclaimed king when he became seven years old. The chief priest Jehoida had Athaliah killed and the temple of Baal (which she had established) torn down. Athaliah had ruled for several years (842–837 B.C.), the only person not of the Davidic line to sit upon the throne of Judah.

The fortunes of Judah roughly paralleled those of Israel, for in the eighth century at the time of the resurgence of Israel (owing to Assyria's momentary weakness) Judah too experienced a time of prosperity. In Judah the kings associated with this era of good times were Amaziah (800–873 B.C.) and Uzziah (783–742 B.C.). New territory came under Judah's control and industry flourished.

The renewed interest of Assyria in the area meant that changes were momentarily to be made. Israel had by this time already felt the strong hand of Tiglath-Pileser III, but in ca. 735/4 B.C. the kings of Syria and Israel joined together in an alliance, the Syro-Ephraimitic alliance, to fight against the Assyrians. They wanted the smaller nations to join with them (by force if necessary) to deter the Assyrian menace. The king of Israel at this time was Pekah.

In the south Ahaz had now ascended to the throne in Jerusalem; when pressured to join the Syro-Ephraimitic alliance, Ahaz did not wish to do so. He did not want to fight and therefore contemplated appealing for aid (i.e., to become a political vassal) to Tiglath-Pileser III. In those days becoming a vassal of a more powerful state meant at least nominally adopting the gods of that state, something that religious purists in any country would vehemently resist. But appeal to Assyria he did, and Judah became a vassal of Assyria. It is possible that Judah's continued existence at this time was a result of her vassalage to Assyria when Israel was finally destroyed.

When Hezekiah became king in Judah (715 B.C.), the nation remained in a position of subservience to Assyria. But in the land there was the hope that a new David would emerge to lead the people to great heights once again, both politically and religiously. It is obvious that the idealization process had been at work in the matter of David's character! At this time Egypt had begun again actively to encourage revolt against Assyria among the small nations in Palestine. Some did rebel but were crushed.

In 705 B.C., for example, Hezekiah of Judah instituted sweeping reforms, throwing out the Assyrian gods—in reality an act of defiance and independence. This was the year that a change in the kingship in Assyria had come about. The new king Sennacherib, did not take this revolt lightly. By 701 B.C. he had come into the land of Judah, ravaged the countryside, destroyed forty-six walled cities, and besieged Jerusalem. The terms of peace were quite harsh. Hezekiah was required to pay large amounts of tribute and to give some of his daughters as concubines to Sennacherib. Jerusalem, however, did not fall, and this great deliverance gave at the moment a cause for celebration, but later it caused among the people a false sense of security and safety. Their reasoning was that if the city had been delivered from such a great host as the Assyrian army, Yahweh would protect it against any army.

There is some discussion among historians as to how many times Sennacherib besieged Jerusalem. In all probability this occurrence took place in the Assyrian campaign of 701 B.C. There is some evidence, however, which causes some historians to speculate that there may have been two different campaigns, one ca. 701 B.C. and another ca. 688 B.C., and that these two have been telescoped into one story as is so often found in the Old Testament traditions. It is more likely, however, that there was only one incident which occurred in 701 B.C. There are, of course, several interesting features connected with the story. First, the Assyrian king himself described the expedition and boasted that he had shut Hezekiah up "like a bird in a cage!" Secondly, there must have been some very unusual circumstances connected with the lifting of the siege of Jerusalem, for even the Greek historian, Herodotus, from a much later time relates the story. His version had it that the rats gnawed the bowstrings of the Assyrians so that they could not fight! The mention of rats and the accounts in 2 Kings and Isaiah concerning this event may well point to a plague which swept through the camp of the Assyrians. Since they had already devasted the land and won huge concessions, the capture of Jerusalem was, to them, irrelevant.

After Hezekiah came the king who reigned the longest in Judah, Manasseh (687/6–642 B.C.). He was considered by the Deuteronomistic Historians as the very worst, however. Also immediately he made it plain that Judah was to be a loyal vassal of Assyria. This, of course, meant reestablishment of the gods of Assyria in the land. There were other gods who were worshiped as well, and many unsavory religious practices were performed during Manasseh's reign: ritual prostitution, divination and magic, astral worship, even human sacrifice.

Manasseh was followed by his son, Amon, who was soon assassinated, and after some confusion, Josiah, a young boy only eight years old, was proclaimed king. He was the son of Amon. His priestly supporters obviously guided him well and actually ruled through the boy until he became his own person. Josiah was in the right place at the right time during the early portion of his rule. Assyria was in the process of disintegrating; Egypt was weak. He extended the territory of Judah and may even have envisioned the reestablishment of the nation as it had been in the times of David and Solomon, at least boundary-wise.

In addition Josiah is most famous, religiously speaking, for the reform, usually called the Deuteronomic Reform, inaugurated during his reign. This reform abolished all worship except for the worship of Yahweh, forbade the practice of magic and divination, and outlawed human sacrifice. Most importantly, however, was the stipulation that all outlying shrines had to be closed. All worship was required to be celebrated in the Jerusalem Temple.

As Babylonia with some assistance began to cause Assyria to disintegrate, Egypt decided to come to the aid of Assyria. Fearing the strong nation of Babylonia, Egypt wanted to keep Assyria, though now in a weakened position, as a buffer between Babylonia and Palestine. This would assist Egypt since it could then be free of foreign domination, but also it would allow Egypt a free hand in Palestine, something it had not enjoyed for many years. Therefore ca. 609 B.C. Egypt marched to the assistance of Assyria.

Josiah, nominally sympathetic if not actually allied with Babylonia, felt called upon to fight the Egyptians. Therefore at Megiddo in 609 B.C. the Judeans fought the Pharaoh Necho (Neco), and for his trouble Josiah was killed. His son Jehoahaz succeeded him, but the Egyptians deposed him and placed his brother Eliakim, on the throne as a vassal of Egypt. His name was then changed to Jehoiakim.

The Egyptians were soundly defeated at Carchemish in 605 B.C. and Palestine came under the control of Babylonia. Jehoiakim remained as king in Judah but was thoroughly pro-Egyptian, however, and took the opportunity when it arose ca. 600 B.C. to rebel against Babylonia. That was a fatal mistake. Nebuchadrezzar marched into the land in 598 B.C. Before the fall of the nation Jehoiakim died, whether by natural causes or otherwise is not known, and his son, Jehoiachin, became king only to be the one to surrender to the Babylonians (598/7 B.C.). He along with many high ranking persons was carried off into exile to Babylon. Surprisingly enough the Babylonians were very generous with the people of Judah. The city of Jerusalem was not destroyed, the people were treated very leniently, and a Davidic descendant was placed on the throne. An uncle of Jehoiachin was made king, Mattaniah, renamed Zedekiah.

Unfortunately for the people of Judah, Zedekiah was a very weak ruler. He knew what was right for the people, but he was not strong enough to resist the pro-Egyptian faction in the ruling heirarchy. Egypt, up to her old tricks, continued to encourage the smaller states in Palestine to rebel against Babylonia, promising help it could not really deliver. A rebellion almost broke out in 594 B.C. but did not get off the ground.

In 589 B.C. the final revolt of Judah came against Babylonia. The Babylonians came into the area, and this time they did "the job right." Jerusalem was destroyed, the Temple was destroyed, and most of the people of any consequence were carried off into Babylonian exile. All this took place ca. 587/6 B.C. At this point Judah ceased to exist as a nation and became part of the Babylonian administrative district of Samaria.

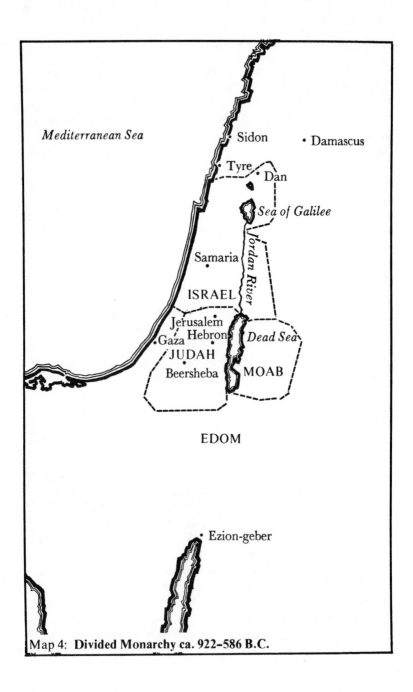

Mediterranean Sea

• Sidon

• Damascus

• Tyre

• Dan

Sea of Galilee

Jordan River

Samaria
•

ISRAEL

Jerusalem
•
Hebron
Gaza•
Dead Sea

JUDAH

Beersheba
•

MOAB

EDOM

• Ezion-geber

Map 4: **Divided Monarchy ca. 922–586 B.C.**

The people from Judah, called "Judahites" by the Babylonians, whence then the term "Jews," were settled near Babylon and obviously allowed to live in relative peace. Though there was initially an undercurrent among the people to return, they ultimately settled down and became very comfortable living in this strange land. Some people from Judah had also moved into Egypt during this same period. Hope for the restoration of the land lay with the people in Babylon, however, for these were the leaders—trained in political, but more especially religious affairs.

After Nebuchadrezzar, there was no political leader in Babylonia who was really up to the job. The Babylonian Empire slowly began to crumble and in 539 B.C. was conquered by the great Persian leader, Cyrus. A most enlightened ruler, Cyrus allowed exiled peoples to return to their original homelands, and to return to the worship of their gods. In 538 B.C. the Jews were allowed to return home. But after all two generations had now gone by, and most of the people had never known any home but Babylon, their livelihood and roots being there. In short, many did not want to return, and in fact did not.

Some did want to go, however, and led by a man named Sheshbazzar they did return. Sheshbazzar is an interesting study, for after the people return he is heard from no more. At this point a governmental official emerged in Judah, a descendant of the Davidic line, named Zerubbabel. These names indicate how much the Babylonian culture had permeated Hebrew thought patterns. Technically speaking, the area of Judah was now part of the Persian administrative district of Samaria and not an independent nation or state. Hopes were high for a restoration of the nation and these hopes seem to have centered on Zerubbabel. Shortly thereafter, Zerubbabel disappeared from the scene. The people in Judah were then basically organized and structured around the Temple and the high priest for some years to come.

Interestingly enough when the people returned they began to rebuild the Temple but seem to have accomplished only the building of the foundation. Times were harsh, even cruel. Survival was the order of the day and the completion of the Temple was postponed. Under the urging of two prophets, Haggai and Zechariah, work on the Temple was begun anew in 520 B.C., and the restored "house of Yahweh" was completed ca. 515 B.C. It served as the focal point of the new community for some time.

What was happening to the people of Judah during these years following the return? The truth is that very little is known about what was happening to them. A few pieces of data can be gleaned from some of the Old Testament writings and from some references by later writers, but for the most part very little specific information exists to enable the historian to reconstruct the history of these people in Judah from ca. 500 B.C. until about 175 B.C. The most certain item was that these people were poor and powerless, subject to the "ebbs and flows" of world history, and at times subject to the whims of less powerful states and peoples in neighboring areas. For example, one theory has been proposed which suggests that the nation of Edom overran the area and destroyed the Temple again in ca. 485 B.C. Very few interpreters have accepted this hypothesis, but not enough is known to argue for or against the idea with any degree of certainty.

The people of Judah were suspicious of most of their neighbors, especially the people of the north. The people around Samaria made offers to help the Judeans, but these offers were rejected. After all, those people were considered to be "impure." Contact with them could cause the Judeans to lose their identity. The post-exilic period then was a struggle to survive, and at the same time to preserve the uniqueness and the integrity of the Jews as they understood themselves to be the unique people of Yahweh.

Literature

Any discussion of the literary problems connected with this second division of the Hebrew canon must be separated into at least two different compartments. And even then each of the individual books can be analyzed further. At this point, however, the discussion will center on the books known as the "Former Prophets" (Joshua, Judges, Samuel, Kings) as one entity and the books known as the "Latter Prophets" (Isaiah, Jeremiah, Ezekiel, and the Book of the Twelve) as another.

It is impossible to discuss the first of these segments without reference also to the problems related to the Pentateuch, for there are some scholars who believe that the sources used in the first four or five books of the Bible actually continued and were used by compilers in the composition of the Former Prophets. This type of thinking was espoused by a number of older scholars but most scholars presently, however, upon closer examination do not find evidence that the J, E, and P sources continue beyond Joshua, if indeed even that far. There was, therefore, much talk earlier about the Hexateuch, a work which originally would have included the Torah plus Joshua. The reasoning was that when the Torah was considered to be authoritative, Joshua was then detached from it. But this theory left Deuteronomy which is quite different in sources and theology as an almost separate entity within the Pentateuch. How was one to explain this?

In 1943 a German scholar, Martin Noth, proposed a theory that has gained wide acceptance (though not universal acceptance). Noth proposed that Deuteronomy was simply the beginning of a larger work which began with Moses and continued through the fall of the southern kingdom of Judah, concluding with the people in exile in Babylon. These are the books of Deuteronomy, Joshua, Judges, Samuel, and Kings. He argued that the style and the religious teaching of all this material was so similar that it must have been the work of a person living in Palestine. The original work was much less full than it now is, however. Since there have been additional passages added to the original writing, there was a Deuteronomistic school which continued to edit and refine the material. This history then is known as the "Deuteronomistic History" and the person/persons who compiled the work as the Deuteronomistic Historian(s). Noth divided the work into basically four sections: the career of Moses; the time of the conquest; the era of the judges; and the period of the kings.

Many of Noth's specific points have been challenged and/or modified in the course of scholarly discussion and investigation. For example, most interpreters now think that the work was carried out in Babylon among the exiles instead of in Palestine. There are other scholars who have never been convinced that there ever was a unified literary history and therefore dispute the idea of the "Deuteronomistic History" as Noth proposed it. While there are problems to be resolved and scholars are still working on many aspects of this overall discussion, it does appear to be likely that the books from Deuteronomy through Kings (with the possible exception of Joshua) were originally intended as a unified history of the people of Israel from Moses to the exile and were written and/or edited from a particular theological viewpoint.

The assumption in this presentation of the material, therefore, will be that the books of Deuteronomy, Judges, Samuel, and Kings constituted at one time a "history" of the covenant people of God from the time of Moses to the middle of the Babylonian exile, at which point the work was probably compiled in something like its present form. Many scholars also include the book of Joshua in the Deuteronomistic History, but it is considered here to be the original conclusion to the Priestly composition, the Tetrateuch. When it was separated from that work, probably at the same time Deuteronomy was separated from the Deuteronomistic History, it was further edited by the Deuteronomistic Historians and substituted for the book of Deuteronomy as the introduction to the entire history. While any reconstruction of these matters is highly debated among Old Testament scholars, this theory explains many of the problems encountered with these writings, though by no means all.

The various sources used in the composition of the Deuteronomic history were varied and many. But again what these were originally, how they came into existence and why, how they were passed down through the years, and how, where, and why they reached the form (either written or oral) in which they were utilized by the Deuteronomistic Historians are all matters of high-level (and sometimes heated) debate. It is clear, however, that there were many different sources used and that several of these were written documents. The biblical texts themselves refer to such sources: the Book of Jasher (cf. Joshua 10:13 and 2 Samuel 1:18), perhaps a book of poetry; the Book of the Acts of Solomon (cf. 1 Kings 11:41); the Book of the Chronicles of the Kings of Israel (cf. 1 Kings 14:19 et al.); the Book of the Chronicles of the Kings of Judah (cf. 1 Kings 14:29 et al.). That there were many others becomes obvious to the careful reader of these accounts. There are lists of cities and territories, ancient poems, accounts and lists of judges, separate saga type stories (such as the Samson cycle), cycles of stories about Samuel, Saul, David, and the ark, old historical accounts such as the Succession History (cf. 2 Samuel 9—20, 1 Kings 1—2), and many others. More specific mention will be made of some of these at the appropriate points in the study of the individual books.

Suffice it to say at this point that during the exile of the Hebrew people in Babylonia there was considerable emphasis placed upon the effort to compile a history of that group. This was being done not simply to delineate an ancient story but to show in and through that story just how God's people were supposed to live and to demonstrate what happens when they do not live as they should. These "historical" works, therefore, were intended to challenge the people to become what God had intended them to be when he made the covenant with them long ago. The promise and the covenant obligations are both still valid—that is the message.

When turning to the books which are more popularly known as "prophetic" (i.e., Isaiah, Amos et al.), one encounters collections of sayings and narratives relating to certain individuals who felt "called" to be spokesmen for Yahweh. These are the writings designated as the "latter prophets." Early in Old Testament research these prophets were labeled "writing prophets" since books existed of their collected sayings along with accounts from their lives. But it was soon recognized that these curious but powerful men were not really writers but proclaimers. Therefore the books which are known by their names were not written down by them but are the products of a period of preservation of material related to their teachings and lives, the passing along of that material, and finally the collection and editing process which produced the books as they now exist.

The phenomenon of prophecy was not unique to Israel, but it was found in many of the cultures of the ancient world. There seem to have been at least two "types" of prophet, an ecstatic type frequently associated with the fertility cults and a "seer" type often connected with nomadic peoples. Some scholars have argued that these two types merged together to form the prophetic movement in Israel. That understanding, however, appears to be much too narrow, for many other elements are also involved in the distinctive makeup of the movement as it emerged and developed. There were elements of the priestly segment of Israel's life; in fact there are those who believe that the prophets, far from being the arch-enemies of the priests (an earlier theory relating to the two groups), were themselves priests and intimately associated with cultic practices. There also appear to be elements of the "wise men" and the wisdom movement and its teaching in the prophetic teaching.

The wisdom movement was present during this period of Israel's history even though its full flowering did not occur until later. Further, some prophets served as court counselors to the kings in the early days of Israel's history. All of these elements combined together at a precise moment of Israel's history to give rise to the prophetic movement. In fact, one sees very clearly in studying this phenomenon in Israel that the prophets came to the fore during the period of the Kingdom (both united and divided), but after the exile the movement gradually faded away. As with most of Israel's eras of religious development and understanding, this one too was historically conditioned.

As it became increasingly clear that the prophets were primarily proclaimers rather than writers, interpreters began to examine the prophetic oracles to ascertain what form these people utilized in the presentation of their messages. Originally it was suggested that the basic form of the prophetic oracle was the "threat" (the announcement of judgment on the people), closely followed by the reproach (the reason for the judgment). In addition to these basic forms were such others as exhortations, judicial challenges, dialogues, laments, and many more. More recent scholars have emphasized the importance of the form known as the "messenger formula" which developed two types of addresses, one a judgment speech against an individual, and secondly a judgment speech against a nation. As with most form-critical studies there are varied views as to the exact forms in which the prophetic oracles were delivered. Even more diversified are the theories as to the exact settings in which these messages were delivered originally.

There is no question that many types of material can be recognized among the prophetic collections. There are "call" stories, stories of visions and/or auditions, threats, stories about the prophets in either first or third person form, hymns, funeral dirges, drinking songs, taunt songs, stories which depict a "law-suit" against the people (usually designated as a *Rib)*, and even love songs. The categorization of all these elements is still being pursued, but there is no real unanimity of opinion in these areas.

As important as it is to recognize and study the individual forms of the prophetic material, however, it is even more important to attempt to deal with the biblical texts as they have been compiled and edited and passed along. It is generally agreed that initially the prophets delivered their messages orally. Then these sayings were remembered and passed along until they were written down. For example, one highly debated point in scholarly circles centers in the question of just how long it was before these materials were committed to writing. Some say very soon after they were delivered, while others argue that many years passed before this step was taken. Quite probably the answer is that in some instances (Jeremiah, for example) the prophetic teachings began to be written down even during the lifetime of the prophet, but in other instances the material was passed along in oral form for lengthy periods before being committed to writing.

Who preserved these sayings? Some have conjectured that priests at various sanctuaries preserved the material. Others argue for "schools" of disciples of the prophetic personages who learned the teachings of the "master" and then preserved the data from generation to generation in oral form, a practice that was not at all unusual for those people in that period of history. As the historical circumstances changed, the material was applied to new situations which process could have modified the sayings somewhat. Finally, these materials were edited together into the books which are now known to us as the collection of sayings and incidents of the life of each individual prophet.

Whatever theory one finds most congenial, it is clear that these prophetic personalities exerted enormous influence over their disciples and eventually over the development and course of Hebrew religion.

Joshua

Whether the book of Joshua is to be considered as the last book of a Hexateuch, or as the beginning of the actual "history" in the Deuteronomic History, or as the culmination of the Tetrateuch, or as simply an isolated work which ultimately became connected with other works to form a history of the Hebrew people and nation until the exile is still highly debated among Old Testament scholars. Each of these conjectures remains a possibility, but it seems very likely that the book itself should be understood as the final section of the larger work which began with Genesis, continued through Numbers, and culminated with the taking and division of the land in Joshua. The reasons for this view are several: the fact that many scholars still distinguish the continuation of the Tetrateuchal sources (J, E, P) in the book of Joshua; the finalization of the promise of a land made in Genesis to the patriarchs is completed here and the emphasis on covenant and covenant renewal found in the Tetrateuch seems to reach a natural conclusion in the final chapters of the book of Joshua.

Historically speaking, one of the chief problems which scholars have wrestled with for many years concerns the question as to why the book of Joshua depicts a unified, militaristic invasion of the land with great successes which culminated in the wrestling of the area from the Canaanites, while the book of Judges depicts a slow and painstaking settlement which only gradually led to the establishment of a nation. Earlier interpreters quite frequently understood Joshua to be the "idealized" portrait of the settlement and Judges to be the more "realistic" view. It appears, however, that the issue is more closely related to literary and religious motifs than to psychological or historical reasonings. The book of Joshua appears to be composed of some ancient sources many of which still carry the aetiological explanations so characteristic of the older source-strata already encountered in the Tetrateuch. And these traditions were edited together in such a way as to demonstrate that Yahweh keeps his promises to the people. This is the religious thesis of the book.

One of the major problems which is encountered in the study of this book, however, lies in the arena of archaeology. Joshua tells about the invasion of the land, battles with its inhabitants, and victories at various ancient cities. Archaeologists have found, however, that many of the sites described as having been destroyed in the invasion of those who came from the Exodus (dated ca. 1250 B.C.) had been destroyed much earlier. Jericho and Ai, for example, were simply not in existence at this time. Other cities mentioned in the account (such as Hazor and Bethel) were, and show definite signs of having been destroyed during this particular period of history. But some of the archaeological findings indicate that not all the cities which appear to have been destroyed during this time were destroyed by people like the Hebrews. The uncertainty of the archaeological evidence when compared with the stories of Joshua constitute, therefore, a puzzle.

The probable answer to this puzzle perhaps lies in the Hebrew tendency to telescope and concretize events, movements, motifs, etc., in one person or one era. What has probably happened is that ancient traditions concerning the taking of certain areas and cities over a long period of time and by all the groups which finally became Israel have been telescoped into the period immediately following the Exodus and concretized in the "unified" campaigns of one of the great leaders of Hebrew history, Joshua. This "telescoping" process definitely served a literary and religious purpose but not a historical one (in the absolute sense), but such a method of approaching history was so typical of the Hebrew culture and mind-set that it seems clear that something like this occurred with these traditions also, being finalized in literary form in the book of Joshua.

It appears likely from reading the text of Joshua that this work was edited and redacted at a time when the "all Israel" motif had become a fixture in the thinking of the Hebrew people. This motif is simply the result of assimilating all the old disparate and separate traditions from the various entities which finally came together as Israel and fusing them together into a tradition in which the people were depicted as having all come from the same background. This process has already been noted with the traditions of the Tetrateuch especially with the patriarchal traditions of Genesis.

Turning again to a cultural phenomenon, one notes that there is in this collection of stories an emphasis upon the concept of holy war. This idea was quite prevalent in the Semitic world and was characterized by the thought that the god of the tribe or nation had directed the people to fight or that the people had gone out to fight and, to insure victory, had dedicated the war to the god. In either case the god was supposed to grant victory to the people, and in turn the victorious people were to dedicate all that was conquered to the god, killing all the conquered people and burning all the material possessions. This sacrifice of the spoils is usually known as being "under the ban" *herem* or ("devoted" to the god). When this requirement was not carried out, it was viewed as a serious transgression which caused severe consequences.

One further problem should be addressed, and this relates to the background and dates of the major sources or portions of sources for the book of Joshua. Much debate continues about this matter, but it is generally agreed among Old Testament scholars that the basic material found in chapters 2—9 related to the tribe of Benjamin and was in all probability originally preserved at the shrine at Gilgal. In addition the material contained in chapters 13—21 which contains lists of various kinds may be, in part at least, older than earlier scholarship had assumed. In these chapters there is the listing of towns, but some believe that this listing refers to administrative districts which were in effect during the reign of Josiah. The second listing is called the "boundary" lists, and many scholars now believe that these lists could well be traced back to the actual period of the judges.

It should be kept in mind that whatever the sources and origin of the book, the writing has undergone a very thorough editing from the Deuteronomic traditions.

Joshua: Outline

   I. Stories About the Conquest 1—12
  II. The Division of the Land 13—21
 III. Conclusion and Covenant Renewal 22—24

As one reads this collection of stories, it becomes evident that one of the chief features of the book lies in the area of aetiology and how the elements in the story directly relate to the religion of the people. This is most clearly seen in the story of the crossing of the Jordan and the erection of a memorial built of stones (where the memorial was built seems to have been something of a problem, cf. 4:3–4; 4:9; 4:19–20). The purpose of the stones was to cause the children to ask, "What do these stones mean to you?" (4:6). The answer was to be given in terms of the recalling of the crossing of the Jordan (4:7) or the remembrance of the deliverance at the sea when the people had escaped from Egypt (4:23).

One of the most familiar of the stories in Joshua is that of the taking of Jericho, but quite frequently the motif of holy war in that story is ignored. All Jericho was destroyed (cf. 6:21), but when Israel went out to fight again they were defeated. It was learned that someone had not been faithful to the *herem* obligation and had kept part of the spoils (7:1). The culprit was found to be a person named Achan, and he and his entire family were stoned to death. The story vividly illustrates how apostasy caused problems for God's people. Even here, however, the aetiological motif is still quite prominent, for this story seems to explain a great mound of stones and the name of the valley, the Valley of Achor (Trouble).

One other incident should be examined, again partly because it is so well-known and probably misunderstood. This concerns the battle which the people of Israel had with the coalition of five kings who had joined together to fight against the Gibeonites who had (by trickery) made a covenant with the Hebrews. When the Gibeonites learned of the attack, they sent word to Joshua to come to their aid. This he did and the coalition was defeated. The interesting feature is that more light hours were needed to complete the victory; this need was expressed in the poetic lines calling upon the sun and the moon for assistance (10:12b–13a). Most scholars are agreed that the composition came from some type of poetic epic. The poetry here simply states that the sun and moon cooperated. It is interesting to note that a later prose writer or editor had heightened this poetic account into a stupendous miracle which it originally was not understood to be except at the point of Joshua's great victory—miracle enough!

After having fought in the central and southern areas, the scene shifts to the northern part of Palestine which the book of Joshua also depicted as having been conquered by the people of God. This portion of Joshua concludes with the glowing report of how the great leader, Joshua, empowered by the hand of God, had been able to take the "whole land" (11:23a). Chapter 12 summarizes all that has happened to this point.

The second section of the book, chapters 13—22, contains a collection of lists which include tribal boundary lists, town lists, lists of cities of refuge, and lists of settlements for the Levites. As already noted, these lists probably came from various moments in Israel's history. The oldest may be the enumeration of the cities of refuge, places where someone could seek asylum from an "avenger." The concept of the *go'el,* or avenger originated in very ancient times. When someone was killed or wronged or slandered, it was the duty of a kinsman to avenge the death or wrong done to the person. These cities of refuge provided a place of haven for persons who had killed someone accidentally.

Finally, the last two chapters of the book of Joshua contain speeches by Joshua challenging the people to keep the covenant. Chapter 23 seems to be the work of a Deuteronomic editor, while chapter 24 appears to have been originally a part of the older Pentateuchal traditions but edited somewhat by a Deuteronomic redactor. This second account in chapter 24 depicts a covenant-renewal ceremony which Joshua initiated with the people. The setting for this was Shechem, one of the oldest religious centers in the land. Many scholars feel confident that this tradition does in fact describe an old ceremony related to the establishment or renewal of an ancient covenant.

There are a number of important elements to be noted in this passage. This episode seems to represent a formal covenant renewal which took place in ancient Israel and which bound the divergent groups into a form of loose confederacy or coalition. Such a group is called an amphictyony. The basic motif in an amphictyony was that some common concern (usually religious in nature) would bind the various groups together, in this case a common allegiance to their God, Yahweh. Another feature of such an agreement was that if any one of the groups should ever need assistance, the others would be bound to come to its aid. Many scholars feel that just such a loosely-knit arrangement evolved after the tribes had "officially" settled in Canaan and had begun to develop closer relationships with other peoples of similar need and outlook.

A second feature of this ceremony centers in the challenge to the people to put away all the other gods which they had previously known and worshiped. Connected with this is the probability that in this ceremony there was a broadening of the concept relating to the covenant people which provided now for the inclusion of others who had not previously belonged to the group.

One of the key elements in this entire story, however, seems to be the solemnity and depth of challenge associated with this covenant. Yahweh was presented not as just another god, but a God who demands that the people obey and keep the covenant. If they would not, serious consequences will definitely result (24:19ff.). Yahweh was not a God who could be controlled or manipulated, a God who acted without thought or reason. Yahweh was a God different from and more awesome than any others!

Thus the story begun with the promise made to the patriarchs had come to a close. The people were settled in the land, and this stage of their history was now complete.

Judges

In contrast with the book of Joshua which depicts the settlement of the people in the land of Canaan as rapid and unified and basically complete, the book of Judges depicts the settlement as slow, basically localized in separate areas emphasizing individual tribes rather than the "whole" people, and this process of settlement was far from complete. This book was probably originally the second segment of the Deuteronomic History which began with Deuteronomy and which continued through Kings.

It is generally conceded by most scholars that the book of Judges contains some very ancient traditions, some of which may have been collected together before the Deuteronomistic Historians utilized them in their writing. Other sources seem to be separate entities, similar to the sagas of Genesis (e.g., the Samson narrative), and brought together by these later editors in an attempt to illustrate God's dealing with his people. Whatever the exact origin of these various traditions, it is clear that they have been used and edited and placed into a theological framework by the Deuteronomistic Historians. The structure of apostasy—judgment—repentance—deliverance can be recognized quite easily in this book.

One problem which has puzzled interpreters of the book revolves around the figure of the "judge." Just what kind of office or function did the judge have? What kind of person was the judge and how was he elected? No real certainty can be assured with regard to the questions, but several theories (naturally) abound. Some think that the office of judge was that of a local person of authority who interpreted the laws for the clan or tribe and who when necessary led or commanded the group in war. This type of office would have been required almost anywhere since order and authority have to be exercised by someone to insure the well-being of the group. Others feel that the judge was basically a charismatic military leader who only appeared on the scene when the situation called for such a person to lead the people against oppressors. Still others argue for both types being existent in ancient Israel.

In the book of Judges itself there are some judges who are simply listed by name with the only identification being given as where he was judge and where he was buried. These people seem to have been usually associated with a specific place and are usually designated "minor" judges. There are others whose exploits are much more fully recounted and who are called "major" judges. Some scholars have identified the minor judges with the local leaders and the major judges with the more charismatic and dramatic types. Whether this is absolutely correct cannot be determined, but it is clear that the office of "judge" probably incorporated several types of duties, tasks, and responsibilities.

The artificial structure of the book of Judges is typically Deuteronomistic and quite easily distinguishable. The people sin; God sends oppressors as punishment for their apostasy; the people repent; God sends deliverers to release them from their judgment. The cycle occurs very frequently, and each episode concludes with the formula, "And the land had rest for forty (or eighty) years." One recalls that the number "forty" is only a general designation for a long period of time. This, naturally, makes it impossible to structure any kind of chronological system from the material contained in Judges, though many still attempt to do so.

One of the main themes of this book concerns the emphasis upon loyalty to Yahweh alone, but the historical pressures which the people were subjected to by their neighbors led some of them to the conclusion that what they really needed was a king. This situation became very acute later in the period with the establishment of a strong group of people along the coast who were known as the Philistines. These people had probably come from somewhere in or around Greece during the latter part of the thirteenth century B.C. through Palestine and into Egypt. The Egyptians referred to them as the "Sea Peoples" and repelled them (ca. 1175 B.C.). At that point they settled along the coast lands of Palestine, their society centering in five major cities (Ashod, Ashkelon, Ekron, Gaza, and Gath). Since these people were culturally superior to the Hebrews and most of the Canaanites at that time, they naturally exercised a great degree of influence in the area. One of their chief means for maintaining superiority was their ability with making iron implements, and they forbade the Hebrews to do so.

The threat from this new group of people to the Hebrews was very real. Many began to understand that if Israel was to be able to stand free in the face of the Philistine menace, she must be united and strengthened. This could be done, they reasoned, only through a strong central government under a king. This view, however, was challenged by a large and obviously influential segment of Israel. To their way of thinking to have a king was to commit an act of idolatry; Yahweh was to be the only king for Israel. Older scholarship tended to think of the pro-monarchial material in the Deuteronomistic History as reflecting the older more ancient traditions, while the anti-monarchial material reflected a later interpretation which had developed after it was seen what kings could do; this latter view basically presented a negative view of kingship "after the fact." It is, however, much more reasonable to believe that both currents of thought were present in the period under consideration. The materials preserved in the Judges seem to reflect both motifs quite realistically.

Some scholars argue that the book of Judges may well have concluded originally with the material found in the Samson saga. This cycle of stories seems to have been originally a separate collection dealing with a local hero who had fought with some success against the Philistines. Some scholars find in the episodes dealing with Samson a connection with mythological stories relating to sun worship, and some striking points have been noted. It is much more likely, however, that this cycle centering in the figure of Samson is simply a collection of stories about a local hero. One notes that Samson is not called a judge but rather he is identified as a *Nazirite*. This designation describes a special group of persons who were dedicated to God for a prescribed period of time. Some Nazirite "vows" seem to have been for one's entire lifetime, and some seem to indicate service for only a short period of time. Whatever the length of time involved, it was incumbent upon the person taking the Nazirite vow to abstain from eating or drinking anything connected with the "fruit of the vine," and it was further understood that one's hair was not to be cut (cf. Numbers 6:1–21). A Nazirite's life was to be dedicated to the service of Yahweh. Samson was supposed to have been a Nazirite for his entire lifetime, but the stories demonstrate just how "human" he was. Interestingly enough, the life of Samson is quite Deuteronomistic in its cycles.

The final two episodes which conclude the book of Judges as it now stands relate the story of the movement of the tribe of Dan from the coastal area to the northern section of the land (17—18) and a story about a shameful act by the members of the tribe of Benjamin (19—21). The probable intent of the inclusion of these stories at this point in the Deuteronomistic History was to emphasize the weakness and anarchy affecting the people of Israel without strong leadership. These stories depicting political weakness and moral bankruptcy served as a strong foundation for the recurring theme, "In those days there was no king in Israel; every man did what was right in his own eyes" (cf. 18:1; 21:15).

Such stories demonstrated the reason why there was a strong movement toward the establishment of a monarchy in Israel. Political weakness, economic instability, and immoral behavior had led to chaos and anarchy. Something had to be done to remedy the situation.

Judges: Outline

    I. Introduction 1:1—2:15
   II. The Activities of the Judges 2:16—12:15
  III. The Samson Story 13—16
  IV. Two Appendices
      A. The Story of the Tribe of Dan 17—18
      B. Problems in Benjamin 19—21

The book of Judges begins with a brief recapitulation dealing with the settlement in the land which reflects a quite different situation from that which was found in the book of Joshua. It is stated very straightforwardly that the people of Israel did not drive out all the inhabitants and did not conquer all that they would have liked. Further, the scene is set for a story in which the people of God are not depicted in the best possible light (cf. 2:11ff.). They were far from loyal and faithful to Yahweh, and in fact quite frequently openly worshiped Baal!

One of the most interesting of all the traditions included in this book is an old poetic work usually called the "Song of Deborah" (chapter 5). This may be the oldest piece of Hebrew literature of any length in the entire Old Testament. Some argue that it also reflects a cultic and liturgical background and may have been part of some type of covenant festival, but it appears more likely to be an ancient poem which reflects upon the events which it attempts to describe.

Both chapters 4 and 5 deal with this circumstance where two tribes (Naphtali and Zebulun) fought in the region of the Plain of Esdraelon against a Canaanite group which was a source of oppression for the Hebrew people in this area. According to the ideals of the amphictyony the other tribes were supposed to assist them. Many did not. The charismatic leader who inspired the people for battle was Deborah, called both a prophetess and a judge. The victory was won, the people being greatly assisted by some sort of rainstorm. The leader of the Canaanite forces, Sisera, fled from the battle and came to the tent of a woman named Jael, the wife of a Kenite (one is reminded again of the constant references to "Kenites" in the older biblical traditions). According to the prose account of chapter 4 Jael gave the man food and drink which caused him to relax (one recalls the regulations regarding hospitality here). After he had gone to sleep Jael drove a tent peg through his head.

The old "Song of Deborah" recounts in poetic style the victory over the Canaanites on that occasion and also the courage of Jael who risked the consequences for breaking the taboo associated with hospitality in order to aid the Israelites. The poem also reflects the chaotic and anarchic state of affairs which existed sociologically at that time (cf. 5:6–7); certain tribes were chastised for not responding to the call to assist their kinsmen (5:15b–17). The description of Jael's murder of Sisera is a bit different in the poem, indicating that Sisera was still standing rather than asleep when she hit him in the head. The piece culminates in a typical literary type found in such settings, a taunt song (5:28–30). And the entire work concludes with a condemnation of all Yahweh's enemies!

Following this episode one finds a lengthy story about Gideon (another local hero) who delivered the people, and also about Gideon's son, Abimelech, who made an unsuccessful attempt to be king. Gideon was also known as Jerubbaal—the latter name reflecting the way in which the newer Hebrew peoples were becoming socially acclimated to their new environment. It is interesting to note that the later explanation of the Baal name attempts to explain this fact away (cf. 6:32).

After Gideon had delivered the people from the danger, there was a movement to make him king (8:22). Gideon, however, flatly declined the offer, pointing out that only Yahweh was to rule over them (8:23). His son, Abimelech, was not so shy about wanting to be king and encouraged the people at Shechem to proclaim him as such. He is supposed to have killed all his brothers except one (a very large number, 9:5) and to have ruled for a brief period. There were rebellions against him, and he was finally killed at Thebez. A woman dropped a large millstone upon his head, thereby crushing his skull but he asked his armor-bearer to kill him with a sword so that it would not be known that a woman had killed him!

The Samson stories are delightful stories which constitute a hero-saga about a man who was as much a man-of-the-world practical joker as he was a serious religious or political personage. There are many mysteries and problems surrounding the stories themselves and the reason why the Deuteronomistic Historians incorporated them here. It seems clear that one of the primary reasons was to present the Philistine threat to the existence of the people of Israel, thus laying the groundwork for the selection of a king as a response to that threat.

The last two episodes (17—18; 19—21) reflect the need for strong leadership in Israel since things were simply in a state of anarchy. As one reads, the tension of the sources becomes clear: Israel should have no king but Yahweh—but a king was needed to insure the continued existence of the people by giving some form of stability to their society and by making them militarily strong.

The Books of Samuel

Originally the two books of Samuel were probably a part of the larger Deuteronomistic History work. Later, when the work was divided into books, the books of Samuel were considered to be only one book. When the Greek translation of the Hebrew Scriptures (the Septuagint) was completed, the books of Samuel and Kings were divided into four separate books called the "Books of Kingdoms." The division of the two books, which are now known as 1 and 2 Samuel and 1 and 2 Kings, came about at the time of the Septuagint (ca. 200–100 B.C.), but the first two had come to be associated with the figure of Samuel. Some obviously felt that Samuel wrote these two books, while others perhaps understood and recognized that Samuel's influence was very effective during this particular period of Hebrew history.

It is obvious to the reader of these writings that they were, in fact, intended to be a natural sequel to the book of Judges. The way had been prepared with the references to the Philistine threat, the discussion about the wisdom of having a king, and the general situation current among the Israelite tribes at that time. The book(s) of Samuel then is the logical and sequential continuation of the story of the history of the people in Canaan.

There were, obviously, many different sources which were utilized by the editors and writers of this work. Some were probably written; others were oral. Some were local and separate; others were probably more inclusive and continuous. The scholarly debate over these matters is, as one can imagine, quite vigorous and wide-ranging. Most scholars agree that several sources were used by the Deuteronomic authors. One of these is found in 1 Samuel 4—6 and 2 Samuel 6 and is a narrative dealing with the ark. Many believe that this tradition originated in and was passed along by those who were involved most directly with the cultus.

There is also a source which seems to be directly related to the person of Saul and how he rose to a position of leadership in Israel. Most connect 1 Samuel 9:1—10:16; 11; 13; 14 with this source. Interwoven with this source and story can be detected another with a different emphasis, i.e., 1 Samuel 8; 10:17–27. The first source is more positive toward Saul and the idea of kingship, while the second is much more negative in its approach.

Naturally there were traditions which told of the rise of David to a position of power and popularity. Most of these stories are contained in 1 Samuel 16:14—2 Samuel 5. It is interesting to note that the stories, while obviously very positive toward David, do not really attempt to hide his faults.

Another source contains an account of the intrigues and subterfuge that were attendant to the succession to the throne after David. This report is found in 2 Samuel 9—20 and 1 Kings 1—2. It is known as the "Court History of David" or, perhaps more appropriately, the

"Succession History." Many have argued that this work appears to have been written by an eyewitness and that it is perhaps the oldest piece of historical writing of any length which is known. Whether these conjectures can be substantiated may be debated, but there is probably no question as to the approximate date (very close to the events described) and significance of the writing. As with every writing in the Old Testament, however, this one is certainly not devoid of religious and theological orientation and intepretation.

Numerous other smaller units were incorporated also into this historical retelling of the establishment into a United Kingdom of the Israelite people. Since there are numerous doublets, there must have been various traditions which were merged into the one story. It was under the genius of David, however, that the unification of these diverse groups was accomplished. Partly by brilliance, partly by sheer good fortune, and partly by shabby political expediency and at times even immorality, David built a United Kingdom of north and south. The dates for the years of Saul are usually agreed to be ca. 1020–1000 B.C., and for David, ca. 1000–961 B.C.

The Books of Samuel: Outline

1 Samuel
- I. Stories Revolving Around Samuel 1—7
  - A. Samuel's Early Years 1—3
  - B. Stories About the Ark 4—6
  - C. Samuel and the Philistines 7
- II. Samuel and Saul 8—15
  - A. The Selection of Saul to Be King 8—11
  - B. Samuel's Farewell Address 12
  - C. The Wars of Saul 13—14
  - D. Samuel's Rejection of Saul 15
- III. Stories About Saul and David 16—31
  - A. David at Saul's Court 16—20
  - B. David as a Mercenary 21—27
  - C. Saul and the Witch of En-dor 28
  - D. David Established in the South 29—30
  - E. Saul's Death 31

2 Samuel

The books of Samuel begin with an account of the birth and development of Samuel. His mother, Hannah, was childless (considered a great disgrace and shame in those days) and prayed very hard for a child, even agreeing to dedicate him to Yahweh as a Nazirite for his entire life. The prayer was heard and while he was yet very young, Samuel was given to the priest, Eli, to be reared at the central shrine then located at Shiloh. Since Eli's sons were not properly behaved to be priests, they were rejected from succeeding their father in the office. This emphasis is quite Deuteronomic.

The person of Samuel is interesting to examine. He was dedicated as a Nazirite by his mother, trained as a priest, called by Yahweh to be a prophetic type person (cf. 1 Samuel 3:13ff.), and functioned at times as a judge! He is truly a transition figure in the history of Israel and certainly exercised considerable authority and power.

At this point in the narrative the reader is reminded about the Philistine menace through the stories connected with the ark. The Philistines were triumphant over Israel even though the ark had been brought into the camp of the Israelite soldiers (one is reminded again of the holy war motif). Israel was defeated, however, and the ark captured by the Philistines who for some reason did not destroy *the* religious standard of Israel. Rather they carried it to their own cities, but strange events began to happen. They were engulfed in a plague (probably a form of the bubonic plague) which they (and the Deuteronomic editors) were convinced had come from the presence of Yahweh among them. Whereupon, the Philistines decided to return the ark to Israel, and they did exactly that with great care and precision (cf. 1 Samuel 6:1—7:2).

It is interesting to note that the ark was returned along with golden images of tumors and rats. The bubonic plague is carried by the fleas on rats and the sending of the images was probably a form of sympathetic magic designed to insure that both the rats and the plague, having been sent away, would stay away. The fact that the ark was not returned to Shiloh has led some to think that Shiloh had been destroyed by the Philistines. Though this is possible the archaeological evidence reveals that Shiloh may not have been destroyed until ca. 600 B.C. (the prophet Jeremiah refers to the destruction of Shiloh, cf. Jeremiah 7:12f.).

At this point in the narrative, the historical situation of Israel looked grim. Even though under the leadership of Samuel (in his capacity as "judge" at this point) there was some respite from the Philistine threat, it was obvious that something had to be done to counter the Philistines. The solution—a king. This is what the narrative has been leading toward since the beginning of the Deuteronomistic History.

As already noted there are two accounts of Saul's being appointed king. In chapter 8 the people asked Samuel to give them a king. This request was viewed here as a rejection of Yahweh as their king (1 Samuel 8:7), but nevertheless Saul was chosen by lot to be king (1 Samuel 10:17–27). In chapter 9, however, there is a different version. Here Samuel is portrayed as a local "seer," somewhat akin to a clairvoyant, who was sought out by Saul to assist him in locating his father's lost livestock. At this point Samuel was commanded *by Yahweh* to anoint this man Saul to be "prince" over Israel (1 Samuel 9:16). Anointing carried in those days a very special significance indicating that the person thus designated had a special duty to perform on behalf of God and the people of God. Kings, priests, and perhaps sometimes prophets were among those who were anointed. It is of some significance to note here that the term in Hebrew for "anoint" is *msh* from which comes the well known word, Messiah, "anointed one."

No matter which account one follows the issue was certain—Saul had become the leader of the largest unified group in Israel until this time. And obviously his efforts met with some, though not total, success. The accounts which tell of Saul and his exploits are basically unsympathetic to the man. Even though he did some very positive things such as to encourage Yahweh worship and to purge that worship of some unsavory elements (i.e., divination, etc.), Saul was in the eyes of the

Deuteronomic editors basically sinful. There were two incidents which were highlighted to serve as illustrative of Saul's deficiencies.

First, there was the incident at Gilgal where Saul had gathered the troops from various places to lead them in battle. He was supposed to wait for Samuel who was to preside over a sacrifice for what was obviously a holy war type military engagement. When Samuel did not appear by the appointed time and when his troops began to leave, Saul presided over the sacrifice himself. Samuel finally arrived and was furious because (in Israelite tradition) the king was not supposed to be allowed to perform priestly functions.

The second incident also occurred at Gilgal. As one recalls, in holy war all the spoils and captives were to be put "under the ban," i.e., they were to be totally destroyed in dedication to the god who had given the victory. After defeating the Amalekites, Saul did not follow through on that custom, believing that the animals and even the ruler (Agag) could be of more value if kept for some future use. When Samuel came and found the animals and Agag, however, he again was beside himself. One simply could not disobey the commands of God! Therefore Samuel himself ". . . hewed Agag into pieces before Yahweh in Gilgal" (1 Samuel 15:34b)! Samuel had come to the conclusion that Saul could not be the king who was to bring God's people together and win a victory over their enemies.

There are many moderns who become concerned with such passages as the one just mentioned. How could God, they argue, ever command the needless slaughter and destruction described in these stories? One must remember that the world of that day and the world of today are very different culturally, religiously, politically, and scientifically. Their thought world is far from ours, and therefore it is very hard to understand such actions from our perspective. If one attempts to understand the stories from their perspective, however, more intelligent use can be made of the accounts. One of the major themes one encounters in the development of Old Testament religious ideas is the recurring revelation that Yahweh, God of Israel, was different from the other gods. What the people of those times considered to be in keeping with the will of the gods was not always accepted as the command of Yahweh. Some ideas thought to be Yahweh's will were even rejected! Under normal circumstances, however, it was understood that one should be completely obedient to Yahweh; if a certain action was what any god might require, then that action was normally carried out. The fact that some of these old ideas were culturally conditioned would not have occurred to them. Later as they learned more about the nature of this Yahweh, there were many things which the peole had thought were required to be done or not done which they realized they were mistaken about. The realization that Yahweh did not require the sacrifice of the firstborn child or the slaughter of all enemies and their possessions are just two examples of this type of "developing" understanding.

At this juncture in the Samuel narrative David enters the picture. He is first of all a soldier in Saul's army who distinguished himself in battle. Whether he actually killed Goliath (one of his most famous exploits) is not certain. In 1 Samuel 17 it is David who does the deed, but in 2 Samuel 21:19 it is reported that Goliath was killed by one of David's soldiers, Elhanan.

David had become very popular with the people. His reputation as a great warrior and leader was known throughout the area. The account depicts Saul as becoming jealous and attempting to arrange for David to be killed while collecting a dowry for the purpose of marrying Saul's daughter, Michal (cf. 1 Samuel 18:20–29). When David succeeded in this endeavor, however, and was married to the girl, this did not negate the bitter feelings between the two. The situation became so bad that David became a fugitive mercenary who at times allied himself with the Philistines!

As the conclusion to Saul's life comes rapidly to a climax, there is an unusual story inserted into the narrative. This story relates how Saul, when he could receive no direction from any source available to him, consulted a medium (which practice he had outlawed) to conjure up Samuel, since he believed that Samuel would know God's will and purpose and be willing to declare it to him directly. These passages are difficult to translate and therefore it is difficult to understand this account clearly, but several points can be noted with some interest. There is clear evidence that Saul had indeed outlawed such activity in Israel indicating his efforts to purify the land of certain unsavory practices. Further, there is the implication that when the woman knew that Samuel was the one Saul wanted to see, she realized that this person must be

Saul in disguise. There is also the interesting implication that Saul did not see the apparition; only the woman did. Also involved is the curious wording used to describe the "shade" of Samuel; it is called *elohim*, "god" or "gods." Whether this description refers to some concept unknown to us or to the "spiritlike" quality of the apparition cannot be determined with certainty. Finally, note with interest the utter shock and surprise of the woman when Samuel really did appear! This element may have been included in the story for the purpose of raising a question about the validity of what the woman was doing. The fact that she was supposed to be able to communicate with the dead did not really mean that she could. Thus when Samuel appeared, she was astonished!

Saul, after hearing his fate, nevertheless went out to meet it. The story of Saul is very similar in many respects to a Greek tragedy with Saul as the tragic hero. He was killed fighting the Philistines, and it can be noted that some of his people were committed enough to him to risk their lives to rescue his body and the bodies of his sons from the walls of Beth-shan in order to give them proper burial, a most important matter to people of those times and even today.

The death of Saul opened the way, however, for David to become king. He had been allied and joined with the Philistines but did not take part in the battle against Saul, because the Philistines did not trust him. A fortuitous sequence of events occurred which together made it possible for David to become king and yet come out of the dubious situation "smelling like a rose." The sequence of events went something like this: Saul and most of his sons had been killed in battle, leaving the people without authorized leadership. David was then proclaimed king in the south at Hebron. Abner, who was the chief of Saul's army, exercised political authority on behalf of Ishbosheth, Saul's son, in the north. Abner was then treacherously slain by Joab, David's Chief of the Military, with David making a great display of concern over Abner's death. David has Michal, his first wife and daughter of Saul, brought back to him even though she had remarried and was quite happy where she was (2 Samuel 3:13–16), thus giving him another claim to kingship. Saul's remaining descendants, who could claim the throne, were slain, with David again lamenting their death. All these actions took place rather quickly, and all of them together presented David with an even stronger claim to rule over Israel. Finally, the people of Israel came to David at

Hebron asking that he become king over them. Having made the necessary agreements, David became king over all Israel. Thus the United
Monarchy began (ca. 993 B.C.).

Shortly after these intriguing events, David accomplished a stunning
military victory by taking one of the old Canaanite cities which had not
been captured by the Hebrew invaders, the city of Jerusalem. Then he
made a shrewd political maneuver; he established the new capital of the .
united peoples at Jerusalem and had the ark brought there so that Jerusalem became both the political and religious center for the new nation.
It was basically a neutral site from the standpoint of both the northern
and southern tribes and was a very easy city to defend against attack.
This maneuver was very helpful in the development of the United
Kingdom, and Jerusalem has been an important city ever since.

This brings the reader to an account in the Samuel narrative which
has been much researched of late, i.e., the promise to David of a dynasty
to follow him and to rule over the people "for ever" (cf. 2 Samuel
7:4–17). There are a number of interpreters who see in this account the
beginning of a second major theme in Old Testament understanding and
history, i.e., that of the making of a David-Zion covenant motif based
upon the promise of God alone. This motif is frequently contrasted with
the Moses-Sinai theme which is understood to have been centered in the
old federation concepts and which required obedience from the people
in order to be valid. There are some scholars who see in these two
contrasting themes the basis for a struggle between the factions for
supremacy within the confines of the development of the religion of
Israel.

A hope and belief based upon the promises of God is definitely
within the stories dealing with the Davidic dynasty and the city of
Jerusalem. Whether the interpretation that these promises carried *no*
obligations and could *never* be abrogated no matter what kind of actions
the king and the people might take is valid is another matter. It is of some
importance to note that this dynastic promise to David is found in the
midst of the Deuteronomic History which has as its chief theological
motif the judgment of God upon those who refuse to do Yahweh's will!
While the history itself was written within the time of the exile with the
Hebrew people looking forward to restoration in the land of Judah with
a new king of David's line (probably), it is also true that the Deu-

teronomic interpretation was that the sins of the king and the people had caused the kingdom to be divided, the majority to be exiled and lost in other lands and the southern minority to be languishing in exile in Babylonia. This is not exactly promise without proper response.

Another aspect of this discussion deserves some attention also. This revolves around the question as to whether there is in the Old Testament a concept of "for ever" in the Greek or modern sense of the term. The word underlying this translation is the Hebrew *'olam* which means literally "an age," or a specified period of time. The term, *l^e 'olam*, "to the age," is sometimes translated and understood as "for ever," but there is enough question here to warrant some degree of caution. This phrase is used of coming to the end of a period of history or of living out one's lifespan to the full, neither carrying the idea of "eternity," only indicating a long and sometimes determined period of time. It is quite possible that the establishment of the house of David, recorded as it is in 2 Samuel 7, and promised to be "for ever" may just indicate a long period of time, i.e., until its days are completed. This is quite a different understanding than that which would see in this a promise with little or no obligation and forcing a meaning onto a Hebrew term which it does not usually bear. It is interesting also to note that the reference in the passage to David's house could be understood as a reference only to his successor, Solomon. However one wishes to interpret this chapter, as unconditional promise or otherwise, it was understood to be of great significance within the history of the Hebrew nation. The passage does contain a promise to the house of David, but the Deuteronomic challenge to be faithful and loyal—or else—seems still to be a part of the picture as well.

There is one other feature of Old Testament studies which is frequently discussed along with this passage. This debate revolves around the question of whether there was in Israel an enthronement festival each year in honor of the God but for the purpose of reaffirming the king, declaring him to be the "son of God," and attached to some sort of atonement ritual usually celebrated at the time of the New Year. Such ceremonies were part of the culture of the ancient world. There are many who believe that such a ceremony existed in Israel also, but many others find the elaborate theories connected with such a concept little supported by the evidence which can be gleaned from the Old Testament writings themselves. It appears logical that there would indeed be a certain ritual and festival attached to the ascension of a new king to the throne, but whether that would be annually repeated can be doubted. Certain aspects of an enthronement festival do seem to be indicated in certain psalms (cf. Psalms 2; 132; also 47; 93; 96—99) and in this particular segment of 2 Samuel.

With the establishment of David's house as the political authority in the land, the Deuteronomistic Historians then incorporated the larger source-strata usually called the "Succession History" (2 Samuel 9—20; 1 Kings 1—2) into the continuing account. This piece of writing does not place David in the best possible light, to say the least! Most of these earlier sources do not, but later as time went on there was a decided movement to idealize David and look upon him as the epitome of rectitude and uprightness.

There are those who would begin the "Succession History" with chapter 7, but most scholars still prefer to regard chapter 9 as the starting point. David is shown being quite friendly to the last heir of Saul's household, a crippled son of his friend Jonathan, but where better to keep the only person around whom a coup might form than in one's very house? The famous or infamous Bathsheba affair shows David in an exceedingly bad light. Not only did he take someone else's wife (adultery) and have sexual relations with her while she was yet unpurified from her menstrual period, but he tried to cause Uriah to break his vow relating to holy war and ultimately had Uriah murdered. This is not exactly the image of moral rectitude! Nathan delivered the Deuteronomic judgment on these actions with his moving story of the poor man and his pet lamb (12:1–7a).

The intrigue and turmoil which then began within David's family is told quickly and matter-of-factly. Amnon, David's son, rapes his half sister, Tamar; Absalom, Tamar's brother, kills Amnon and leads a revolt against David's kingship, especially taking advantage of the obvious neglect which the northern peoples were aleady beginning to feel in this new alliance. The revolt was put down by Joab, and Absalom was killed. Other revolts also occurred.

The conclusion to the story is found in 1 Kings 1—2 where David was near death and obviously in no condition to act as king nor even to remember clearly what he had earlier stated. In this very crucial time it is interesting to note how the prophets were again involved in the selection process. Nathan supported Solomon and entered into a "deal" with Bathsheba to trick the ailing monarch into declaring Solomon king, whereas the legitimate heir (i.e., the eldest remaining son), Adonijah, was supported by Joab and Abiathar the priest. The conclusion of the tale is that Adonijah and Joab were murdered, Joab while holding on to the horns of the altar, supposedly a place of safety! Abiathar the priest was exiled from Jerusalem to Anathoth in the land of Benjamin.

The last chapters of 2 Samuel contain several isolated accounts and poetry, the most interesting of which concerns the census which David ordered for the land (2 Samuel 24). This census so angered Yahweh that a plague swept through the land! And finally, the site for the new Temple was purchased, but it was first used as a place of sacrifice in order to ensure that the plague would leave the land.

The Books of Kings

The books of Kings, like the books of Samuel, originally comprised only one volume, but they were separated into two roughly equal books with the translation of the Hebrew text into Greek. As with the books of Samuel, the books of Kings constitute a part of the larger work known as the Deuteronomistic History. These books actually conclude that work. The last recorded event in the larger work is the releasing from prison in Babylon of the Judean king, Jehoiachin, which took place in ca. 561 B.C. By placing this incident at the conclusion of the entire work, the editors may have been attempting to demonstrate some hope to the people for a restoration of the people and the Davidic line back in their land.

There were several sources used in the compilation of these writings, the book (annals) of Solomon, the book (annals) of the kings of Israel, and the book (annals) of the kings of Judah specifically mentioned. In addition to these probably several other sources and traditions were utilized also. There was the tradition(s) relating to the prophets Elijah and Elisha; there were traditions relating to other prophets also, such as Ahijah, Micaiah, Isaiah, and more. The books, therefore, are a composite from numerous sources but undoubtedly were edited from the Deuteronomic viewpoint.

To be noted is the chronological arrangement which the books of
Kings present for the length of the reigns of the various kings of Israel
and Judah and the correlation of these reigns one to another. Attempting
to obtain a clear chronological history from these books is a complex and
complicated problem, and the plain fact is that one cannot really obtain
a straightforward and logically sequential order from the accounts as
they stand. The best one can do is to structure a chronology using both
extra-biblical as well as biblical sources. The reasons for the discrepancies may be varied since we do not know enough about the way the
"king years" were counted in this period. For example, did the king's
first year begin at the time of taking office, or at the beginning of the
New Year immediately following? When there were cases of co-regency
(because of illness) were the years of co-regency counted as part of the
entire reign or not? These and other problems cause difficulty in interpreting the chronological data found in these books. But the evidence is
satisfactory enough for us to build a fairly accurate picture of the kings
and their times.

The Books of Kings: Outline

    I. Solomon Becomes King 1 Kings 1—2
   II. Stories About Solomon and His Reign 1 Kings 3—11
      The Building and Dedication of the Temple 1 Kings 6—8
  III. The Division of the United Monarchy 1 Kings 12
  IV. The History of Israel and Judah as Separate States
      1 Kings 13—2 Kings 25
      A. The Elijah Stories 1 Kings 17—19, 21; 2 Kings 1—2
      B. The Jehu Rebellion 2 Kings 9—10
      C. The Fall of Israel 2 Kings 17
      D. The Reforms of Hezekiah in Judah 2 Kings 18—20
      E. The Evil Reign of Manasseh 2 Kings 21
      F. The Reforms of Josiah 2 Kings 22—23
      G. The Fall of Judah 2 Kings 24—25

There has already been some discussion about the account of Solomon's becoming king (cf. above, pp. 128f.). As far as the Deuteronomistic Historians were concerned, Solomon began on the right

path but strayed from it. Because initially he pursued the way of wisdom, he and his nation were blessed. When he strayed later, however, this marked the time for a judgment which materialized as the split of the United Kingdom into two kingdoms. This resulted because Solomon acted as a typical oriental ruler who exercised power sometimes ruthlessly and married foreign wives as a way of cementing political and economic alliances, but the worst thing he did was to build places of worship for the gods of the foreign women whom he had married. This practice was customary in those days, but it was not to be allowed among God's people! This was his most grievous sin according to the Deuteronomistic Historians.

Solomon's grandeur is well known to most persons, even those who are not students of the biblical writings. He engaged in large public works building programs, established a standing military force, and encouraged the official beginning of a movement in Israel which did not fully flower until the post-exilic period. This involved the establishment at the court of a group of "wise" men whose duty it was to pass along the wisdom of the world, to prepare persons for duty to the king and the state, to make lists of certain important data (such as animals, trees, kings, etc.), and generally to advise the king on important matters. This type of wisdom movement and tradition was already well established in certain other great nations of antiquity (such as Egypt, old Babylonia, Assyria, and others), but it was given its impetus among the Hebrew people in the court of Solomon. (A fuller discussion of the flowering of this movement will be given below, cf. pp. 225ff.).

Of course, the most important and significant of the many accomplishments of Solomon was the building of the Temple at Jerusalem. Two full chapters of Kings detail the arrangements for the building and one lengthy chapter is devoted to the dedication of that structure. The ark is again one of the central features in the story. Another interesting bit of information which demonstrates something of what was happening culturally to the (formerly) wandering people after having settled in the land of the Canaanites is the fact that the Temple was built along the lines of a typical Canaanite temple! Solomon's prayer at the dedication was typically Deuteronomic, however!

Solomon's grandeur and building programs were carried out, but at a high cost. To pay for these extravagancies he divided the land into twelve new administrative districts (not congruous with the old tribal boundaries, incidentally) for the purposes of taxation, military service, and forced labor. As one can readily recognize, the brunt of such programs fell upon the people from the northern area since they had the most people and were the most prosperous. This caused them to be increasingly restless. Nothing happened during Solomon's reign to disrupt the unity of the nation, however, but the seeds of discontent were sown and the way was paved for something drastic to occur.

About this time a prophet had met Jeroboam, one of Solomon's leaders of the forced labor detail and performed a peculiar act usually known as a "prophetic sign." This prophet had taken a new garment and had torn it into twelve pieces, giving Jeroboam ten of them and announcing that Jeroboam was to be the leader of a separate northern nation. It is interesting that while ten tribes are given to the north, the text states that only one is left for David. Does this mean that there were only eleven at that time? Or that one from the eleven (other than Judah) would remain a part of the southern group? If the latter is the correct understanding, then Benjamin (or the southern part of Benjamin) could be the tribe referred to here. The numbering here is a minor problem, however.

After Solomon's death his son Rehoboam journeyed to the ancient northern shrine at Shechem, expecting to be proclaimed king by the northern tribes. Rehoboam was approached at Shechem, however, by the elders of the north among whom was Jeroboam requesting that some of the burdens of the Solomonic administrative districts be removed. Having consulted with his advisers both old and young, Rehoboam accepted the advice of his younger advisers, telling the northern leaders that he would be even more harsh than Solomon. With that report the people of the north had had enough.

> What portion have we in David?
> We have no inheritance in the son of Jesse.
> To your tents, O Israel!
> Look now to your own house, David. (1 Kings 12:16)

The union between the northern and southern tribes and people had been uneasy from the beginning and did not last long. The United Monarchy had begun ca. 993 B.C., and the division came ca. 922 B.C. The time spent together, however, probably strengthened both groups, for the Northern Kingdom lasted for another 200 years and the Southern for about 335 years.

Rehoboam wanted very much to force the union back together, but about this time the Egyptian Pharaoh, Shishak, invaded Palestine and this prevented any possibility of reuniting the regions. It is questionable whether Rehoboam could have done it even if the Egyptians had not invaded at that moment.

Jeroboam lost no time in attempting to solidify the northern people into a new nation. He founded the capital of the new nation in the old cultic center at Shechem. And to rival the religious centrality and focus of the Jerusalem Temple which housed the ark, he established two cultic cities at Dan and Bethel. At those cities he erected golden bull images which were probably intended to represent the throne of Yahweh and were not intended as images of him. They may even have been his substitution for the ark of the covenant which remained in the Jerusalem Temple. Since Baalism was still quite prevalent in the land and since the image for Baal was the bull and since these images smacked too much of idolatry, the Deuteronomic editors refer constantly to these as *the* "sin of Jeroboam." The prophets who had supported Jeroboam in leading the northern people out of the alliance themselves turned against him (cf. 1 Kings 13).

For about fifty years Israel and Judah, as the Northern and Southern Kingdoms were now known, remained about equal in stature, but it was inevitable with the resources and geographical positioning which Israel had that it would become a far superior state economically and politically. Israel perhaps could have been even stronger had it not been for the lack of a solid dynastic base (as was not the case in Judah with the Davidic line) which led to many coups in the history of that land, and thus periods of political weakness.

One of these coups took place ca. 876 B.C. when Omri became a powerful and able ruler. He gave some political stability to the land. He established the capital at a new city called Samaria, one quite similar in many respects to Jerusalem in the south. Omri was given short space by the Deuteronomic Historians since he is described as having continued walking in the ". . . way of Jeroboam." After Omri died, his son, Ahab, became king, and there is a large amount of space devoted to him. This is not because he was favored or good but because the prophet Elijah, considered perhaps to be the first of the great prophets, lived during the reign of King Ahab and had many contacts with him.

The reader of the Deuteronomic History detects an emphasis and concern for the prophetic movement from the beginning. For example, it is in Deuteronomy that Moses was called a prophet, and guidelines for determining the identity of a true prophet are given there as well. Within the other books in this larger history one finds prophets in the most crucial places especially when the monarchy was established. Samuel himself was looked upon as, among other things, a prophet, and he was the one who anointed both Saul and David to be kings. The prophets were portrayed as king-makers, advisers to the kings, critics of the kings, and at times king-breakers. Thus the prophetic influence in the Deuteronomic writings is quite profound especially when the monarchy was established and especially at crisis points in the history of the nation.

The first major prophet seems to have been Elijah, a native of Gilead which was the area closest to the desert. At this point in Israel's history the religious and cultural battle between the old traditions and Yahweh, on the one hand, and the Canaanite traditions and Baal, on the other, seemed to have reached a turning point. Ahab's wife, Jezebel, was a devotee of the Tyrian Baal and used her position to press for this type of worship in Israel. Elijah is the one who stood for the old ways and the worship of Yahweh. The point of the Elijah stories, and the Elisha stories too, seems to be the superiority of Yahweh over Baal. The episodes reflect a real struggle over which god was to be worshiped in Israel, Yahweh or Baal. Since Baal was viewed as the giver of the fertility of the land, it was at this strength that Yahweh challenged Baal. All the stories relating to these prophets, the giving of the rain, the giving of life, increasing of oil and meal, and the ascending to heaven, all supposedly areas in which Baal was supreme, clearly show that it was through the power of Yahweh that these things were accomplished.

The account of the confrontation of Yahweh and Baal on Mt. Carmel is a famous story. The issue here was the giving of the rain, and the pouring out of the jars of water was probably originally intended as a prophetic sign, an outgrowth of the ideas related to sympathetic magic. The presence of fire in the story indicates that there was in the episode the element of theophany. From the time of Elijah and Elisha, therefore, it seems clear that Yahweh was the supreme God in Israel. But elements of Baalism were quite frequently incorporated into the worship of Yahweh, which caused later prophets great consternation.

One of the most famous revolutions of the entire period of Israel's history occurred during the time when Elisha was prophet. These events began when Elisha anointed Jehu to be king over Israel and commissioned him to destroy the house of Omri. This Jehu did with zeal and perhaps even some relish (cf. 2 Kings 9—10). But the slaughter of the ruling house and its advisers left the nation with little or no experience for leadership and with old alliances broken. Therefore, while the nation was "purged" of the evil of the Omrids and Baalism, weakness was the characteristic of the government.

About this time the Assyrians began to direct their power toward this segment of the ancient world. One significant factor for Israel's history was the fact that Assyria had soundly defeated Syria, Israel's northern neighbor and frequent adversary (ca. 802 B.C.). Because of the weakness of Egypt at that moment and the fact that the Assyrians did not penetrate further into Palestine than Syria, Israel enjoyed a resurgence of political and economic growth during the reign of Jeroboam II (786–746 B.C.). Boundaries were extended, and economic prosperity was enjoyed, at least for some, but the prosperity was to be short lived, for Assyria began to move westward again and with that movement the fate of Israel was sealed especially if she resisted, which she did.

In 735 B.C. the nations of Israel and a resurgent Syria joined together in an alliance to attempt to put together a force which would keep the Assyrians out of Palestine. This was called the Syro-Ephraimitic alliance, and this alliance tried to force the smaller nations of the area to join in the coalition. Judah was pressured to join but did not.

By this time political anarchy was the order of the day in Israel, however. Confusion, a rapid succession of rulers, a crushing defeat of Israel, and the fall of Samaria tolled the death knell for the Northern Kingdom. The people were carried away into other lands, and other peoples were brought into the land to repopulate the area (cf. 2 Kings 17:24–28). These new people mingled with the remaining Israelites and were viewed as unclean by the Judeans. The words of Amos are quite appropriate to describe the situation:

Fallen, no more to rise,
   is the virgin Israel;
forsaken on her land,
   with none to raise her up. (Amos 5:2)

The history of southern Judah is not really so turbulent, probably a result of a stable monarchy. A Davidic descendant sat upon the throne of Judah for all but a few years of its history. That circumstance came about as a result of the Jehu revolution in the north. Ahab had tried to improve relations with Judah and had given his daughter, Athaliah, to be married to the son of Jehoshaphat, Jehoram. In the rebellion Jehu was supposed to eliminate all male members of the house of Omri which would have included the sons of Jehoram and Athaliah. When Athaliah learned about this matter, she attemped to have all the royal family of David destroyed, which included her own grandchildren. But one infant, Joash, was hidden and later was proclaimed king. Athaliah, who had ruled until that time, was put to death (cf. 2 Kings 11).

Even in the Southern Kingdom, however, there were periods of religious reform and religious decadence according to the Deuteronomistic Historians. The two kings who are praised the most are Hezekiah (715–686 B.C.) and Josiah (640–609 B.C.). It is of more than passing interest that both instituted cultic reforms which were centered around the Temple and a covenant renewal. To the Deuteronomists this kind of activity was proper and right.

The reform of Hezekiah was needed because his predecessor, Ahaz (735–715 B.C.) had appealed to Assyria for aid when pressured to join the Syro-Ephraimitic alliance. In those days to appeal for aid meant more than paying large amounts of tribute and being subject to the commands of the stronger nation. This also included the nominal acceptance and worship of that nation's gods. Thus when an attempt was made to reject the worship of the other nation's gods, this was not just a religious matter but in essence a declaration of independence. Hezekiah did just that and the consequences were quite severe. The Assyrians came into the land, overran the counryside, captured forty-six fortified cities, and besieged Jerusalem.

Hezekiah had to pay heavy tribute and give his daughters to the king of Assyria in compensation for this rebellion, but nevertheless Hezekiah received high marks from the Deuteronomists. Jerusalem was not destroyed or taken even though it came under heavy attack, and the escape of the city from ruin left a lasting impression upon the people. It also planted the seed in the minds of the people that somehow, no matter what the odds, Yahweh would never allow his city to be captuerd. This later turned out to be a very hopeless delusion.

The second reform occurred under Josiah who came to the throne at the age of eight (640 B.C.). Between the kings Hezekiah and Josiah there was the hated Manasseh. Generally presented by the Deuteronomic Historians as the worst king Judah ever had, Manasseh reigned for fifty-five years! (This circumstance caused the Deuteronomic Historians great embarrassment!) Pagan worship of different types flourished during his reign. Some interpreters believe that Manasseh must have actively persecuted the prophets of Yahweh, since there are no prophets connected with this period of Judean history. The sacrifice of children obviously was practiced also (cf. 2 Kings 21).

According to the Deuteronomic account a reform movement was begun during Josiah's reign and while repairing and cleaning up the Temple a "book of the Law" was discovered. Whether this book was really discovered or was a "plant" by some religious group has been debated, but the outcome was that the "book" was read to Josiah who was so moved by it that he made the document the foundation for his reform movement. The aspects of the reform as given in 2 Kings (cf. 22—23) so closely resemble the stipulations found in Deuteronomy 12—26, 28 that many believe that at least this part of Deuteronomy (if not more) was the book found in the Temple. For this reason the reform is usually called the Deuteronomic Reform. The requirements were very pointed: all pagan practices were outlawed; the sacrifice of children was abolished; the passover was reinstituted; but most important to the Deuteronomists all worship was abolished except in the Jerusalem Temple. (So as not to put local priests out of work, a plan was devised for each priest to officiate at Jerusalem for a designated time each year.) In addition, Josiah was attempting to expand Judah's political influence and territorial claims.

On the larger historical scene, the Assyrian Empire was on the wane and a new power was beginning to flex its muscles in lower Mesopotamia, namely Babylonia. While the Egyptians did not really like Assyria, they nevertheless did not want them to be completely destroyed, because they were concerned that this would give Babylonia too much power. Therefore when Assyria was being attacked by Babylonia, Egypt sent aid to its old adversary. Josiah was nominally allied with Babylonia at this moment and attempted to head off the Egyptian forces at the Valley of Jezreel at Megiddo, the scene of many important battles in Old Testament times. This foolish action issued in the defeat of the Judean forces and the death of Josiah.

One of Josiah's sons, Jehoahaz, succeeded to the throne but did not reign for long, because the Egyptian pharaoh placed a pro-Egyptian son of Josiah, Eliakim, on the throne. His name was changed to Jehoiakim. This king was not exactly of the same moral fiber as his father, and shortly after he came to the throne it was obvious that the reform movement of his father was dead. The Deuteronomic Historians give him very short space.

We know from other sources that Judah remained a vassal state of Egypt until ca. 605 B.C. In that year the Babylonians defeated the Egyptians at Carchemish and swept down into Palestine. In 604 B.C. Jehoiakim became a vassal of Nebuchadnezzar, the famous Babylonian ruler.

Jehoiakim, nevertheless, remained basically pro-Egyptian, and encouraged by a withdrawal of Babylonian forces from the frontier (ca. 600 B.C.) he rebelled. The Babylonians were somewhat slow to move but when they did, their army marched into the area of Judea ca. 598 B.C. At this moment, Jehoiakim died (whether naturally or by assassination is not really clear), and his son, Jehoiachin (also known as Jeconiah or Coniah) came to rule. This rule was very short, for he was forced to surrender to the Babylonians; this was in 597 B.C. The king and numerous court officials and leaders were deported to Babylon, but Nebuchadnezzar allowed Judah to remain in existence. Zedekiah, another of Josiah's sons, was placed on the throne (cf. 2 Kings 23:17ff.).

Zedekiah was a poor excuse for a king. Most of what we know about him comes from the book of Jeremiah rather than the account in 2 Kings. He was weak, too easily swayed by the pro-Egyptian agitators, and lacked moral courage and plain common sense! He knew what was right for the country but was too weak to do battle with the pro-Egyptian party which exercised some political clout. Naturally the Egyptians encouraged those smaller nations lying between Egypt and Babylonia to rebel against Babylonia. There seems to have been at least one near fatal blunder by Zedekiah in 594–593 B.C., but again this had no lasting effect. In 589 B.C., however, rebellion broke out again and spurred on by promises of aid from Egypt and encouraged by promises of victory in Yahweh's name by some of the prophets and other religious leaders, Judah joined in the activity. That proved to be a fatal mistake. The Babylonian army moved into the land and by the middle of the summer of 587 Jerusalem fell for the second time to the invaders. Zedekiah attempted to escape but was captured and forced to witness the execution of his children. He then was immediately blinded, taken to Babylon, and died there. Jerusalem was burned and its walls were torn down. Many more persons were deported to Babylon and many others were simply executed. The few people who remained in the land were basically the poor and uneducated.

The area was then organized as a province within the Babylonian empire, and a certain Gedaliah was named as governor, but shortly thereafter, Gedaliah was murdered by a subversive group headed by a man named Ishmael. There was a large group of Judeans which left Judah and settled in Egypt to escape further Babylonian wrath. Some scholars argue that another deportation took place in 582–581 B.C., but this cannot be demonstrated unequivocally. Judah then became a part of the province of Samaria. The land was decimated by war and deportation, the victim of its own folly.

The books of Kings conclude with Jehoiachin having been released from prison (ca. 561 B.C.) and dining at the king's table in Babylon. Some see in this incident, recorded at the end of the Deuteronomic History, a figure of hope. The Davidic line had not been extinguished; the former king was free and living well in Babylon. Could it be that Yahweh might yet reestablish the line? Only time would tell.

CHAPTER III

Nebi'im (continued)

History and Literature

The second section of the second division of the Hebrew canon consists of four books or scrolls known as the "Latter Prophets": Isaiah, Jeremiah, Ezekiel, and the Book of the Twelve (which contains those shorter prophetic books usually known by the designation of the "minor prophets"). These are the books which are popularly known as "prophetic." The prophetic movement exercised a strong influence upon the development of the religion and the religious traditions of Israel.

Prophecy was not an isolated phenomenon in Israel alone, however; many other cultures and societies had prophetic movements also. But none of them seems to have reached the lofty heights of ethical concern and the depths of understanding of the nature of God as the movement developed among the Hebrew people. As with almost all of the religious developments in Israel, the prophetic movement was specifically connected with a particular period of history. Prophecy received its impetus and continued its growth along with the development of the monarchy in Israel. After the kingdoms were destroyed, the prophetic movement continued but eventually ceased to sustain any real momentum. Early in the post-exilic period (ca. 538 B.C. ff.) the voices of the prophets were heard less and less frequently, finally yielding to other modes of revelation and communication between God and his people.

Just how did prophecy begin and develop among the Hebrew people? Older scholarship formerly detected three basic stages through which the movement passed. First, there was the oldest stage where prophecy was primarily concerned with divination, the persons involved being called "seers." Then there came a second stage where the prophets were grouped together (usually) into bands of people who were connected with shrines or who simply roved about the countryside. The persons in these groups were characterized by ecstatic seizure which was supposed to demonstrate that the person had been taken over by the spirit of the god. In such a state some message of the god might be communicated either in a vision or by means of ecstatic speech. By either means the message could be explained when the person recovered from the possession. Such roving bands in Israel were called *nebi'im*. These two stages were then superseded by the final stage of the "writing" or classical prophets who were not so concerned with divining the future or ecstatic activities as they were with proclaiming the message from God to the people.

More recent interpreters, however, believe that there were only two basic types of prophets in the ancient world, a "seer" type primarily related to nomadic tribes and the ecstatic type primarily connected with fertility cults. The theory espoused here is that in Israel these two types gradually merged together under the influence of the religion of Yahweh which transformed both into the significant character and force which the prophets exercised among the Hebrew people.

In all probability these two schemes, as neat as they are, do not fully reflect the complexity of the background of the prophetic beginnings. As one studies Hebrew prophecy carefully, one finds elements of the old "seer" and the ecstatic, but other tributaries have also fed into the main stream. There is evidence that the priests made a contribution to the movement. It is obvious from reading the prophetic words that "wisdom" thinking also played a part in the total picture. Prophets sometimes served as court counselors as well. What one finds, therefore, is a complex mingling of various traditions and functions which ultimately issued in the prophetic movement as it evolved in Israel.

Most moderns have the preconceived idea that prophecy means "predicting the future." This is not really the understanding presented by the prophetic books nor the prophets themselves, however. The office of the prophet is portrayed as that of persons who felt under a divine call to proclaim the message of Yahweh to the people of the nation in a given situation. Any prediction which emerged from this situation was a prediction of the *immediate* future, not a long range future.

As already noted, the Deuteronomic History has prepared the way for the prophetic literature. Historically speaking the period of the monarchy provides the basic background for this movement. There is really no need to rehearse the history of the era which includes the pre-exilic prophets, as this has already been recounted (cf. above, pp. 92ff.). The history of the exilic and post-exilic periods will be presented at the appropriate place.

The prophets were, therefore, primarily messengers for God to the people of Israel and Judah. In fact, this emphasis upon delivering a message to the people is such an important aspect of the prophet's ministry that many scholars believe that the basic prophetic oracle was presented in the form of the old "messenger formula." This form follows a fairly set structure with the one who has sent the message identified, the reason for the message given, the pronouncement of the message, and any consequences deriving therefrom. (Most of these include either a threat or a promise of deliverance.) The student will recognize this formula quite readily in the reading of the prophetic materials. Not all of the prophetic teachings can be classified under this form, however.

It is also necessary for the student of the prophetic books to be aware that a large majority of the prophetic teachings was originally delivered and subsequently preserved in poetic form. This point should be kept in mind because not all English translations present the prophetic teachings in poetry (the RSV has, however), and it is obvious to the student of literature that poetry is not interpreted exactly like narrative history. The implications of this will become clear as one studies the biblical books *per se*. The prophets, then, are to be understood as poetic proclaimers of the word of Yahweh to the people of Israel and Judah in specific concrete situations.

One additional matter should be kept in mind in examining the teachings contained in the prophetic materials: this concerns the sometimes peculiar actions of the prophets usually called "prophetic signs." For example, one reads in Jeremiah that he took a flask and shattered it into pieces on the ground in the presence of the elders of the city (cf. Jeremiah 19). This seems an unusual action to modern interpreters, but one should recall the idea that was prevalent in the ancient world of the efficacy of certain actions in being a part of bringing to completion what the action was intended to portray. This type of action probably evolved from the ancient belief in sympathetic magic and was used by the prophets quite frequently (cf. Introduction). In Israel's prophetic movement, however, there was no thought that the action tied the hands of Yahweh to do the bidding of the prophet. Rather it was truly believed that the prophet was acting on behalf of and *at the command of* Yahweh, but nevertheless the culture of the time understood the "sign" as actually a part of the accomplishment of whatever the sign was intended to portray. This is one of the reasons why the prophets were hated so vehemently by the people and the political authorities; once a word of doom or an act that pointed toward doom had been spoken or enacted the forces to bring that doom to completion had been set into motion.

The books which bear the names of the prophets were assembled and came into being as the result of a long period of passing along the teachings of the prophets orally and in written form, by gradually collecting the oracles together, and at points reinterpreting and rearranging some of the sayings. Upon close examination it also appears that other prophetic oracles from other periods were included along with those of the prophets from the past. In addition to specific teachings there was also prose material about certain prophets which ultimately came to be included in the final editions of the prophetic books. These two types of material collected together usually formed the basis for the various prophetic collections, and this collection of sayings and incidents is placed at the very beginning of the books. Other units of tradition were also collected and included in the various prophetic books. As well as the sayings directed toward the people of Israel and/or Judah, oracles were directed against foreign nations as well, and these were usually collected together thus forming a second major portion of the prophet's work. In addition to these two collections, there was quite often an attempt to conclude (especially the longer works) with a historical incident or reflection which usually depicted some hope for the future of God's people. One can, therefore, understand something of the complexity one faces in attempting to trace development of the prophetic teachings until they were written down in their final form.

One other aspect of the final editing of the prophetic books should be noted here. In the pre-exilic prophets one notes a definite tendency for the basic theme of the prophetic proclamation to be *doom*. The basic message was that the people of Israel and Judah had sinned, and therefore they deserved and would receive punishment for their breach of God's commandments. (This basically reflects typical Deuteronomic theology.) In the post-exilic period, however, the judgment had taken place, and the basic thrust of the prophetic message then was for hope and restoration. Older scholarship took these two categories, doom and hope, and made them into a guideline for understanding and distinguishing between pre- and post-exilic prophecy. If an oracle of hope or restoration was found, therefore, in a pre-exilic prophetic collection, it was automatically assumed to be a later post-exilic insertion into the text and not to be interpreted as part of the pre-exilic prophet's teaching.

This type of schema can be helpful to the student in attempting to understand the prophetic literature, but as is obvious the formula can be too rigidly interpreted. To deny *any* positive teachings to the pre-exilic prophets seems quite arbitrary. As one examines them, the hope passages found in the pre-exilic prophetic material, the best course of action is to examine each teaching on its own to determine if there was perhaps some hope in the original prophetic message. Generally speaking, however, the characteristic teaching of the pre-exilic prophet was doom, while the distinguishing feature of the post-exilic prophet was hope for restoration of the nation in the land.

Perhaps the most appropriate method which could be employed to understand best the prophetic teachings would be that of examining the prophetic books and/or personages in chronological order. This approach, however, is complicated by the fact that the books themselves are not arranged in chronological order, and further by the fact that at least two of the books (Isaiah and the Book of the Twelve) are composite works which incorporate several prophetic personalities or traditions into one book. The prophetic personalities (and the appropriate book or portion thereof) will be presented here in chronological order, insofar as this can be determined.

The Pre-Exilic Prophetic Books
Amos

Amos was a Judean southerner who spoke in the northern kingdom of Israel. He described himself as a keeper of sycamores (some type of fig, probably), and the superscription to the book indicates that he was also a shepherd. During the reign of Jeroboam II (786–746 B.C.) in Israel, both Egypt and Assyria were weak or dormant, and since Syria to Israel's north had suffered defeat earlier at the hands of the Assyrians this was a time of relative peace and some degree of prosperity for the nation. Things were going right; they must be doing God's will.

But this scene was very misleading; the depth of the religious convictions of the people was shallow indeed. The laws were not being kept; the powerless were not being protected under the law; selfishness was the order of the day. Peace and prosperity seemed to abound, but the covenant of God was not being honored by the people. To this situation Amos spoke somewhere between 760–750 B.C.

The book itself appears to have been formed from two major collections which numerous scholars argue may go back to Amos himself, a collection of oracles of doom (chapters 1—6) and a series of visions 7:1–9; 8:1–3; 9:1–6). In addition other shorter units including sayings, doxologies, and oracles round out the material collected together in the book.

If there is one major theme which seems to run through the material and hold it together, it is the concept of righteousness and its close associate, justice. To Amos Yahweh was a God of righteousness, i.e., he does what is right, acting in accordance with his nature. Because Yahweh is a God of righteousness, he demands that his people conduct themselves in the same manner. Doing what was right meant abiding by the law given by God, especially rendering justice in the courts of law.

As one recognizes these emphases, it becomes exceedingly easy when reading Amos' preaching to view him as simply a great social reformer. Among earlier scholars he was quite frequently depicted as just that. But upon closer examination one finds that Amos is first and foremost a man of religious conviction. Whatever social ideas he held, they were directly related to and an outgrowth of his religious convictions and his understanding of Yahweh's nature and requirements. To interpret Amos apart from these understandings is, therefore, to miss the essence of the man.

When Amos came to Israel, he found a people who believed themselves to be truly "religious." They supported and frequented the shrines, and the outward forms of religious ideology were certainly present. The substitution of form, however, for essence was the crucial problem. The prophets, Amos included, had no real quarrel with religious forms *per se*. Older interpreters tended to find a grave conflict between the prophets and the priests who supposedly were the advocates of the correct forms only, but this theory is not widely held today. That there was some tension at points between the two groups is obvious, but there seems to be no long lasting hostility between priest and prophet. What the prophets did was to advocate real religious commitment which meant that the life of the people devoted to God had to be a transformed life, different from the life of the world.

Amos has numerous religious emphases which seem to have been applied in ways that were essentially new. It is not that Amos and the other prophets are necessarily great innovators. Again many older commentators held to that view. They argued that the old adherence to the precepts of the law and the external forms of religion gave way to the emphasis in the prophets of a "pure" liberalized religion with social concerns and new interpretations of God and his requirements. Upon closer study, however, one finds that the prophets viewed themselves as "conservatives," looking back to the real meaning of the old laws and the old covenant. They did not view themselves as bringers of something new, but as those who called the people back to the old ways.

Amos emphasized that Yahweh required righteousness and justice from his people. Instead of great privilege which the people felt they had in the covenant relationship with God, Amos argued that they had taken upon themselves a tremendous responsibility. To be the elect people of God was to be burdened with duties almost too great to bear. But the people had not accepted these duties—and this meant that judgment was certain.

Until the time of Amos most of the emphasis in thinking about the relationship of God with foreign nations had centered in how those nations directly affected the course of Israel's history. There was little further thought about how God could or even was concerned to relate to other nations, but in Amos' oracles there is the clear teaching that Yahweh had concern for and exercised jurisdiction over the nations, at least those close to Israel though not necessarily directly related with her at that immediate moment. Those nations supposedly operated under a set of understandings and agreements which were nominally regarded at least as binding on themselves. They did not have the fuller revelation of Yahweh's law, but they were under obligation to conduct themselves in accordance with what they had agreed upon and accepted. Not to do so meant that Yahweh could judge them even if he was not "specifically" their God.

Amos' basic message was for the people of Israel, and unfortunately for them Amos could find no ray of hope. His message was almost totally one of unmitigated doom. The nation would be destroyed, and there was no turning back. Exactly when or by whom (either Egypt or Assyria, cf. 3:9) he did not know. The question that many today ask when confronting such teaching revolves around what happens to the "good" people in the land. Surely there were some who did not deserve to be participants in such a judgment. This is a type of thinking which would not really have occurred to these people. They were so saturated with corporate thinking that thoughts about individuals did not usually come to their mind. And further they were also realists in the sense that they understood that when judgment came, there was no way to separate individuals into those who did and those who did not deserve to be punished. The nation as a whole was either rewarded or punished.

In almost every prophet who pronounced the coming judgment of Yahweh the judgment was portrayed as a time of military conquest. This probably results from the fact that in the course of human history the most horrible events occur in times of war. Destruction, famine, and the human capacity for devising unthinkable atrocities against other humans and all living things make war a most appropriate symbol of judgment. It was also because in the course of human history, war seems to be the way in which nations were judged and brought low when they overstepped the bounds of God's law.

Amos: Outline

I. Oracles Against Nations 1:3—2:5
II. Oracles Against Israel 2:6—6:14
III. Series of Visions 7:1—9:4
    A.   Vision of Locusts 7:1–3
    B.   Vision of the Fire 7:4–6
    C.   Vision of the Wall and the Plumb Line 7:7–9
    D.   Interlude: Amos and the Priest at Bethel 7:10–17

The book of Amos begins (after a short identification of Amos) with a collection of oracles against foreign nations, proclamations of doom against evil nations, especially the enemies of God's people. Most of the prophets obviously participated in such activity; in fact, there are some scholars who argue that this is the way prophecy in Israel (and in some other places) began, i.e., with oracles directed against the enemies of the nation. (One recalls the belief in the efficacy of the spoken word in ancient society.) In the shorter prophetic books such sayings are not always present, but in the larger collections there is usually a long section which contains oracles against foreign nations. The point of interest here in the book of Amos is that these oracles are placed first when usually they are found after the collection of oracles against the prophet's own nation (cf. Isaiah 13—23 for example).

As these denunciations of Israel's neighbors are placed here, however, they reflect a definite editorial rationale. The nations around Israel were known to the people of Israel and Judah; therefore their breaches of covenants and their sins could serve as an object lesson. Whoever broke the established and understood codes of conduct recognized even among the "pagan" nations would not escape the judgment of Yahweh. In other words, they were expected to keep the understandings between themselves even though they may not have the special revelation of the law and were not the special people of God. When the nations broke these covenants, they stood under judgment. And even though they did not acknowledge the lordship of Yahweh, Yahweh would judge them anyway. His power was obviously not confined only to Israel! Interestingly enough, there is an oracle against Judah included in the list (2:4–5). Whether this came from Amos himself or was a free-floating oracle against Judah which was felt to be appropriate for inclusion here is debated by some interpreters. Wherever it originated, it is clear that the oracle was felt to be the perfect "lead-in" to the major portion of the book, the oracles against Israel.

The first of these oracles contains an indictment of the nation in general because it had taken advantage of those who attempted to do right and it had exploited the poor and the powerless. Elements of Baalism had crept into the cultic practices of Yahwism (2:7b–8). The arrangement of the material then depicts Amos as he recounted the great deeds by which Yahweh had delivered the people from Egypt and brought them into the land they now possessed. (It was quite typical of the prophets to look back to the Exodus experience as the "honeymoon" period between Yahweh and his people.) Because Yahweh had done all these things for the people, Amos understood that the nation was under great obligation to keep the covenant requirements:

> You only have I known
>   of all the families of the earth;
> therefore I will punish you
>   for all your iniquities. (3:2)

The prophet appears to be certain that some type of military destruction was in store for Israel, but he did not seem to be sure what nation would deliver the death blow (either Assyria or Egypt, cf. 3:9). Amos does not seem to have any degree of hope that somehow the nation might be delivered. Some have interpreted 3:12 as indicative of a remnant hope, but upon close examination that passage does not appear to contain such a teaching. The figure is reflective of the culture of the times when a hired shepherd had to bring to the sheep's owner as much of the carcass as could be rescued from the wild animal to validate the claim that the animal had really been killed and not stolen. The idea was to present the remains to show that this had once been a sheep. Sometimes what could be rescued was skimpy indeed; "two ankle bones and a piece of an ear" are not much! To Amos' mind the destruction of Israel would be almost as complete. Whatever was left would only be enough to ascertain that once there had been a nation there—"a corner of a couch and part of a bed."

The majority of Amos' teaching, however, centers on the sins of the people, especially those in positions of authority who used their offices and power for purely selfish reasons without any thought about the people who were being exploited. He spoke about "summer homes and winter homes" (3:15), labeled the women who pressure their husbands for "more!" as "you cows of Bashan" (4:1), chastised the merchants for their false weights and inferior but overpriced merchandise (8:4–6), and was amazed that they could not be perceptive enough to see where all this was leading (cf. 4:6–11; 6:1–7).

The people had taken refuge in their religious activities as a talisman, a form of protection from any disaster which might come upon them, but Amos made a parody of their misplaced trust: "Come to Bethel [a central sanctuary], and *transgress,* to Gilgal [another shrine], and *multiply transgression . . ."* (4:4a)!

And in the most famous and moving of his attacks on misplaced security based on religious forms, he thundered:

> I hate, I despise your feasts,
>   and I take no delight in your solemn assemblies . . . .
> Take away from me the noise of your songs;
>   to the melody of your harps I will not listen.
> But let justice roll down like waters,
>   and righteousness like an ever-flowing stream. (5:21–24)

From the book of Amos one finds that there was current among the people an idea popularly known as the "Day of the Lord," perhaps a holdover concept derived from the days of the holy war. Obviously the people of Israel considered that day to be a time of judgment for all of Israel's enemies and of exaltation for Israel, but Amos put the needle into that balloon also by saying,

> Woe to you who desire the day of the LORD!
>   Why would you have the day of the LORD?
> It is darkness, and not light . . .
>   and gloom with no brightness in it? (5:18–20)

This type of preaching naturally brought some strong reactions from the religious leaders of Israel. The priest at Bethel ordered Amos to leave the land (whether he had the approval of the king is not clear), for he said ". . . the land is not able to bear all his words" (7:10c). The words were harsh and often uncompromising. There are some persons who when studying the prophetic books become somewhat alarmed because they feel that these men were psychological misfits who somehow relieved their own guilt and fed their own egos by blasting out at the nation. Such an interpretation of these persons, however, does not take into account the culture and understandings of the times and does not take seriously enough the prophet's identification of himself with the nation and the people. Amos, for example, interceded on behalf of the people (7:3, 6), but he also realized that there comes a time when the justice of God must take precedence over the sad condition of a people who ought to know how to live as God required but were not doing so. This is plainly the teaching of Amos' vision of the plumb line beside a wall which originally had been built correctly but was now hopelessly out of plumb!

There is yet another interesting matter to be examined when studying the prophetic books. This involves the understanding of the nature of the prophetic vision. Whether these visions should be understood as types of ecstatic or mystical experience is not certain, but it is interesting that the prophetic "visions" are usually common sights seen in everyday life which were interpreted by the prophet as a revelation from God. Frequently, the visions consist of a "play-on-words," something the Semitic mind was fond of doing. In the vision of the summer fruit (8:1–2), for example, Amos saw a basket of summer fruit. In Hebrew, where there are no vowels written, only consonants, "summer fruit" is spelled *qyts* (pronounced *qayits*), but Amos saw here a message from God about the nation Israel, since the word for "end" in Hebrew is also spelled *qyts* (pronounced *qêts*, however). From this meditation on the basket of fruit Amos understood that God was about to bring an end to the nation of Israel.

As already indicated, Amos saw no hope for the nation. Its sins were such that it could not be spared. The last authentic words of Amos are probably, "I will destroy it from the face of the earth" (9:8b, paraphrase). How, then, does one explain the "happy" ending of 9:8c–15? If this saying were not from Amos, why was it placed here? One needs to recall that these materials experienced a long period of transmission, and when they were finally edited, the people of Judah had experienced the exile and had returned to their land. To them they were still Israel, the people of God. Israel, the Northern Kingdom, however, was gone and had not been restored. Therefore, the oracle of hope that is attached to the harsh (and absolutely true) words of Amos was probably placed there to relieve somewhat the harshness of the message, but more especially to indicate that there was a future for God's people in the land. In a sense both Amos and the prophetic editors were correct: Amos in that Israel did not return as a political entity, and the editors in that God's people had been restored after their judgment.

It is clear from 9:11 that this portion of the oracle was originally directed to the Southern Kingdom of Judah, and that passage fits the time after the destruction of that nation (586 B.C.). The thrust of the teaching is that the line of David would be reestablished followed by a period of great prosperity and happiness. This kind of prophetic teaching was very prominent in the post-exilic times, and one of the most common figures used to emphasize God's presence was that of the increased fertility of the land. This is exactly the idea expressed here in these verses at the conclusion of the book of Amos. The hope was that a king like David would arise again and establish a new kingdom even more glorious and powerful than the old one. This time of resurgence was depicted by the poetic figure indicating great prosperity and increased yields of crops. The verse which states in part the "plowman shall overtake the reaper" illustrates the idea. There would not be ample time to harvest the crop from one season or year until it would be time to prepare for the next planting. (One must keep in mind that these "hope" passages are *poetic* in nature.)

This editing process in the book of Amos illustrates the way the prophetic material was used. For the most part the sayings of the prophets were remembered rather carefully and passed along in the same manner, but the people who handled the material did not think it illegitimate to use the material not only to reflect the prophet's word to his own generation but in ways which could and would speak to new generations. Judgment had been experienced among God's people, but there was among those in Judah, at least, the opportunity to rebuild and to reestablish a nation. Since the prophetic books were edited in that type of cultural setting, it was considered quite appropriate to present those teachings in a way that would speak to people in the present generation who were struggling in the resettlement process.

The prophet Amos, however, did not see a hope for the nation, Israel, and he was quite correct in his assessment. Having been originally constructed in accordance with the plumb line of Yahweh's righteousness, Israel now was so far out of alignment that it was useless and hopelessly corrupt. It would be totally destroyed—and it was.

Hosea

The prophet Hosea was also a spokesman to the Northern Kingdom but, unlike Amos, was a native of that land. He probably exercised his prophetic ministry during a longer period of time than Amos, somewhere between ca. 750-725 B.C. Whereas Amos found among the people of Israel a lack of the righteousness of God, Hosea found that the problem lay basically in their religious convictions which had become so intertwined with elements of Baalism that the true faith of Yahwism was no longer extant. The people had become apostate, corrupted with the worship of Baal.

During Hosea's ministry there was no real political stability in the land, and the threat from the great nation of Assyria was very real. These were times of anarchy and chaos, and some of this can be seen reflected in the sayings of Hosea. As for Hosea himself, we know very little of his background, but he must have been from a culturally privileged background since his knowledge and wit reflect someone trained beyond the ordinary for that time. He must have had some contact with the "wise" because wisdom motifs and sayings are quite common in this material.

What is known about Hosea comes basically from the book which bears his name. In chapters 1 and 3 there are two accounts of Hosea and his wife, one biographical and one autobiographical. As a prophetic sign, Hosea was commanded to marry a harlot to signify the relationship between Yahweh and his people, and their children were given names which were also "signs": the last one designated *Lo-ammi*, "not my people."

Scholars have debated for years about the "women problem" in Hosea. Are the women mentioned in chapter 1 and chapter 3 the same person, or are they different? Was Gomer, the wife, a harlot before Hosea married her, or did she adopt that style after the marriage? Or was she, perhaps, a woman who served her time in the practice of cultic prostitution? No matter the answers that may be reached concerning this problem, it is clear that the stories were told to illustrate the point that Israel had been unfaithful to Yahweh and had gone "awhoring after other gods."

The basic underlying thesis of Hosea's message was that the people did not "know" Yahweh, that is they were not in the proper relationship with God. This situation was clearly demonstrated in that they had broken the covenant relationship, and they did not adhere to the obligations they took upon themselves in the covenant. The word in the Hebrew for "covenant loyalty" is *hesed,* quite frequently translated as mercy, love, steadfast love, or the like. It connotes more the idea of loyalty and obligation, however, than it does emotional feeling. The problem with Israel was that they were not in the proper relationship with God, and therefore they were unable and unwilling to keep their covenant commitments.

In interpreting the message of Hosea one encounters two difficulties. One results from the condition of the Hebrew text of this book which is probably the least well preserved of all the books of the Old Testament. The reasons for this are unclear and probably varied, but the text is difficult at points to translate clearly and therefore difficult to interpret. The second problem is quite similar to that of most of the prophetic books, namely settling the question as to which of the included oracles are from Hosea and which may have been added later. There seems to be some hope in Hosea's teaching, but exactly how much remains a question not always agreed upon by interpreters.

Hosea: Outline

   I. (Auto-) Biographical Material 1—3
   II. Oracles Concerning Israel 4—14

One notes immediately that there is no collection of oracles against foreign nations in the book of Hosea. The little Hosea had to say about other nations (most frequently Egypt and Assyria) is usually connected directly to the fortunes of Israel.

The first three chapters of the book are concerned with Hosea's personal life, but more importantly what this signified in terms of Yahweh's relationship with the people of Israel. Chapter 1 is told in prose and in third-person narrative, while chapter 3 is also in prose but in first-person narrative. The second chapter is a poetic composition which depicts the relationship between God and Israel as like that between a faithful husband and an unfaithful wife, specifically one who has become involved in Baalistic practices. In fact, the passage itself reflects the form of a legal proceeding!

The interesting portions of this section are concerned with the possibility of restoration. In 2:14ff. and 3:1–5 there seems to be some element of hope, whether from Hosea originally or from the post-exilic editors cannot be determined with certainty. The sensitivity of this prophet, however, leads one to the conclusion that there may have been some hope indeed in his teachings, though probably supplemented and augmented by post-exilic redaction (specifically the comment about David, 3:5).

Interpreters differ in their understanding of chapter 3 as to whether the woman referred to is the same as the wife of chapter 1. If the passage refers to the same woman, the idea may be that after the judgment there could be a possibility for the restoration of the nation. If it refers, however, to another woman, it is just possible that the teaching understands the first woman to have been put away for good and that a restoration will have to take place with someone else (perhaps Judah?). This is a difficult passage to interpret.

The remainder of the book consists primarily of oracles directed against the sin and stupidity of the nation Israel. Within these sayings one detects quite frequently elements of the wisdom tradition. These elements are easily discernible in the short pithy sayings, figures of speech to make comparisons, the use of word-plays, and the like. Hosea is especially fond of using figures to describe Israel, i.e., a silly dove (7:11), a stubborn heifer (4:16), a cake not turned (i.e., a pancake burned on one side, gooey on the other!). In a skillful and clever manner, therefore, the message of the prophet emerged.

Religiously speaking, however, Hosea emphasized the break in the covenant relationship between Yahweh and the people. This break was understood basically to be the consequence of the people's faithlessness, and this condition led to serious consequences in human relationships as well as in the divine-human realm.

> There is no faithfulness or kindness,
>   and no knowledge of God in the land;
> there is swearing, lying, killing, stealing, and committing adultery;
>   they break all bounds and murder follows murder. (4:1c–2)

This type of situation results directly, according to Hosea, from lack of a right relationship with God. "My people are destroyed for lack of knowledge" (4:6a). The times were ripe for God's judgment to come upon the nation. Many scholars, for example, interpret 5:8ff. as having originated during the period of the Syro-Ephraimitic war, with the basic idea being that dealing with Assyria would invite destruction no matter what those dealings might be! And that destruction came ca. 722 B.C.

Sadly enough, part of the problem lay in the conduct and morality of the religious leaders. The priests and the prophets came under indictment for their failure to lead the people aright. "And it shall be like people, like priest . . . " (4:9a, cf. also 9:7–9). The teaching of Hosea was quite pointed. Empty religious display avails nothing unless there is substantial change in the actual hearts of the people; religion was not to be used as a magical shield to avert disaster.

> For I desire *hesed* [covenant loyalty] and not sacrifice,
> the knowledge of God, rather than burnt offerings. (6:6)

The most difficult problem in interpreting the book of Hosea lies in ascertaining the exact meaning in the hope passages. One of the most famous is the poignant figure in chapter 11 where Israel is described as Yahweh's child who, in spite of all good things God did for him, rebelled and went astray. The passage depicts God's struggle in his own mind as to what should be done with the rebellious child. Because of the sin, judgment must come: that was obvious. But what happens then? Was there to be a restoration of the nation? This question is sharply debated among interpreters of Hosea, and the resolution of the problem is not certain. Some argue that the comment in 11:9, "I will not again destroy Ephraim" presupposed a restoration in the land, thereby making that verse a post-exilic addition to the teachings of the pre-exilic prophet. Upon closer examination of the text, however, one finds that the idea of restoration to the land is not really the focal point. The main thrust lies in the restoration of the covenant, and this seems to be envisioned as occurring in a new relationship with Yahweh such as that relationship which existed in the wilderness. The teaching may be, then, that in the exile of the people, scattered as they will be, Yahweh could still enter into a *hesed* relationship with them. It is interesting that the literal translation of the Hebrew in 11:9 is not "I will not come to destroy" but rather "I will not come into the city." This may well indicate that the time and the place for whatever restoration there could be for Israel and its people would have to come *apart* from their land and nation. This concept is also present in 12:9. Given Hosea's understanding of God and his own experience, he understood that there could be some hope for the people, but that hope could only come after the destruction of the nation and the reestablishment of a new covenant relationship with God apart from the land, as it had been during the time of the wanderings where even though the people had no nation they still had Yahweh as their God. (This teaching reflects also the basic teaching of chapter 3, the conclusion of the first portion of the book!)

Isaiah

One of the most revered of all the prophets was the person known as Isaiah. This esteem was exemplified in several ways. The book of Isaiah was placed first among the "latter" prophets; it is the longest of any single prophetic book; and it contains oracles and teachings from different times and places which point to the existence of an Isaiah "school" (cf. 8:16) which continued from Isaiah's own time into the post-exilic period.

The prophet himself appears to have been a native of Jerusalem, a highly educated man, one who served as court counselor to the kings, and he may even have been a member of the priestly circles as well. His period of activity lasted from the days of King Uzziah (ca. 742 B.C.) until the reign of Hezekiah was over (ca. 687/6 B.C.) During this lengthy service the social and political conditions changed drastically at times, but through it all Isaiah remained a tower of strength and consistency.

Isaiah's primary teaching centered around the concept of faithfulness. In the biblical tradition faith is usually better defined as "faithfulness" or perhaps "trust." The basic idea emphasized that the people were to trust God and to entrust their lives to God. Whenever this "trust" takes place, there is real religion, i.e., a relationship with God. Isaiah's teaching focused on such an understanding of Hebrew religion. In addition he had an exalted concept of God as magnificent and "other than" humankind and the created order. His favorite term for God reflected this understanding, as he continually referred to God as "The Holy One of Israel."

It is interesting to note in conjunction with the examination of the prophet Isaiah the idea of "Messiah." The word "Messiah" means in Hebrew "anointed one." In those days there were three groups who could be anointed (signifying being set apart for a special duty), prophets, priests, and kings. The most usual understanding of the procedure, however, was definitely that of the anointing of a king. The king was a "messiah" because he had been anointed to serve in that very responsible capacity. Therefore during periods of intense trouble brought on by a bad king, the prophets began to look foward to a new and better time brought about by a good king. Since this idea seems to have originated in Judah, it was therefore not unusual that the expected king would be from the line of David. In other words Messianism originated as a religio-political idea.

Some Old Testament scholars have argued that the concept of Messianism did not originate until after the exile of Judah, during the times when the people were longing for a restoration in Judah under another king from the line of David. This is, of course, quite possible, but there are others who believe that the idea really began earlier than the post-exilic period. It is even quite probable that the concept is pre-exilic and originated during periods of bad rulers when the nation was suffering under their reigns. Such a historical circumstance seems to fit the situation of Isaiah's time (or part of it), and it is interesting that Isaiah definitely does seem to look forward to a new ruler who would govern properly. As far as one can determine, it was during this period of Judah's history that the concept of Messiah began to emerge.

Perhaps the most puzzling of all the problems relating to the book of Isaiah, however, concerns how the book was put together. As it stands, it contains sixty-six chapters, all included under the teaching of Isaiah. Upon even superficial observation, however, it appears that the historical background for several sections of the book seems to be quite different. Chapters 1—39, generally speaking, reflect the eighth century B.C. when Assyria was the great power in the world, followed by Egypt. Chapters 40—55, however, are set in the sixth century B.C. with God's people in exile in Babylon, while chapters 56—66 seem to reflect the resettlement of the people into the land after the exile was over in 538 B.C. If this assessment is true, and almost all reputable interpreters agree basically with it, then the book of Isaiah contains not simply the teachings of one prophet but a prophetic tradition which stretches for over two hundred years.

Another problem of similar nature revolves around the material contained within the three major divisions of the book, and there is some uncertainty involved in the interpretation of the various units of material incorporated within them. For example, the heart of the prophetic message of Isaiah (1—39) seems to lie in 6:1—9:6(7), which as it presently stands in the text interrupts another collection of material found in 5:1–30 and 9:7(8)–20. And other collections are found in this section as well. The interpreter is faced, therefore, with various collections of materials which have in turn been collected together and finally were redacted into the book of Isaiah as it now stands. A closer examination of the outline and content of the various divisions will help the interpreter understand some of the teachings and problems better. At this point, however, only chapters 1—39 will be examined, the remaining chapters 40—55 (sometimes called Deutero-Isaiah) and 56—66 (sometimes designated Trito-Isaiah) will be discussed at the appropriate chronological juncture.

Isaiah 1—39: Outline

   I. First Major Collection 1—12
      A. Introduction to the Oracles of Isaiah and the Book 1
      B. Collection of Oracles from Isaiah's Earlier Ministry 2—4
      C. God's Relationship with His People 5—11
      D. Concluding Doxology for the Collection 12
  II. Collection of Oracles Against Foreign Nations 13—23
 III. Collection of Doom and Hope Oracles 24—35
      A. Post-exilic Collection 24—27
      B. Sayings of Isaiah 28—33
      C. Collection of Doom on Edom and Hope for Zion 34—35
 IV. Historical Epilogues 36—39

The first chapter of Isaiah in a sense sets the tone for the entire book (2—66) in that it describes the sin of the people, the destruction which that sin brought, and the conditions for restoration. The themes seem to be woven together in 1:18–20:

Come now, let us reason together,
  says the LORD:
Though your sins are like scarlet,
  will they become as white as snow?
Though they are red like crimson,
  will they become like wool?
If you are willing and obedient,
  you shall eat the good of the land;
But if you refuse and rebel,
  you will be devoured by the sword. (paraphrase)

One of the most famous passages in the book of Isaiah is that found in 5:1ff. These verses contain a poem usually designated the "Song of the Vineyard." Here the nation was compared to a vineyard which had been cared for very carefully but had produced only wild grapes. Having given the vineyard every opportunity to produce good grapes, the owner decided to allow it to be destroyed. There is in the passage another of those word-plays for which the Semitic mind is noted:

. . . and he looked for justice [*Mishpat*],
  but behold, bloodshed [*Mishpah*];
    for righteousness [*tsedaqah*],
    but behold, a cry [*tse'aqah*].
      (5:7cd)

The most significant section of Isaiah 1—39, however, is the collection of materials in 6:1—9:7, for in this composite of oracles and biographical data one finds three of the most important themes and episodes of the entire collection. The first is an account of Isaiah's "call experience." This type of event played an important part in the careers of most of the prophets even though accounts of a call for each prophet have not survived. Isaiah received his call in the Temple in Jerusalem in a theophany experience (cf. Moses) and was given a commission to prophesy to the people of Judah.

One of the major interpretive problems connected with this passage (chapter 6) centers in the purpose of the call. From an initial reading of the text it appears that the reason for the call of Isaiah to preach was to establish the people in their sin so that judgment would be certain. This seems strange to persons today who view the message of God to a people to be that of repentance, a call to return from their evil ways so as to escape the crushing judgment. In the world of the Old Testament, however, not as definitive a line was drawn between purpose and result. If something occurred, they reasoned, then the event must have been purposed to result in such an occasion, and if a certain result occurred, then the purpose must have been intended to bring about that result. The prophetic preaching was seen as God's word to the people to call them to repentance or to warn them of judgment if they did not repent. Since the people did not usually repent and the judgment came, then this must have been the purpose of the preaching, to ensure the judgment upon them. Since Judah did not ultimately repent and was destroyed, then that must have been the purpose of the prophet's ministry. Such reasoning seems a bit unusual for us, but that was their way of thinking.

The second incident which is recorded in this section of Isaiah demonstrates several motifs of the prophet's ministry and teaching. One finds in 7:1—8:8 an incident which occurred ca. 734 B.C. during the Syro-Ephraimitic war. The first matter of interest is that Isaiah, like Hosea, had given his children names which would serve as prophetic signs. Secondly, the religious emphasis in this section is upon trust in Yahweh. "If you will not believe, surely you will not be established" (7:9b) is Isaiah's warning to the king and to the people.

What was happening, historically speaking, was that Israel and Syria had formed an alliance (and were pressuring all the small nations in the area to join them) in order to keep Assyria from invading Palestine. Judah did not wish to join, but Ahaz who was king of Judah felt that the appropriate gesture was to call upon the Assyrians for aid in the face of this military coalition. While the king was pondering this move, Isaiah went to him to warn him not to call upon Assyria for assistance. One of the reasons why the prophets were so opposed to military alliances was that when one allied oneself with a superior power, it was nominally agreed that the gods of the foreign nation be worshiped along with the native god. For the true Yahwist this was unthinkable.

Isaiah told Ahaz that the two lands, Syria and Israel, would be destroyed within two to twelve years (cf. 7:14–16). This was to be made concrete in a sign with the birth of a child by a woman already pregnant and almost ready to deliver. By the time that child was old enough to know how to discern between right and wrong (in those days about two to twelve years old), Israel and Syria would be gone. And they were! By

722 Israel had fallen; Syria had succumbed before that. The name of the child was to be a prophetic sign, Immanuel, which means "God is with us." (The same teaching is recorded again in another name, cf. 8:1–5). The emphasis of the entire story is upon God's deliverance of his people.

The plea of Isaiah was for the people to trust in Yahweh. Ahaz did not trust; he appealed to Assyria for assistance and Judah became a vassal of that country. Isaiah was later proved correct in his assessment since the two nations were soon destroyed, and devastation was ultimately brought upon Judah when it attempted to break the alliance and agreement with Assyria which Ahaz had made (cf. above, p. 136).

Out of this experience with Ahaz, a king who did not trust Yahweh and who led the people in the wrong paths, Isaiah began to look forward to a king who would be faithful to God and lead the people in the right ways. This hope led to the beautiful and well known passage which describes the ideal king (9:2–7). Some scholars have argued that this oracle was given upon the succession of Hezekiah to the throne (715 B.C.), or perhaps upon upon the occasion of his birth. Whatever the original setting the thought is clear. Judah needed a new king who would lead the people as David had done in the past. (One notes that the idealization process with regard to David had indeed begun, since in reality David was not as wonderful as Isaiah and some others believed in their reflections.) Nevertheless, the longing was there for a new king who would be strong and faithful to Yahweh. This would solve the problems of the nation; Isaiah was convinced of this.

In the collection of oracles against foreign nations one encounters a peculiar and fascinating bit of information about an incident in the life of Isaiah. As a sign against Egypt, Isaiah is reported to have walked about Jerusalem naked for three years to demonstrate (and participate in) the captivity of Egypt. (It is interesting to read the scholarly discussions arguing whether Isaiah was stark naked or wore a loincloth!)

The last collection of Isaiah 1—39 contains historical data, the most important being that which relates the story of the Assyrian seige of Jerusalem. The historical setting occurs when Hezekiah had become king and had attempted to carry out certain reforms. One of the most important of these was the refusal to pay tribute to the Assyrians. Sennacherib, the king of Assyria, came into the land, however, and devastated it. He captured and destroyed forty-six walled cities of Judah, and then he turned his sights toward Jerusalem. Hezekiah had to pay heavy tribute and to give several of his daughters to Sennacherib as concubines, but Jerusalem had not been harmed.

The story of Jerusalem's reprieve is famous indeed. Isaiah told Hezekiah to trust Yahweh, that the city would be delivered (37:5–7, 33–35). And for whatever reason the city was spared. Some argue that rumors of an attempted coup in Assyria forced Sennacherib to go home (cf. 37:7), while others believe that a plague decimated the army of the Assyrians so that they had to return (cf. 37:36). Interestingly enough the Greek historian, Herodotus, gives an account of the story saying that the rats ate the bowstrings of the Assyrians so that they were unable to fight. The mention of rats gives some credence to the theory about the plague.

Naturally the people of Judah interpreted this event as a great deliverance by their God, which indeed it was. Unfortunately, however, they also began to think of Jerusalem as inviolate, believing that Yahweh would never allow anything to happen to Jerusalem no matter what. This proved to be a false hope. This final portion of the book of Isaiah (1—39) prepares for a time when the nation would be carried away captive, but that event was to be postponed for a while.

Micah

The prophet Micah was a native of southern Judah who lived in the countryside southwest of Jerusalem. He was a contemporary of Isaiah (and of Hosea also since he directed some of his oracles against Israel which had not yet fallen when he began his career). His ministry continued into the period of Hezekiah, perhaps even continuing after the invasion of Sennacherib in 701 B.C.

Micah primarily was concerned with the sin of the nations (Israel and Judah) and believed that both would be punished for their wickedness. Being from the countryside, he located the root cause of the problem in the cities, especially Samaria and Jerusalem. Whether his interpretation at this point came as a result of the natural enmity between urban and rural folks or whether he understood the city to be the seat of government which had led the people into the serious situation they now confronted cannot be precisely determined. Apparently both of these elements contributed to Micah's interpretation of the events of his time and place. The basic thrust of his invective was directed at the leaders, be they religious, social, or political.

Few of the prophetic books are as difficult as Micah in ascertaining exactly what oracles originated primarily from his ministry and time and which were later developments of his thinking. It is generally agreed that the collection of oracles found in chapters 1—3 are basically from Micah. After this consensus, however, there is very little agreement! Many scholars argue that the *only* authentic oracles from Micah are in chapters 1—3 and that all others came from a later time. Some argue that the material in 6:1—7:6 should also be considered part of Micah's message. Still others believe that chapters 4—5, even though they may have been edited by later generations, basically go back to Micah also. These passages then are quite disputed as to origin, but it is almost completely agreed that 7:7–20 reflects a post-exilic ending for the final edition of Micah's prophecy.

If one is seeking a central point for the message of this prophet, it appears to be found in his emphasis upon the importance of superior leaders in every area of life—political, religious, business, etc. Where the leadership is corrupt and weak-kneed, people are exploited and ultimately destroyed. And the passage in 5:2–4 which looks forward to a good king from the line of David may therefore have strong claim to be authentically from Micah. After all, Isaiah and Micah were contemporaries, and Isaiah certainly looked forward to a good king to help the people "out of the darkness."

Micah: Outline

    I. Oracles of Doom 1—3
   II. Hope for the Future 4—5
 III. The Nation Deserves Judgment 6:1—7:6
 IV. Hope for Restoration 7:7–20

The first three chapters of Micah are filled with denunciations against both Israel and Judah, primarily Judah. The sins of these two nations are focused in their capitals, Samaria and Jerusalem, and the responsibility for such sin was depicted as resting squarely upon the shoulders of the leaders, political and religious. Such misconduct in high places could only lead inevitably to a society in which people are exploited and horribly abused. One of the most moving of all the prophetic oracles which describes such exploitation is found in Micah.

> Hear, you heads of Jacob,
>> and rulers of the house of Israel!
> Is it not for you to know justice?—
>> you who hate the good and love the evil,
> who tear the skin from off my people,
>> and their flesh from off their bones;
> who eat the flesh of my people,
>> and flay their skin from off them,
> and break their bones in pieces,
>> and chop them up like meat in a kettle,
> like flesh in a caldron. (3:1–3)

Micah's firm belief was that surely judgment would come both upon Samaria and Jerusalem. Samaria did fall within his lifetime, and he obviously thought that Sennacherib would finish Jerusalem just as surely as he had devastated the countryside where Micah lived. Even though this did not happen immediately, ultimately Micah was correct and Jerusalem did fall. It is interesting to note that the saying of Micah about Jerusalem (3:12) is quoted in the book of Jeremiah and probably saved Jeremiah's life.

The collection of hope passages found in chapters 4—5 obviously has been edited from the later viewpoint which emerged in the post-exilic period. But there are some very strong arguments to support the assumption that Micah was responsible for most of these sayings, reworked though they may be. After all, if Micah's ministry lasted into the reign of Hezekiah, as probable, then he would have been quite in approval of Hezekiah's reforms, as was Isaiah, and would have seen some hope in the new awakening of religious reform. It is extremely interesting to note two very close similarities in certain teachings preserved in the books of the two contemporaries.

First, there is the oracle which is so well known even today which appears in both the collections of Isaiah and Micah.

> For out of Zion shall go forth the law,
>> and the word of the LORD from Jerusalem.

> He shall judge between many peoples,
>   and shall decide for strong nations afar off;
> And they shall beat their swords into plowshares,
>   and their spears into pruning hooks;
> Nation shall not lift up sword against nation,
>   neither shall they learn war any more. (4:2b–3, cf. Isaiah 2:3c–4)

Though many scholars argue that this oracle is definitely a post-exilic saying, it is possible that this prophetic proclamation arose from the deliverance of Jerusalem from the hand of the Assyrians. The departure of Sennacherib and his troops could very easily have given rise to the idea of the centrality of Jerusalem and its law as well as to the emphasis upon peace among the nations. Certainty cannot, however, be demonstrated!

The second similarity between Isaiah and Micah focused in the area of looking forward to a better and good king from the line of David to lead the people. It seems clear that Isaiah looked forward to such a person. Many scholars, however, deny the messianic passage in Micah 5:2–4 to Micah, arguing that this is a post-exilic oracle placed here within the Micah collection. It is just as likely that the oracle reflects Micah's thought about a good king who would help to lead the people aright, especially after the Assyrians had left the land (cf. 5:5–6). It is very likely, therefore, that Isaiah and Micah are much closer in their teaching than many interpreters have thought, and that the oracles included in Micah 4—5 may reflect the actual teaching of Micah himself.

Chapter 6 begins a new collection of judgment passages set in an interesting scene. The setting is depicted as a law court in which God brought a charge against his people, and in which the "mountains and the foundations of the earth" were to serve as the jury! This scene then comes to its climax in one of the most well known of all prophetic sayings.

> He has showed you, O man, what is good;
>   and what does the LORD require of you
> But to do justice, and to love *ḥesed* (covenant loyalty),
>   and to walk humbly with your God? (6:8)

This is the kind of religion which Micah understood to be required by Yahweh. No amount of sacrifices nor external rituals could suffice as substitutes for a genuine relationship with Yahweh and the keeping of his covenant obligations and commands.

The last portion of the book reflects the time of the exile and after. The historical setting here is a time when the nation had been destroyed, but the hope was that the people would be restored in their land. The emphasis is beginning to be made, as reflected here, on Yahweh's forgiveness for his people. There was to be hope after the judgment, a message that the post-exilic community needed to hear.

Zephaniah

From the time of Isaiah and Micah, at the conclusion of the eighth century, there was a lengthy period in which there is no record of any prophetic voice. This period coincides with the reign of Manasseh which lasted for fifty-five years, and that period was considered the worst period in the history of Judah by the Deuteronomistic Historians. Many scholars believe that during the time of Manasseh there may well have been a systematic persecution of the prophets of Yahweh.

After the death of Manasseh, however, the situation became more conducive to the proclamation of the prophetic word, in the sense that these spokesmen were not suppressed. The superscription to the book dates Zephaniah during the reign of Josiah (640–609 B.C.), but the situation reflects a time of real religious apostasy. Since the Josianic reform took place in the 620s, the prophet Zephaniah most likely served in the earlier years of Josiah's reign (ca. 630 B.C.) before the reform movement began. Some have argued that this prophet may have been at least partly responsible for the reform! Some others have argued, however, that the more likely time for Zephaniah's ministry was soon after the death of Josiah, in the early years of Jehoiakim's reign when it had become obvious that the reform movement was no longer to be honored. If this latter date is accepted, Zephaniah would have been a contemporary of Jeremiah. Agreement on this matter, however, is difficult to find.

Zephaniah: Outline

I. Oracles Against Judah 1:1—2:3
II. Oracles Against Nations 2:4—3:8
III. Oracles of Hope 3:9–20

One notes the typical outline of many prophetic books even in this small collection—oracles against the nation, oracles against foreign nations, oracles of hope. The book of Zephaniah has, even so, its own peculiar emphases at several points. Zephaniah proclaimed again the old concept of the "Day of Yahweh" first encountered in Amos' preaching. As did Amos, Zephaniah believed that the day would be one of judgment for the people of God, and he thought that the day was near (1:14). (His belief in the nearness of the day of judgment may well point to the time of Jeremiah rather than the earlier date most scholars postulate for him.)

His plea to the people was for them to repent, to be humble. In fact Zephaniah found hope for the continuation of the nation after judgment in the humble and lowly (2:3; 3:12–13). He believed that a remnant would be left when the judgment came, and it was his conviction and hope that from this remnant a new nation could be made.

One notes that the concluding portion of the book of Zephaniah again reflects the post-exilic view which postulated that Yahweh would restore the people to the land.

Nahum

The book of Nahum is basically a collection of several oracles directed against Assyria. The date of the prophet's proclamation can be limited in that the book refers to a sack of the Egyptian city (Thebes, 3:8) which occurred in 663 B.C., and the city of Nineveh was itself at that moment in danger of imminent destruction. Historically this could have been in 625 or in 612, probably the latter. Thus the entire book seems to be an oracle of doom against a foreign nation, a typical and common type of prophetic utterance.

Because the book is almost completely directed against Assyria, however, there are some scholars who see in Nahum a type of prophet who constantly prophesied good things for Judah. These prophets were real "thorns in the flesh" to the others, such as Jeremiah, who tried to open the eyes of the people to their own sin. This view of Nahum seems to be much too narrow an interpretation of his work, and one notes that there is very little in the book to give any great hope to the people of

Judah in terms of escaping the consequences of their own sin. The book rather depicts a historical situation wherein the nation of Assyria which was the great scourge of the ancient world for several centuries and which had committed unthinkable atrocities against most of the nations of that area was about to "get her due." There was no thought here, however, of allowing Judah to escape her sins.

The book itself seems to have been compiled from two basic blocks of material. The first block in chapter 1 was originally an acrostic poem, i.e., a poem in which each line in succession began with the letters of the Hebrew alphabet. The poem, however, stops with the letter, L, thereby causing one to wonder what happened to the other half, or if another half ever existed. Some have argued that this poem may have originated and been used in a cultic liturgy. The second part of the book consists of poems describing the fall of Nineveh and the satisfaction which Nahum and others felt at the destruction of such a malicious nation.

Nahum: Outline

    I. Proclamation of Yahweh's Judgment on the Wicked Nation 1
   II. Descriptions of the Fall of Nineveh 2—3

From the very beginning of the book the nation which was to be judged is described as greatly deserving of God's punishment. The prophetic message leaves no doubt that the source of the judgment is Yahweh, God of Hosts. The nation to be judged was evil and idolatrous and had been especially harsh on the people of God (cf. 1:14–15). But God's punishment on this wicked nation had finally come, and not only Judah but the nations of the world were rejoicing to see such atrocity destroyed. This thought graphically concludes the book:

    Your shepherds are asleep,
      O king of Assyria;
      your nobles slumber,
    Your people are scattered on the mountains
      with none to gather them.
    There is no assuaging your hurt,
      your wound is grievous.

All who hear the news of you
clap their hands over you.
For upon whom has not come
your unceasing evil? (3:18–19)

Numerous allusions to Nineveh and its beliefs are scattered throughout the poems. The patron goddess of Nineveh was Ishtar, a fierce war
goddess and also goddess of love and lust who was frequently depicted
as riding upon a lion. Thus the lion was quite often used as a symbol for
Assyria. Passages such as 2:10–12 and 3:4 reflect this background.

There are those who question the place of such an outright proclamation of glee at human destruction and feel that there is no "redeeming
value" in Nahum's outburst of utter hatred. But to argue thus misses the
real point of the book. The basic teaching seems to be that Yahweh does
judge the evil of the world. Nations which cruelly and mercilessly inflict
unthinkable suffering upon others do stand under the judgment of God.
While one may well be repulsed by Nahum's *total* joy at the destruction
of Nineveh, the question might well be asked if there is not some place
in God's order of justice for "righteous indignation" when evil runs
unchecked. Obviously Nahum and the editors of the prophetic messages
as well thought that there was a place for such feeling as long as God
was executing the vengeance.

Habakkuk

Very little is known about the prophet Habakkuk, and there is very
little in the contents of the book which can give clues as to the time of
his ministry. Conjectures have been made which date this material from
the mid-seventh century to the time of Alexander the Great (ca. 330
B.C.). The reference, however, to the Chaldeans (i.e., the Babylonians)
seems to give a fairly definite clue to the dating problem, placing the
material in the late seventh century or perhaps the early part of the sixth.
The question at that point then becomes the identity of the "wicked" who
were to be destroyed by the Babylonians. Some have argued that the
Assyrians were intended; if so the date would be somewhere between
626 and 612 B.C. It is more likely, however, that the wicked here are to

be identified with Judah. This would mean that the most probable date would be somewhere during the latter part of the reign of Jehoiakim (605–600 B.C.).

The prophet Habakkuk appears to have been associated with the cult somehow, since there are several references in the material which seem to point in that direction. In fact some have even argued that chapters 1 and 2 constitute a cultic liturgy!

Another problem has to do with chapter 3. It has its own super-scription and appears to be a hymn which may have been used in a cultic service. Some have argued that this hymn, therefore, was not a part of Habakkuk's original message but was added later because of the similarity of teaching between the two blocks of material. Some support for such a view was found in the Dead Sea Scroll collection from Qumran where there was a text of Habakkuk which consisted only of chapters 1—2. Others, however, still argue for the material in chapter 3 as part of Habakkuk's message.

Habakkuk: Outline

I. A Dialogue Between Habakkuk and God 1—2
II. Concluding Hymn or Prayer 3

The prophet Habakkuk is somewhat different from his fellow proph-ets in that he appears to be more reflective in his proclamations than they were. He realized, for example, that the people of Judah had broken the covenant with their God and deserved to be punished, but he was concerned about the age old question of *theodicy,* i.e., the justice of God. Habakkuk could not understand why God would use an evil people to exercise judgment on a less evil people (1:13). His question has been asked by many persons, and still is! Stationing himself in a tower in order to receive a response to this concern, Habakkuk was finally told that the "righteous person shall live by faithfulness" (2:4, paraphrase). As one can immediately recognize, this was not really a direct answer to his question.

By asking such questions, this prophet proved to be the forerunner of another movement which developed and flourished in the post-exilic period, i.e., the speculative dimension of the Wisdom tradition (cf. below, pp. 226ff.). There was great strength in the man, however, for in spite of his lack of understanding he trusted in the power and ultimate righteousness of God. The hymn in chapter 3 does indeed reflect the basic message of the book, especially verses 17–18:

> Though the fig tree do not blossom,
>   nor fruit be on the vines,
> the produce of the olive fail
>   and the fields yield no food . . .
> Yet I will rejoice in the LORD,
>   I will joy in the God of my salvation.

Jeremiah

Jeremiah, one of the greatest and most tragic prophetic figures, was a native of Anathoth, a small village north of Jerusalem in the land of Benjamin. Many interpreters try to link Jeremiah with the priest exiled to that place at the time of Solomon's ascendency to the throne, namely Abiathar. There is no real evidence for any connection, however. The time for the beginning of Jeremiah's ministry is usually placed ca. 626 B.C., but of late several interpreters have questioned that date. Since Jeremiah does not mention Josiah except as a king of the past and does not refer to Josiah's reforms, some believe that Jeremiah's ministry actually began shortly after Josiah's death in 609 B.C. It is interesting that Jeremiah felt that his call to begin preaching, which is described in chapter 1, came while he was as yet unborn! Therefore some argue that the date 626 B.C. is the date of Jeremiah's birth rather than the date of the inauguration of his ministry. Whatever view one accepts, it is without question that Jeremiah's ministry basically took place during the reigns of Jehoiakim and Zedekiah.

With Jeremiah, and also Ezekiel, a new emphasis arose in the prophetic message. Since the judgment had now come upon Judah, there needed to be a shift in emphasis away from oracles of doom to oracles of hope. One finds just such a shift in these two prophets. They uttered many words of judgment because the nation was still in the midst of the historical downfall, but they looked beyond the fall to the future. More will be said about this matter later.

The book of Jeremiah consists of several different collections of material which were edited together into the form which now exists. The text must have had an interesting history, for the Greek version of Jeremiah is one-eighth shorter than the Hebrew text and also is arranged differently. The initial point of departure for a literary study of this book resides in the story found in chapter 36 where Jeremiah called his scribe, Baruch, to him and dictated a large number of oracles against the nation of Judah. This scroll was taken to the Temple and read, and thence to King Jehoiakim. When the king heard it, he cut the scroll into small pieces and dropped them into the fire. Whereupon Jeremiah dictated again to Baruch and even added some additional sayings! This incident probably occurred ca. 605 B.C. and most scholars believe that this scroll probably formed the basic if not the essential content for chapters 1—25 which contain oracles of Jeremiah most of which seem to fit into the time of Jehoiakim.

A second collection of the prophet's oracles is found in 46—51, a series of oracles against foreign nations. It is interesting that in the Septuagint these chapters are located after 25:13a, following the usual pattern of the prophetic books, but in the Hebrew they have been moved to the end of the collection.

Another block of material appears in chapters 30—33, sometimes called the "Book of Consolation," a collection of primarily hope passages. Some even divide these chapters into two separate sets, 30—31 and 32—33. Additionally, chapters 26—29 and 34—45 contain a collection of basically prose stories and accounts dealing with the life of Jeremiah and which reflect certain Deuteronomic style and thought. Some have conjectured that Baruch was responsible for this collection, at least initially before the Deuteronomic editing process.

All of these collections were then placed together to form the book of Jeremiah. It is possible for one to find traces of some other collections within these larger collections, the most famous of which is the sequence of personal laments from Jeremiah usually called the "Confessions." These passages are found in 11:18—12:6; 15:10–21; 17:12(14)–18; 18:18–23; and 20:7–18. In them much can be learned about the life of Jeremiah and his personal feelings in the light of all that was happening to him. The bottom line is that persons were plotting to kill Jeremiah and to inflict serious harm upon him. Naturally the prospects of such actions

by his enemies did not set too well with this emotional man, especially
when he would rather have been doing something else!

Jeremiah: Outline

   I. Oracles Against Judah and Miscellaneous Data 1:1—25:14
  II. Oracles Against Foreign Nations 25:15—38; 46—51
 III. Episodes from the Life of Jeremiah 26—29; 34—45
 IV. Oracles of Hope 30—33
  V. Historical Appendix 52

Jeremiah's ministry may well have begun with an incident reported
in the account of his famous "Temple Sermon." This was considered a
major event in his life as is evidenced in the fact that there are two
accounts of it in the book (cf. chapters 7 and 26). Jeremiah was told to
go and to say in the Temple that the Temple could not deliver the nation
from judgment. This message was indeed startling to the people and
especially to the leaders. The reader is reminded that one of the key
features of Josiah's reform was to centralize all legitimate worship in the
Temple, emphasizing the presence of Yahweh in that place. Coupled
with the remembrance of what had occurred in Isaiah's time when the
Assyrians were not able to capture Jerusalem (though they captured most
of the remainder of Judah), the emphasis on the importance of the
Temple led the people and its leaders into believing that Jerusalem and
the Temple insured the safety of the nation. For Jeremiah to say in the
gate of the Temple that this was erroneous was a serious accusation. The
account in chapter 26 indicates that Jeremiah came very close to losing
his life; someone's remembering that Micah had said essentially the
same thing almost a century before kept him safe, however. During the
first portion of his ministry under Jehoiakim, Jeremiah was the target of
much opposition. He was beaten and placed into stocks; plots were
devised against his life, and he was generally hated and excluded from
the life of the people.

Jeremiah was set in opposition to the people and the leaders, not
because he wanted it so but because his understanding of Yahweh's
requirements and actions was diametrically opposed to theirs. He had a
running feud with Jehoiakim whose funeral Jeremiah predicted would be

like that of a dead jackass! The actions of the religious leaders were quite at odds with Jeremiah's understanding of their duties and responsibilities. He accused them of being professional religionists whose sole aim was to make as much as they could from saying and doing what the people wanted. Jeremiah found (cf. 5:1–5) that it was not only the leadership of the land that was lax and corrupt; the people also were basically and hopelessly evil.

One of Jeremiah's basic themes related to that very point, that the people needed to have a new nature, a new heart. One of his favorite expressions consisted of calling upon the people to "circumcise their hearts" (e.g., 4:4a). Jeremiah found that the nature of the people had become such that they did not even know how to blush, and washing with lye could not remove their guilt. Just how bad they had become is reflected in the episode during the second siege of Jerusalem when Zedekiah was king. The situation was grave indeed; food and water were scarce, but the law required persons who owned slaves to see to the well-being of the slaves even in harsh times. Therefore, to circumvent this requirement the slaves were proclaimed "freed." Shortly thereafter the armies of the Babylonians left for a short while (to take care of an Egyptian problem) and when that happened the rulers immediately rescinded the decree of freedom for the slaves and took them back again. Such wickedness and hypocrisy Jeremiah felt was too much to be forgiven (cf. chapter 34).

Many prophetic signs were connected with the ministry of Jeremiah—the breaking of the flask to demonstrate God's judgment upon the nation (19), the hiding of the loincloth along a river or body of water (13), as well as several others. But the one which perhaps was the hardest for Jeremiah was his belief that he should not marry (almost unthinkable in that time) as a sign that the judgment of God was definitely coming which would cause intense suffering. Women and children would be slaughtered or worse, and the land would not immediately survive the judgment. His advice to the people was to surrender to the Babylonians to keep the ravages of war to a minimum, since they had no chance of succeeding in resisting this great power. The people, however, looked upon him as a traitor.

The first defeat at the hands of the Babylonians came in 597 B.C. Jehoiakim had died immediately before the fall of the city; his son,

Jehoiachin, came to the throne but was carried away into Babylon (along with a number of the leaders) into exile. Babylonia, as Jeremiah had predicted, was very lenient in spite of the rebellion. Zedekiah was placed on the throne by Nebuchadnezzar, but Zedekiah was too weak to resist the pro-Egyptian group in Judah which constantly agitated for further rebellion against Babylonia. Egypt, naturally, encouraged this sort of behavior in all of the smaller nations which stood between her and Babylonia.

There was constant turmoil in such a situation. Jeremiah urged the people to submit to the yoke of Babylon for that was Yahweh's will (cf. chapters 27—28). Others urged rebellion, for, they argued, Yahweh would break the yoke of Babylonia and bring back the exiles very shortly. The rebellion finally occurred and soon became an open challenge to Babylonia. Such action only brought greater suffering, as Jeremiah had predicted. When the Babylonians came back in 587/6 B.C., they destroyed the city and carried away a large number of people. Jeremiah was asked (by the Babylonians) if he wished to go to Babylon; he chose to remain with the people left in the land, to attempt to be a help to them.

Yet another rebellion was then spawned, in spite of Jeremiah's opposition. After all this time when the teaching of this tragic figure had been proved to be correct, the people would still not listen to the man. This time, those who murdered the governor, Gedaliah, forced Jeremiah to flee with them to Egypt where, as tradition has it, they finally stoned him to death!

One might think that after all the tragedy of Jeremiah's life that he would be bitter and without hope, but his understanding of God was such that all the tragedy of his life could not dispel the hope that he basically understood to reside in this God. In spite of the destruction of the nation, the desolation of the land, and the two deportations of people to Babylon, Jeremiah could see that there would be a restoration of the nation in the land. That restoration would not come soon, however, and therefore he counseled the people in Babylon to settle down, make new lives for themselves, and even pray for the peace of Babylon. Jeremiah felt that it would take about two generations before the Judean people would be allowed to return, but he definitely felt that the hope for a new nation lay with the exiles in Babylon. The people who had been left in the land would be of no value in reestablishing a new nation. They were, as he saw in a "vision," bad figs (cf. chapters 24—25).

To demonstrate his own confidence in the restoration of the nation Jeremiah performed another prophetic sign. On this occasion he bought a piece of property as a sign of hope that some day fields could again be bought and sold and that stability would return to the lives of the people (cf. chapter 32).

The heart of Jeremiah's hope, however, is found in chapters 30—31, especially in the famous passage 31:31–34. There are some interpreters who argue that these passages are post-exilic additions to Jeremiah's oracles and teachings. This may be true, at least in the sense that these passages may have been edited by a post-exilic Deuteronomic redactor. But Jeremiah is somewhat different, as is Ezekiel, in that he stood not only before the judgment, looking toward that event, but also after the judgment. This enabled him to see that same event from a new and different perspective. Thus it is questionable as to whether the hope passages in Jeremiah, particularly those in 30—31, should be denied to him.

The primary teaching is found in 31:31–34 which is frequently called the "new covenant" passage. Perhaps the examination of this passage would assist in determining its meaning and Jeremiah's connection with it. One interesting feature is that the passage (while translated as prose in the RSV) might well be poetic.

> Behold, the days are coming, says the LORD, when I will make a new covenant with the house of Israel and the house of Judah, not like the covenant which I made with their fathers when I took them by the hand to bring them out of Egypt, my covenant which they broke, though I was their husband, says the LORD. But this is the covenant which I will make with the house of Israel after those days, says the LORD:
> I will put my law within them,
>   and I will write it upon their hearts;
> and I will be their God,
> and they shall be my people.
> And no longer shall each man teach his neighbor
>   and each his brother, saying,
> "Know the LORD,"
>   for they shall all know me,

from the least of them to the greatest, says the LORD;
for I will forgive their iniquity,
and I will remember their sin no more.

One is struck with the number of specifically Jeremianic phrases and thoughts incorporated into this passage. The central issue is that of covenant which the people had broken, an emphasis found in Jeremiah's teaching. This breach of covenant as Jeremiah understood it resulted from an "uncircumcised heart." The new covenant is solidly based upon a new heart upon which the law of God has been written. The hope is that all people, from the least to the greatest, will "know" (i.e., be in the proper relationship with) Yahweh—another of Jeremiah's concerns. Finally, the entire scenario is based upon one indispensable pre-requisite—God has to forgive the people before a restoration can take place. This again is part of Jeremiah's genuine teaching. Thus, if this passage does not come directly from Jeremiah, it certainly does reflect accurately his basic religious understandings.

For all his trouble Jeremiah never gave up hope for the nation because he understood that God could and would continue to exist even if Judah and the Temple fell. Yahweh was not confined to this people only, but his power extended over many nations and his presence could be a factor in the lives of the people no matter where they might be. From the tragedy of his own life he left a great legacy to the descendants of the people who did not like him, sought to kill him, and never heeded his words.

The Exilic Prophets

Ezekiel

Ezekiel was a member of the group which was carried away from Judah into exile in Babylonia ca. 597 B.C. It is clear that he was a priest and obviously exercised a great deal of authority among the people. The fact that he was a priest explains the emphasis in this book upon the proper form and order of worship, the consequences of not fulfilling proper worship, and finally the projected new community which was to revolve around a new Temple with its orders of worship.

Most think that the call to be a prophet came to Ezekiel when he was thirty years old in the year 593 B.C. (cf. 1:1–3). Something of the bizarre nature of this person is revealed immediately in the call account. The weird symbolism and the strange actions which are part of the reminder of the account of Ezekiel's ministry are clearly depicted at the beginning. The call came to Ezekiel during a thunderstorm in which he saw a throne-chariot in the midst of the air upon which the glory of Yahweh resided. The religious interpretation of this account is clear. Yahweh had not been destroyed nor had he remained behind in Judah, but he was present with the people in Babylon. What is portrayed here is another of the familiar theophany accounts, even though this one differs because of the wild images and figures included in it.

Ezekiel was called to be a prophet, and this ministry was understood to be similar to that of a watchman. The watchman's duty was to warn people of danger even if they did not respond to the warning. This was to characterize his ministry. The favorite expression for Ezekiel in the book centers in the term, "Son of Man," which occurs over ninety times within the book. The term means in Hebrew simply "man," usually designating "man" in the sense of his finiteness and weakness.

There are several very difficult questions which are connected with the book (and life) of Ezekiel. On cursory examination the book appears to be a model of order; many of the oracles are even dated, giving a semblance of structure to the book. The last dated oracle seems to be from ca. 571 B.C. Various scholars detect at certain points carefully constructed redactional editing, and dates for the material have ranged from the time of Manasseh (ca. 650 B.C.) to the late post-exilic period (ca. 230 B.C.). Whatever conclusion one reaches on this matter will definitely affect the dating of the book and whether Ezekiel was responsible for most of its contents. There seems to be, however, no reason to deny that most of the material found in this book did in fact originate with the prophet himself.

A second problem frequently debated is that of the geographical location in which Ezekiel carried out his ministry. The reader is told that the prophet was in Babylon, but there are various scenes (cf. chapter 8 for example) which are set in the land of Judah and in the city of Jerusalem. Did Ezekiel actually carry on a ministry in both places? Was he really a Judean prophet who was simply set into the Babylonian milieu later or perhaps himself only came to Babylon at a later date? Was his ministry carried out in Babylon with the prophet receiving detailed and frequent reports of the events happening "back home"? Or has the work of two or more prophets been combined into the one figure now known as Ezekiel? The theories are many, but the most likely answer is that the book is a collection basically from one man, Ezekiel, whose ministry was spent in Babylon, but who kept up with the events from the native land. From Jeremiah's book one learns, for example, of the open communication between the two communities.

Since the final destruction of Jerusalem and the final deportation of the people had not yet taken place when Ezekiel began his ministry, it is not surprising to learn that he was very interested in Judah. And also he was interested in attempting to understand why these calamities had overtaken his people and how they could be prevented in the future.

The final problem lies with the man himself. Having studied the book, the reader is struck by the weird and sometimes bizarre behavior of this man. What does one make of the unusual behavior so typical of this prophet? Was he ill, either physically or mentally? Did he simply have a flair for the dramatic and by acting in such an extremely bizarre manner assure attention to his message? Or was he a person who was simply a "weirdo"? Or could it have been a combination of all these elements? The jury is still out on Ezekiel at this point, but whatever explanation may be given to the question of Ezekiel's personality, the message of the book remains the same.

It is interesting that there are some very real similarities between the teaching of Ezekiel and the priestly material found in the Tetrateuch, especially in some of the requirements and teachings of the Holiness Code (cf. Leviticus 17—26). Could it be that Ezekiel influenced (or was perhaps influenced by) the group which later was responsible for the P material? It is possible since both Ezekiel and this group were centered in Babylon, but most scholars who find a parallel feel that the P material is more fully developed, the product of a longer and more refined tradition.

Ezekiel: Outline

I. Oracles Against Judah and Jerusalem 1—24

II. Oracles Against Foreign Nations 25—32
III. Oracles of Restoration 33—48
   A. Preparation for Return 33—39
   B. Restoration of the Cult in the Temple 40—48

The book of Ezekiel is structured very precisely and neatly. There are oracles dealing with Judah and Jerusalem in chapters 1—24, oracles against foreign nations in 25—32, and oracles dealing with the restoration of the community in and around Jerusalem in 33—48. Interspersed within these sections, especially the first, are many weird and unusal signs, but all of the teachings and signs were directed at the sin of the nation and emphasized the inevitability of the judgment which God had brought upon the people.

As already noted Ezekiel understood his own ministry to be that of a "watchman" warning the people about their sin and challenging them to new life in proper relationship with God. Ezekiel's basic religious understanding evolved directly from his concept of Yahweh, already prefigured in his call experience, as a God transcendent and holy and majestic. It is possible that some of his peculiar actions may have stemmed from this concept and may have been intended to emphasize God's "otherness."

Several of his actions and symbolic stories are quite famous and reflect his basic theological understanding. One is found in chapter 4 where Ezekiel took a brick, sketched a city on it, and surrounded it with camps of soldiers and military paraphernalia (much as a child would do with toy soldiers) as a sign against both Israel and Judah. Then he was commanded to lie on his left side for 390 days to symbolize (or actualize) the punishment of Israel, and on his right side for 40 days to symbolize the punishment of Judah. The point was that the days of their exile would be one year for each day he lay on his side!

It is interesting to note at this point a growing tendency on the part of the prophets to envision the reuniting of Israel and Judah. This was already anticipated in Jeremiah and was carried further by Ezekiel. The question arises as to how and why there would now be a renewed interest in the reunion of the two peoples. In all probability this idea was given impetus in the time of Josiah when the Assyrians were under heavy attack from the Babylonians and were unable to control Palestine as they had previously. During this period Josiah had been able to exercise some degree of control over part of what was formerly the Northern Kingdom. This gave rise to a feeling that the two nations would be reunited again. Believing this, however, did not necessarily mean that it was thought that Israel would come back from captivity, i.e., that the "lost" tribes would be restored. What it did portend was an expansion of the political power of Judah and Jerusalem over the area that had formerly been held by the United Monarchy. This seems to be the teaching of Jeremiah (Jeremiah 30—31) and Ezekiel (especially Ezekiel 37).

Another of the famous episodes of the book of Ezekiel is found in chapter 8. Here is a description of what was going on religiously and cultically in the period between the first deportation and the second. It was found that the people were worshiping the sun, various idols and even the fertility god of Babylonia, Tammuz. All this seems to have been going on with the knowledge and consent of the elders and priests! Because of such activity Ezekiel saw the glory of Yahweh leave the Temple—the meaning needs no explanation.

Earlier interpreters of the Old Testament writings understood the religion of the Bible to be basically evolutionary in nature from lower, more primitive forms to the higher forms. To a degree they were correct in that certain understandings and practices certainly did develop and change. One of the changes which these older scholars thought they discerned in the development lay in the early emphasis on the group which evolved into an emphasis solely upon the individual believer. Most interpreters today do not see a development from corporate to individual; most understand that the teachings, both early and late, involve elements of emphasis on both the group and the individual. Earlier commentators, working with the presuppositions just stated, found the transition from corporate to individual in the prophets Jeremiah and Ezekiel. Upon close examination, however, that interpretation does not hold up. In the Jeremiah passage, 31:31-34, it was the nation which was to be restored and a new covenant formed with it. In Ezekiel one finds the same situation; the community was to be restored.

But many interpreters still look at Ezekiel 18 as the great chapter on individualism in the entire Old Testament. The background for the passage lay in the fact that the people who were in exile in Babylon were complaining that they were suffering unjustly for the sins of their parents. Their cry was, "The fathers have eaten sour grapes, and the children's teeth are set on edge." Ezekiel spoke to this situation and delivered one of his most logical and cogent teachings. In this passage Ezekiel did not argue or dispute the point that the people may have been in exile because of the sins of generations past. What he attempted to set out was that in spite of circumstances, one can still be faithful to Yahweh and his commands. The person who is faithful shall live, i.e., have a good life; the one who is not faithful shall die, i.e., destroy him/herself by not being obedient to Yahweh's commands. In fact, Ezekiel felt that these people should have learned that lesson from their forebears. The prophet depicted Yahweh as urging repentance for all who had sinned and continued steadfastness for all who had remained faithful. "I have no pleasure in the death of anyone, says the Lord GOD; so repent, and live" (18:32, paraphrase).

Another of Ezekiel's well-known figures is found in the allegory of the two harlot sisters, Oholah and Oholibah. These sisters, of course, represented Samaria and Jerusalem, both of whom had played the harlot. The first, Oholah, was destroyed because of her wicked ways, but the other sister did not learn from her example, and she too was destroyed. This passage could have been a warning to Judah close to the time of the second deportation or perhaps a commentary on that fall soon after it had occurred.

The oracles of restoration and hope found in this book are usually divided into two sections, chapters 33—39 and 40—48. The first portrays God's concern for his people and emphasizes that even though the political rulers had no real feelings for the people, God was to them as a Shepherd who cares for his flock. The chapters depict a restoration under a new David, who, interestingly enough, is only called a "prince" not a king (34:24).

In a teaching quite similar to that of Jeremiah 31:31–34, Ezekiel envisions a new covenant between God and the people in which the people are given a new heart made of flesh, to replace their old heart of stone (36:26ff.). Part of this process would necessarily entail a ritual cleansing, something one would expect from a person of priestly background.

His most famous and well-known vision, however, is that of the valley of dry bones (chapter 37). Ezekiel saw a valley full of bones separated from each other, lying scattered on the land. When the Spirit of God moved upon those bones, they were brought together in order and covered over with flesh so that they lived again. This was a vision of the resurrection of the nation, not of individual people, but of the corporate group. Ezekiel believed that the restoration of the people in the land would lead to a nation as great as that formerly presided over by David. This would be made possible by the destruction of God's enemies, here depicted under the name, "Gog and Magog" *or* "Gog from Magog" *or* "Gog even Magog." The precise identification of the origin of these names is not known, but it is clear that they represent Babylonia. When these enemies were destroyed, the people could again be restored in their own land.

Restoration in their own land also would bring with it a restoration of true and proper worship of God. This new society was depicted by Ezekiel as a theocratic state, i.e., one centering in religious precepts and revolving therefore around the role and person of the priests. Naturally such a society in Israel would center in the restored Temple, and most of the remainder of this section describes the new Temple and the cultic activities connected with it. Note the care and precision with which all elements and articles of this new place were described. When all the elements were properly in place, the glory of Yahweh was seen to enter the Temple (cf. chapter 10 where the glory left the Temple). One of the most graphic symbols connected with this material depicts a river flowing out of the Temple which would even cause the Dead Sea to come to life. It should not be necessary to point out that this is poetic license. The important matter is that Yahweh is there; in fact the name of this city will be changed to "The LORD is there" (48:35b).

Isaiah 40—55

The second major section of the book of Isaiah contains chapters 40—55 and is frequently referred to as Second or Deutero-Isaiah. The reason for understanding these chapters as being from a different person than the Isaiah of the eighth century lies in the fact that these chapters presuppose that the people of Judah were in Babylon in captivity. The basic thrust of the message is that Yahweh was about to release the people and allow them to return to their land. This historical setting would then be ca. 550–540 B.C.

One may wonder, then, why these oracles were not collected together under the name of the prophet of the exile into a separate book. There are numerous answers which could be given, but the most likely is that these oracles originated within the circle of those persons who were preserving and transmitting the oracles of the Isaiah of the eighth century. To them there would be nothing wrong in having the collection together, in fact that would have been the natural order of procedure. The same process probably was operative in connecting the last section, chapters 56—66, to the book as well.

It was in 1892 with the work of B. Duhm that the most vigorous arguments for the idea of separating chapters 40—66 from the eighth century prophet were presented. Some had argued for this idea earlier, but Duhm was the one whose name is usually connected with this division. He also propounded the idea, which has become a highly controversial item of debate among Old Testament scholars, of the "Servant Songs." There are in the material of Deutero-Isaiah four poetic sections which deal with the figure of a "servant." These passages are 42:1–4; 49:1–6; 50:4–9, and 52:13—53:12. It was argued that these passages originally existed separately and apart from the other portions of Deutero-Isaiah and were composed by someone other than the prophet of the exile.

Through the years perhaps more scholarly ink has been spilled over the issues connected with the servant than any other one element in Old Testament study. Who was the servant? An individual, a group, or a combination of both? Was the servant a historical person or a mythological figure? If he was a historical person, who was he? Moses, Jehoiachin, Jeremiah, the prophet himself, a leprous teacher of the law? If the servant was a collective entity, was he Israel, ideal Israel, a group within Israel? What was the role of the servant? Was he a kingly figure, a prophetic figure, a messianic figure, a priestly figure?

Unanimity of opinion on these problems will not be found soon or easily but several points should be made. First of all, it is generally thought that even if the servant songs existed separately originally, they do nevertheless reflect the same style and vocabulary as the remainder of chapters 40—55. This would at least point in the direction that would enable these passages to be interpreted as by the same author as the remainder of 40—55. Secondly, one cannot help but notice that the figure of the servant is not limited to the verses in these four sections but appears also in various other places in the text. In these other places the servant is directly identified with the nation, Israel, something that occurs also in one of the servant passages (49:3). The problem in 49:3 is that the phrase identifying Israel as the servant is viewed by some scholars as a later insertion into the text since it disturbs the poetic meter where it now stands.

Is there a solution to this knotty problem of the identity of the servant and the question as to where these poems originated? There is certainly not one which will be agreed upon by everyone, but the following proposal seems to fit most of the data as they appear. It seems clear that the servant was intended to be identified as Israel. This identification is made in the text itself. The fact that persons can find reflections of some of the figures of Israelite history in the descriptions only indicates something of the background and thinking of the one who used this image as a symbol for the nation. Further, it appears that the same person (or persons) responsible for the material in the remainder of Isaiah 40—55 is responsible for these passages also. The style and content are so much the same that to separate only these passages from the rest seems quite arbitrary.

The question remains, however, concerning the portrayal of the servant as an individual and a group at different points in the material. There is also the question as to how Israel can have a ministry to Israel if the servant is Israel! These matters are in reality of little consequence if one recalls the tendency toward the corporate personality motif in the thought of Israel, where an individual can represent the group and the group can represent an individual. The issue as to how Israel can have a ministry to Israel can also be explained by this same motif.

Other matters of concern are also debated rather strongly. What is the setting for the oracles of this great prophet? Could it be in the cultic setting of the worship for the people in Babylon? Or do these poetic pieces appear to have been written down rather than spoken originally? What about the historical setting for the book? It is obvious to the careful reader that there are two basic sections, 40—48, 49—55, but are both from the same historical period? Some have argued, for example, that

40—48 must come ca. 550–540 B.C. (Some date them more precisely ca. 546 B.C.) The second division, 49—55, cannot be dated with any precision since there are few historical clues to give any direction for exact dating. To illustrate the ambiguity of these matters, one is reminded of a theory which argues that 40—48 came from the time of the Babylonian captivity but that these chapters are arranged in reverse chronological order! The further argument is that 49—55 came from a later time, after ca. 485 B.C. This theory simply serves to illustrate the variety and scope of some of the conjectures which have been formulated in connection with this writing.

Isaiah 40—55: Outline

I. Oracles of Hope for the Exiles in Babylon 40—48
II. Oracles of Restoration for the Nation 49—55

While the material in Isaiah 40—55 is easily divided into two sections under two basic headings, the religious ideas involved within these two sections are not so neatly divided. Various themes are seen to flow through the material, and the religious teachings are varied and wide ranging.

The basic thesis of the message of this prophet lies in his belief that Yahweh is the God of all creation and there is no god except Yahweh. Already the reader of the Old Testament documents has seen that while there was to be no god of Israel except Yahweh, there had not been as yet a clear and consistent teaching which absolutely denied the existence of any gods but Yahweh. With this great prophet of the exile, that teaching was espoused and proclaimed with conviction. It is quite possible that this crystallization of a monotheistic interpretation of Yahweh was stimulated by the emphasis which the Babylonians placed upon their gods, especially Marduk seen as the chief of gods and the one responsible for creation. One recalls that the great Priestly account of creation which has some similarities with the Babylonian accounts was in all probability written either during or soon after the Babylonian exile. The emphasis is upon Yahweh as the Creator, the only God, and there are numerous passages where the prophet ridicules and slanders the gods of the Babylonians.

> Thus says Yahweh, the King of Israel . . .
> "I am the first and I am the last;
>   besides me there is no God." (44:6)

Because of Yahweh's greatness and control over creation and history the prophet could proclaim to the people that they would be allowed to return home shortly. This return was portrayed in the language and imagery of another exodus. God would lead the people through the desert, the mountains would be leveled, the valleys filled in, oases would spring up all along the way, and the new land would be a glorious place indeed. One is cautioned to remember that these are poetic statements not historical-factual statements, something that even many of the returning exiles failed to acknowledge.

Another of the religious themes of Isaiah 40—55 revolves around the idea of "universalism," i.e., the idea that Yahweh and the law and covenant of Yahweh are for all people. Many interpreters have made much of this element, and rightly so, but there is also an element of nationalism and exclusivism which cannot be overlooked in the teachings of this prophet. Nevertheless the mission of the servant of Yahweh (the *Ebed-Yahweh*) was to be focused on the Gentiles. The people of God were intended to be a "light to the nations." The question of what position the Gentiles were to be assigned in the new order was not quite so glorious, however!

It is interesting to note that this prophet, as the others before him, understood Yahweh to be the director of history and the God who surprises the people in that he is not a God who can be limited to or by their ideas and notions. Deutero-Isaiah probably surprised the people by stating quite bluntly that Cyrus was the *messiah* of Yahweh (cf. 44:28; 45:1)! Cyrus, it was argued, had been anointed or selected by God to be the means by which the people were to be released and allowed to return to their home.

Of all the teachings of this collection, however, the most unique and revolutionary is that connected with the last servant song, 52:13—53:12. There are many differing interpretations of this passage, but the basic religious motif found here is that of "vicarious" suffering. By this was meant the type of suffering which is not deserved but which is endured and has the effect ultimately of being of redemptive value for others. Whether the prophet felt that the present generation of Israelites in Babylon were suffering vicariously for others who would come later, or whether someone, a religious leader perhaps, in the community had suffered on behalf of the people as a whole, or whether something else was in mind cannot be determined. The religious meaning is the same; this prophet had introduced into the religion of Israel a relatively new concept wherein an innocent person or persons could by their suffering be a means of salvation and redemption for others. This was not then, nor is it now, a "popular" idea, and it is interesting that this teaching is not found again in the Old Testament writings.

This collection concluded with a call to the people to accept Yahweh's redemption and restoration. Here is a marvelous picture of the greatnesss of God and a promise for release from Babylonian captivity.

> For you shall go out in joy,
>> and be led forth in peace;
> the mountains and the hills before you
>> shall break forth into singing,
>> and all the trees of the field shall clap their hands.
> Instead of the thorn shall come up the cypress;
>> instead of the brier shall come up the myrtle;
> and so it shall be to the LORD for a memorial,
>> for an everlasting sign which shall not be cut off. (55:12–13)

The Post-Exilic Prophets

Haggai

With the destruction of the Babylonian empire by Cyrus in 539 B.C., the world situation changed and so did the situation of the people of Judah in exile. An enlightened ruler, Cyrus proclaimed that all the exiled peoples could return to their homelands and worship their own gods. No wonder that Deutero-Isaiah looked upon him as "messiah." The stage was set for the return of the exiles. But the plain truth was that most of the people did not want to return. Most of these people had never seen Jerusalem and Judea; Babylon was their home. Their vocations and livelihoods were there. Why return?

Some, however, did want to return, and led by a certain Sheshbazzar went back to Judea ca. 538 B.C. Instead of finding glorious and miraculous (poetic) things, they were faced with the grim realities of life. The land had been basically uninhabited for almost fifty years; that part of the land which was any good had been possessed by others not willing now to relinquish their claim upon it. The people who lived in the area of the old Northern Kingdom were worse than foreigners to the returning exiles. The returning exiles were very vulnerable to the attacks of neighboring countries and peoples. This was *not* a dream fulfilled!

Obviously the reality of simply being preoccupied with survival caused the people to be somewhat depressed and disheartened. They were naturally concerned primarily with food and shelter for themselves and their families. Times were harsh, and crop failures added to the hardships. Further, the people of Judah did not have a new nation, they were simply made part of the Persian system of government. There was, however, a brief period upon the death of the Persian king Cambyses (Cyrus' son) when the empire experienced internal problems. At that point the prophets Haggai and Zechariah appeared on the scene in Judah.

These spokesmen of God took this opportunity to rally the people together for what they believed was the first step in the reestablishment of the nation to a place of greatness. Without the Temple, they believed, the nation could not be restored. Therefore the primary focus was upon the rebuilding of the Temple; this would be the inauguration of the new age of greatness for God's people. This hope was also reinforced by the fact that there was on the scene a descendant of the Davidic line, a certain Zerubbabel, a grandson of Jehoiachin.

Thus great hope surrounded the events of 520–515 B.C., the rebuilding of the Temple and the expected new age to emerge under the leadership of Zerubbabel. The situation within the Persian government began to stabilize, however, and it was not long before the power of the government was reasserted over all the areas of the Empire. It was also not long after Haggai looked upon Zerubbabel as the new messiah, the king of the nation, that Zerubbabel simply disappeared; and no more was heard of him. What happened to this person remains a mystery.

Haggai: Outline

I. The People Punished Because They Have Neglected the Temple 1
II. Promises for a New Nation 2

The contents of the book of Haggai are simple enough. In chapter 1 the prophet chastised the people for their neglect in not having rebuilt the Temple. In typical Deuteronomic fashion he told them that their bad condition, poor crops, and failure to progress were all a result of their not having built Yahweh a house in which to dwell. He challenged them to do that and promised that when they did, their fortunes would be restored. In addition there was a clear call for the people to keep themselves ceremonially clean (2:10ff.).

Finally, there is the oracle in which Zerubbabel was designated as the "signet ring" of Yahweh, the servant, the chosen one (2:20–23). Haggai saw Zerubbabel as a messianic figure who would become the new leader of the nation in a new age of political and economic prosperity. The Temple was completed by 515 B.C.; exactly how the people prospered then is not known since so little is known about the specific history of these times. From what is known, however, there is little to demonstrate that any great change was effected, but the foundation had been laid for something new, if the opportunity presented itself.

Zechariah 1—8

Zechariah, like Ezekiel, was a priest in addition to being a prophet. His ministry was contemporary with that of Haggai, to be dated from ca. 520–518 B.C. The major concern of his teaching also centered in the rebuilding of the Temple which he thought would usher in a new age for the people of God. As did Haggai, Zechariah thought that Zerubbabel had an important role to perform in that drama.

To the careful reader it becomes clear that chapters 1—8 of Zechariah belong to this particular period of Jewish history. Chapters 9—14, however, appear to belong to another time, place, and historical situation. These passages, therefore, will be discussed later (cf. below pp. 205ff.). One is struck with the basic motif encountered in chapters 1—8, that of portraying the prophetic message by means of visions. Interpreters are somewhat divided at the point of exactly how to understand these visions. Are these accounts of actual visions seen by the prophet in dreams or ecstatic states? Or are these accounts literary devices by which the prophet was attempting to deliver his message in a dramatic fashion? Whichever method one chooses to utilize in the interpretation of these accounts, the essential message and meaning of the stories remain the same.

One additional point should be made to alert the reader to the interpretation of the text of Zechariah 6:9–15. Most scholars believe that the original text of this passage referred to a coronation of Zerubbabel but was altered to refer to Joshua, the priest, since Zerubbabel did not in fact become the great political leader originally expected for him by the prophets. The fact that Zerubbabel may have acted too quickly and without reasonable foresight could be reflected in 4:6. It could also explain why he suddenly disappeared.

Zechariah 1—8: Outline

   I. Introduction 1:1–6
  II. Series of Night Visions 1:7—6:15
      A. The Four Horsemen 1:7–17
      B. The Four Horns and the Four Smiths 1:18–21
      C. The Measuring of Jerusalem 2:1–13
      D. The Forgiveness of the High Priest 3
      E. The Lampstand and Two Olive Trees 4
      F. The Flying Scroll 5:1–4
      G. The Women Taken to Babylon 5:5–11
      H. The Four Chariots 6:1–8
 III. The Coronation of Joshua (Zerubbabel) 6:9–15
  IV. Requirements for Restoration 7—8

Interpreters are not completely in agreement with each other concerning the exact meaning of each of the visions of Zechariah, but it is agreed that they represented a portrayal of events which were necessary for the restoration of the people in the land and for them to be participant in a new era of life in Judah. One notes that the visionary emphasis in the book of Zechariah is quite reminiscent of Ezekiel who was also a prophet-priest.

In the fifth vision one is told rather plainly that Zerubbabel was the key to the new situation for the people, but by the end of the visions Zerubbabel's name has disappeared from the account. Without a political leader, however, there was a very real emphasis upon the importance of the high priest in this new community. Whether this resulted from the strong position of the priests among the resettled people or whether it came about by necessity since Zerubbabel had disappeared cannot be known with precision. There was a genuine confidence on the part of the prophet, however, that the new age was about to begin.

A comment should be made here about the scene and the characters involved in vision four (chapter 3). In this vision the high priest was standing before Yahweh in filthy garments, these garments symbolizing the sins of the people. God told the priest that the iniquity had been forgiven, and the priest was given clean new garments. The clear teaching here was that the forgiveness of the people had to be the prerequisite for the coming of a new community.

The interesting new feature which is encountered here is that of the figure of Satan, or as the Hebrew has it, "the Satan." This is the first time in the Old Testament writings where the figure of Satan has been encountered. In this place the figure is one of function more than it is of personality. At this point in Hebrew thought, Satan was a member of the court of Yahweh whose duty it was to "accuse" (the word Satan means accuser) the people. Satan's job was, therefore, to report to God on the sins of the human race. The figure of Satan as the epitome of evil, the leader of the demonic forces of the universe, did not emerge until the intertestamental period (i.e., after ca. 150 B.C.) and in conjunction with the rise and popularity of the apocalyptic movement (cf. below, pp. 228ff).

Isaiah 56—66

The chapters of Isaiah 56—66 are in some measure the continuation of Isaiah 40—55, for it appears that these collected oracles are an attempt in part to relate the message of Deutero-Isaiah to the people in Palestine and Jerusalem. It is quite plain that the setting for these prophecies lies in Palestine after the return. Some portions seem to look forward to the building of the Temple, making the date about the same time as Haggai and Zechariah, while other portions appear to look at the Temple as completed and to examine how one properly worships at this sacred place. The oracles can, therefore, be dated from ca. 520–450 B.C.

One of the major critical problems resides in the question as to whether "Trito-Isaiah" is one prophet or whether these oracles are the product of several prophets collected together into one grouping. Upon close study it is probable that the latter idea is closer to the truth, and it is probably safe to argue that these oracles originated with the "school" which was preserving the Isaiah traditions.

There is an element of some surprise in the teachings in this collection. In the post-exilic prophets, generally speaking, one finds primarily oracles of hope and restoration directed toward the community. In this collection, however, one finds several groups of sayings which continue the old prophetic fire of the pre-exilic prophets. Some of these sayings are directed toward people who refused to do justice (cf. chapter 59), certain leaders who were selfish and unscrupulous (cf. 56:9ff.), and perhaps a group of religious leaders who wished to dominate the community with their own interpretations and were emphasizing the cultic purity of the community without likewise emphasizing the moral purity of the people (cf. chapter 58).

While the basic thrust of the teaching of this prophetic collection still looks for hope in a restored nation centering around the Temple in Jerusalem, nevertheless these sayings do not excuse any sins of the people or their leaders. Hard times were not to be taken as an excuse for laxity in matters of right and morality.

Isaiah 56—66: Outline

I. The Place of the Sabbath and the Temple in the New Community 56:1–8
II. Alternating Passages of Judgment, Threat, and Hope 56:9—66:24

As one can ascertain from reading through the collection of Isaiah 56—66, it is very difficult to divide the material into anything like a consistent and original document which makes logical sense or has a unifying theme. Most of the material either challenged the people or

leaders to become what the community of God's people was supposed
to be, or it attempted to depict the greatness of the new age which was
still expected though it had not as yet arrived.

There are several passages which can be cited to illustrate the teachings and to point out certain of the more interesting parts of this collection. One of these is found in chapter 61. This passage is of interest
because it is very similar in style, language, and thought to the servant
passages of Isaiah 40—55. The initial verses remind the reader of some
of the prophetic "call" passages found in some of the earlier prophets,
except that here the prophet is called to proclaim "good news" to the
people rather than a message of destruction. Many interpreters feel that
chapters 60—62, of which this passage is only a part, form the primary
focus for the entire collection because this block of material proclaims
hope to the people.

Another interesting point can be noted in conjunction with this
passage. One finds in 61:5–6 a strong indication that the people of God
believed vigorously that the people of the world would be subservient to
the new community of God's people. This is extremely interesting since
in some other passages in this collection of oracles all people were
looked upon as being candidates for inclusion into the holy community.
These differing elements probably reflect some of the debates which
went on in the post-exilic community in terms of its relationship with the
"outside" world. The question of who could be part of the new community must have been a matter of some heated debate. There are some
interpreters who argue that the teachings of "Trito-Isaiah" definitely
indicate that membership in the new people of God was not be be based
on the accidents of birth but on correct participation in God's cultic
requirements, a very "open" view. But the signals one gets from a
reading of all the material place that theory into the realm of "possible
conjecture" more than an absolute fact.

The second passage of some interest, and which again causes some
concern about consistency in the collection, is found in 66:1ff. Some
have interpreted this passage as being a polemic against the building of
the Temple, which is quite different from the positive emphasis on the
Temple in other portions of the work. Some commentators have argued
that this oracle may have been addressed to the Samaritans when they
began to build their rival Temple on Mt. Gerizim. Others have postu-

lated that these verses contain a condemnation of the Temple and the worship which takes place in the Temple similar to some of the teachings of the pre-exilic prophets. Others have argued that it was simply a warning and a corrective to those who believed (as Haggai had taught) that the building of the Temple was the panacea to cure all the ills the people were experiencing.

Certainty in interpreting the passage here is elusive, but the most probable interpretation seems to be that which sees a warning against placing too much trust and hope in the fact of the Temple's existence. It had been already proven in earlier times that the Temple's presence did not insure protection. What was required was the proper response in daily living by the devotees. Only this could be an appropriate act of worship.

The teaching of these chapters is, then, a mixed assortment of differing views and beliefs. These varied ideas truly reflect the plight of the people in those difficult and tedious days when the community was trying to rebuild and was frustrated by what they felt was the delay in the coming of a new age.

Obadiah

Nothing is really known about the prophet called Obadiah whose book is the shortest of all the Old Testament writings. There is considerable latitude in the assessment of a date to this prophecy, some arguing for a date as far back as the eighth century B.C. and others arguing for a post-exilic date, but exactly when in the post-exilic era is not agreed.

The content of the book is basically that of an oracle against a foreign nation delivered against Edom because of its participation in a humiliating defeat for Judah. Most interpreters understand this to be the time of the Babylonian defeat when numerous smaller nations joined or were forced to join in the battle against Jerusalem. Others believe that the time was later, soon after the deportation to Babylon in 586 B.C., when the Edomites took advantage of the defenseless situation of the people left behind to take some territory (i.e., the Negeb) and to harass and rob. Still another theory has it that the Edomites attacked Judah in 485 B.C., inflicted much damage on the land, and even destroyed the new Temple. Whatever the answer, the date is most likely to have been sometime after the destruction by Nebuchadnezzar in 586 B.C.

Some have detected in Obadiah evidence to argue that he was a cultic prophet, but that idea is simply a conjecture which cannot be demonstrated without doubt. It is also a matter of some interest to note the similarities between Obadiah and Jeremiah 49. Exactly how one explains this curious circumstance is still a matter of some debate.

Obadiah: Outline

I. Oracle Against Edom vss. 1–14
II. Oracle About the Day of Yahweh vss. 15–21

The first segment of the book contains simply a description of the woes which would come upon Edom as the just reward for the treachery which it had perpetrated against God's people. The details of that treachery are quite detailed. The second section announces the old Day of Yahweh concept. In this message all the nations, but especially Edom, were to stand under God's judgment, and there is the recurring hope that the fortunes of the old United Monarchy would be restored (cf. vss. 19–21).

Jonah

This book is unique among the prophetic collection, for it is not a collection of the oracles of a prophet or prophets directed toward the people in their particular current situation. It is rather a story about a prophet named Jonah. There is a prophet with the same name mentioned in 2 Kings 14:25 about whom very little is known. Some interpreters have attempted to identify that prophet with this book, but that approach is now almost universally rejected. Most date the book of Jonah in the post-exilic period somewhere between the fifth and second centuries B.C.

Several good reasons for this are presented. The language and style of writing reflect post-exilic Hebrew literary style, not the style of the pre-exilic period. Further there are indications in the text that the city of Nineveh is a thing remembered from the "old days," not a city currently in existence, at least as described. There is also a question about the purpose in the writing of the book if it dates from the pre-exilic period, for the contents simply do not seem to fit that time period.

The post-exilic community, however, does seem to be better suited for the origin and purpose of this story. One of the problems many persons today have in interpreting the Bible is in recognizing and understanding that there are included within the Old Testament certain "stories" which are simply that, stories told only to illustrate what the writer felt was a religious truth. Such stories became quite prominent in the post-exilic era especially in relation to the wisdom movement (cf. below, pp. 227f.). Some interpreters call this type of story a parable or an allegory, but neither of these designations are really fundamental to that type of writing. The basic idea in such a story is that of *comparison* or perhaps "analogy" in modern day terminology. Parables and allegories certainly are part of that type of presentation but the motif of comparison can be expressed in many different ways and by many different literary types.

One is reminded that in the post-exilic era there was an extreme emphasis on the purity of the community of God's people. This emphasis led to very stringent regulations especially with regard to contact and communication with those not of the community (cf. below the discussion of Ezra-Nehemiah, pp. 234ff.). It appears that the post-exilic Jewish community had begun to turn in upon itself and become more and more exclusivistic. Part of the reason for such an attitude and mode of life was undoubtedly triggered by the need to survive as a unique community, but such thinking inevitably brought a reaction. Some obviously began to question how the community of God's people could fulfill its purpose of election if it excluded itself from the rest of the world. There was an additional question as well: what is the motivation in becoming exclusivistic—survival or something less honorable? The story of Jonah spoke quite pointedly to these matters.

The book of Jonah is, therefore, a *mashal*, i.e., a comparison type story, the purpose of which was to challenge the hearers and readers to compare Jonah with themselves and their group. The basic point of the story seems to be that even pagans can and will respond to God's call if given the opportunity.

Jonah: Outline

I. Jonah Called to Nineveh and His Response 1:1–16
II. Jonah in the Belly of the Fish 1:17—2:9
III. Jonah Goes to Nineveh and Preaches 2:10—3:10
IV. Jonah's Response to Nineveh's Repentance 4:1–11

The story of Jonah is told very succinctly and to the point. Jonah was called to go preach to Nineveh. As all knew in that era Nineveh was the city of the hated Assyrians under whose capricious atrocities most of the nations of the world had suffered. Instead of heeding God's call Jonah bought a ticket to Tarshish (in Spain), the farthest known point in the west, the opposite direction from Nineveh, but Yahweh caused a storm to arise at sea so that Jonah could not escape. In fact, one is struck with the irony of the situation when the author of the story depicted the pagan sailors doing all they could to save Jonah's life!

Jonah was finally cast into the sea and swallowed by a great fish especially prepared for the occasion by Yahweh. For many years different factions have argued over whether the fish is to be understood as literal or figurative. Because this story seems to be part of the comparison type story so prevalent in that time, the fish is probably symbolic, perhaps of the exile of the people of God. The basic teaching of the book of Jonah is the same no matter which "camp" one chooses. Jonah cried out in his distress, was vomited upon the land (even the fish could not stomach Jonah!), and was told once more to go to Nineveh.

The preaching of Jonah to Nineveh caused the people there to repent. Interestingly, even the pagans are capable of changing their ways. At the point that Jonah became very angry, the problem is clearly enunciated: Jonah had run away not because he was afraid, not because he thought he would be rejected or ridiculed, but rather because he wanted the people of Nineveh to perish! "That is why I made haste to flee to Tarshish; for I know that you are a gracious God, merciful, slow to anger, running over in covenant loyalty and that you change your mind about doing evil" (4:2b, paraphrase).

Jonah's anger continued, but he lingered in the area to see if perchance Nineveh might not even yet receive its just due. A plant shaded Jonah, but it was cut down and Jonah became even angrier. God then asked Jonah if he was justifiably angry, and Jonah allowed that he certainly was! The dramatic and abrupt conclusion comes then with God's words: "You pity the plant, for which you did not labor, nor did you make it grow, which came into being in a night, and perished in a night. And should I not pity Nineveh, that great city, in which there are more than a hundred and twenty thousand persons who do not know their right hand from their left, and also much cattle?" (4:10–11).

The narrowness of Jonah and his bitterness shine brightly if not gallantly. The comparison to be drawn given the historical setting of the book in the post-exilic age seems quite clear. Excluding other peoples from the fellowship of God's community is narrow and selfish. God cares about these persons, even about their animals!

Malachi

The book known as that of the prophet "Malachi" is dated with some degree of certainty by most scholars between the rebuilding of the Temple (ca. 515 B.C.) and the reform movements of Ezra and Nehemiah (ca. 450 B.C.). The identity of the author, however, is another matter. There is no real name given to the prophet, the term Malachi being the Hebrew form of the descriptive title given in 1:1 and 3:1, "my messenger." That this was not originally considered a proper name is supported by the Greek translations where the term is translated by "my messenger." Later, however, this was interpreted to be a proper name.

Investigation into the possible authorship of this work leads to a discussion of a critical problem associated with this book and the concluding chapters of the book of Zechariah (9—14). Since the material in Zechariah (1—8) seems to be a complete unit in itself, one is then left in the Book of the Twelve with three units of prophetic oracle, each approximately the same length and each beginning with the word "oracle" (or *massa* in Hebrew). Many scholars believe that these three collections of prophetic material were originally placed at the conclusion of the larger collection which included all the shorter prophetic books, ending with Zechariah 1—8. In the process of time, however, the first two units of this miscellaneous collection were understood to be associated with the book of Zechariah and the last collection was then understood to be a separate book from another prophet.

Whether something like this is what actually happened is exceedingly difficult to say. If it did, however, it probably occurred rather quickly since the title, "Book of the Twelve," was known rather early and because there is the real possibility that the number twelve had significance for the ones who compiled and passed along the material.

One of the problems with such an understanding derives from the fact that Zechariah 9—14 seems to be compiled from oracles from several places and times, whereas the oracles in Malachi seem to be from the same prophet. Since this is true, it is quite possible, even probable, that the books were originally structured as we now have them, but it is also probably true that the collection in Zechariah 9—14 is exactly that, a collection of various sayings simply placed at the conclusion of Zechariah's material because the teaching of 9—14 was interpreted as appropriate for that particular time and place. The material in Malachi could then have been intended as an appropriate "conclusion" to the entire prophetic collection.

Such an idea is quite probable when one remembers that the postexilic community for which the collection was indeed intended was still looking forward to a new age, but that new age had not yet materialized. The hope was still there, however; therefore the prophetic collection was edited to conclude with the promise and hope of a new era wherein the people of God would be indeed a part of that new era and prepared for it by being as ceremonially and morally clean as they could possibly be. This new age would be inaugurated by the judgment of God and by the appearance of "Elijah" who would prepare the people for the new period. The mention of Elijah does not necessarily mean that the prophet thought of the original Elijah as returning. This could have been intended, but it is more likely that the mention of Elijah has to do with Elijah's original mission to call the people back to Yahweh and to challenge them to be faithful. The one who would do this would be one like Elijah, the embodiment of the prophetic movement, just as David was the embodiment of the kingship and Moses of the law.

Malachi: Outline

I. Yahweh Loves His People 1:1–5
II. Oracle Against the People and Priests 1:6—2:9

III. Oracle Against Marriage Violations 2:10–16
IV. Certainty of God's Judgment 2:17—3:5
 V. Reason for Present Troubles 3:6–12
VI. Coming of New Age 3:13—4:6

The book of Malachi begins with an assurance to the people in Judah that Yahweh loved them. The proof of this was actualized in the fact that Edom had suffered some sort of devastation which Judah had managed to escape, but such a deliverance demanded of the people a greater commitment to God. They had been offering blemished animals for sacrifice, and the priests had been accepting them. This demonstrated that Yahweh was not being placed first in their lives.

Another problem appears to have been that the men of Judah had been divorcing their Jewish wives to marry non-Jewish women. The reasons for this behavior are obscure, but some scholars have argued that the Jewish men were attempting to marry into security and wealth since many of the people to the north (from whom the new wives were being taken) were well established and had economic and political connections.

The ones who heard these oracles were told very plainly that the judgment of God is sure and certain, not only on the pagan nations of the world, but also on the people of God (something they should have learned from the fall of the two nations in 721 and 586). In fact, this prophet believed that judgment would begin at the house of Yahweh (3:1)!

At this point the prophet begins to sound like Haggai. He argued that hard times were continuing among the people because they had not been keeping the proper decorum with relationship to God's requirements in the tithe, sacrifices, and offerings.

The collection concludes with a reiteration of the challenge to do what is right and another proclamation that God's judgment is certain. The new age was still in the future, but it would surely come. Some preparation, however, may be necessary for the people to be ready. Therefore Elijah was supposed to come; his primary task would be to restore the family unit, something that had been a problem in that particular historical situation.

This then is the last book of the collection known as the *Nebi'im* even though it is not the last chronologically. But the clear challenge to the community to do what is right, to keep faith with Yahweh, and to keep itself pure so that the new age can come is the central message of this book and the final call for the people of God to be the people of God and to be prepared for the future.

Joel

There are several problems associated with the study of the book of Joel—the dating of the prophet, the interpretation of the "locusts" in the text, and the determination of exactly what kind of prophet Joel was. There is no real unanimity of opinion with regard to the answers given. Dates for Joel range all the way from the ninth century B.C. to the second century B.C. This range of possibilities emerges from several specific motifs in the text itself: Joel's use of the term "Day of Yahweh," overtones of old Canaanite worship, the implication that theTemple had been rebuilt and the walls of the city restored, and the literary imagery (called Apocalyptic) which did not emerge until the Maccabean period of Jewish history (ca. 165 B.C. ff.).

With so many varied historical situations, one can only suggest a possible solution. The fact that the book of Joel contains older ideas and terminology does not in itself assure that the book as it stands is old. Upon close examination the historical setting presupposed is much more relevant to a later time period, specifically the post-exilic period. There is a reference to the exile of Judah (3:1–3), references to the reconstructed Temple (1:9, 14, 16; 2:17; 3:18) and perhaps even the walls which had been rebuilt (2:7, 9). Further, the use of the term "Day of Yahweh" seems to mean in Joel almost the opposite of its intent in the pre-exilic prophets. All of this together seems to reflect, therefore, a post-exilic situation.

The question remains, however, as to exactly when in the post-exilic period the book originated. Since so little is known about the exact history of that era, especially what was happening to the people in Judah, the best one can do is speculate. The book seems to reflect a period of hard times, possibly connected with some sort of military activity which had caused hardship for the people in or near Judah. The most likely time period for such a setting could be somewhere during or shortly after the military conquests of Alexander the Great and the wars which were fought among his successors after his early and unexpected death (in 323 B.C.). The problems of the people of Judah with relation to the successor states of Alexander's Empire continued until the late Maccabean period (ca. 141 B.C. ff.), but such a late date for this book seems unlikely. The view tentatively proposed here is that the prophecy of Joel originated sometime during or immediately after the military campaigns of Alexander the Great in this area. Joel viewed these conquests as the "Day of Yahweh" for the nations; this gave him the hope that after this time the new age for the people of Judah would finally arrive.

A second problem in dealing with Joel relates to the interpretation of the "locusts." Many, in fact most, interpreters view this reference literally. Some type of locust plague and subsequent drought had brought great suffering to the land. There are others, however, who understand the "locusts" as an invading army, a symbol used rather frequently in those days for a military invasion. Whatever decision one makes about this matter, it seems not to alter the intent of the passage. The people had sinned; this is the judgment; repent, so that the new age can come.

As to the matter of what type of prophet Joel was, most scholars now agree that this man belonged to the cultic organization, and that his message and his method both seem to indicate that Joel was a cultic prophet. Some of the liturgies contained in this book may well have been used in the cultic rituals, especially those connected with lamentation and penitence.

One final note should be made concerning the date and arrangement of the book. There are some who believe that the book of Joel is composed of two separate collections, one (chapters 1—2) originating in pre-exilic times, and the second (chapters 3—4; the book is divided into four chapters in the Hebrew text) originating in the post-exilic era. Upon close examination, however, such a theory does not really appear to be necessary though it is certainly one possibility. The fact that earlier material could have been utilized and modified in a post-exilic setting was not at all unusual, but that in itself would not alter the basic time of the writing of the document or of the message it was intended to proclaim.

Joel: Outline

I. Vision of Awesome Destruction 1:1—2:11
II. Call to Repentance 2:12–17
III. God's Response 2:18–32
IV. God's Judgment on Judah's Enemies 3:1–21

The contents of the book progress rather logically and orderly. There is the vision of the locusts and the drought devastating the land which may have been intended to describe something in the past or in the future, or perhaps even something which could have been going on at that moment. Whether this was a natural catastrophe or a military conquest is debated. More likely it is the latter, but this catastrophe was considered to be deserved by the people because of their sin.

The call went out for the people to repent. "Rend your hearts and not your garments" (2:13a) is the key; God's mercy was considered sure if they would repent and remain faithful. And the description of the new age is quite similar to other post-exilic portraits of the restored community. The promise to them was that the spirit of God would be poured out upon them (2:28–29).

As part of the whole process of full restoration for the people of God there was to be a massive judgment upon the nations especially on those immediately surrounding Judah. One of the more interesting passages in Joel is found within this section expecting judgment on the nations. It is the reverse of a passage found both in Isaiah (2:4) and Micah (4:3):

> Beat your plowshares into swords,
>   and your pruning hooks into spears . . . (3:10)

Obviously the prophet felt that this was a time for defense against the invaders of the land. There is a reference in 3:6 to the "Greeks," which may (though not all interpreters agree) be a reference to the time of Alexander and his successors.

The book of Joel, as do the books of the other post-exilic prophets, looks forward to a new era with the people of God happy and prosperous, restored and focused around Jerusalem.

Zechariah 9—14

These six chapters which stand at the conclusion of the book of Zechariah fairly bristle with historical and critical problems. Mention has already been made about one aspect of the difficulties (cf. above pp. 200ff.), but there are many others quite similar in many respects to the problems connected with the book of Joel.

As for dating these chapters, suggestions have ranged from the pre-exilic to the Maccabean eras. Some have argued that chapters 9—11 are pre-exilic; 12—14 post-exilic. As for the question of authorship, some see in these chapters a single unity, while others find a collection of various oracles from various people and times. One interesting side-light is the comment found in one of the New Testament writings, the Gospel of Matthew, that Zechariah 11:12f. is from the prophet Jeremiah! One sees the complexity of the issues!

In terms of dating these oracles, it is generally agreed, despite all the conflicting theories, that these chapters do date from the post-exilic period. The language and historical references all point to that time. For example, the siege of Tyre by Alexander (ca. 332 B.C.) may well be the basis for the description in 9:1–8, and the literary style of parts of chapters 12—14 reflect the apocalyptic motifs which did not develop until later in the third century B.C.

As for authorship, there are certain ideas and themes which do occur in Zechariah 1—8 and which are repeated in chapters 9—14. These similarities along with the historical differences have brought forward the idea of a Zechariah "school" analogous to the Isaiah "school" which produced Deutero and Trito-Isaiah. Some interpreters, therefore, speak of a Deutero and Trito-Zechariah.

The problems cannot be fully resolved, but it is quite probable that these chapters which were attached to the book of Zechariah originated from several different sources, were collected together, and placed at the conclusion of Zechariah 1—8 because the editors felt that this was an appropriate place to preserve these anonymous oracles.

The content and meaning of the chapters are varied: judgment upon the nations, challenge to the people of God for purity, accusations against unscrupulous leaders both in the political and religious spheres, and again a great hope for a new age in which Jerusalem and the people of Judah would be the center of the community of nations. All of these are typical post-exilic items.

Zechariah 9—14: Outline

I. Judgment on the Nations Means Hope for Judah 9—11
II. Deliverance of God's People and the Establishment of the New Age 12—14

While these six chapters divide rather easily into two sections, there are various themes and sub-themes which flow through and are discussed within each larger section. Even though one of the most prominent themes is that God executes judgment on the nations, there are harsh words given to the community of God's people to keep purity and faith, and there are also harsh words directed to the leaders who are disreputable and selfish. In the second section there are references to the cleansing of the community from idols and sin along with a picture of the new age in which Yahweh is the ruler over all. There is a note of universalism (i.e., that God is the God of all nations) in these writings, but within this new society there is no question as to which people will have the "pride of place," and which place will be central for the world (i.e., Jerusalem). The prophet(s) is hopeful that the time for the new age is near.

Summary

The second division of the Hebrew canon, the "Prophets," extends over a long period of history, extending from the taking of the land beginning ca. 1200 B.C. well into the post-exilic period. During these centuries much had happened to the people who had descended from Abraham and the patriarchs and who participated along with Moses in the Exodus event. There had been at first an amphictyonic structure which gave way under political pressure to the establishment of a monarchy. After many years the two segments, north and south, were finally united under David. But this union lasted only for a very short time, and the two areas existed separately for several centuries.

The Northern Kingdom, destroyed and exiled by the Assyrians, never did recover or return. The people who remained mixed with the new people brought in by the Assyrians and were always looked upon as "impure" by the Southern Kingdom. Not having learned a lesson from the north, Judah also fell and the people were exiled, but within that group taken to Babylon lay the seeds for the continuation of the traditions which now reached back for almost a thousand years.

These people kept the traditions alive, modified them to suit their new situation, and looked forward to a restoration in the land which would rival the time of the great United Monarchy under David and Solomon. They were restored in the land; they continued to look for the new and glorious age but it had not as yet come when the final editing was done on this great collection of material. But as a glance at the last chapters (Zechariah 12—14 and Malachi) of the "Book of the Twelve" will demonstrate, that hope had not been given up.

Suggestions for Further Study

The Former Prophets
E. W. Heaton. *The Hebrew Kingdoms*. The New Clarendon Bible Series. Vol. III. London: Oxford University Press, 1968.

J. L. McKenzie. *The World of the Judges*. Englewood Cliffs, N.J.: Prentice-Hall, Inc., 1966.

Eugene H. Maly. *The World of David and Solomon*. Englewood Cliffs, N.J.: Prentice-Hall, Inc., 1965.

Manfred Weippert. *The Settlement of the Israelite Tribes in Palestine*. Translated by James D. Martin. Studies in Biblical Theology, New Series, No. 21. London: SCM Press, 1971.

R. N. Whybray. *The Succession Narrative: A Study of 2 Sam. 9—20 and 1 Kings 1 and 2*. Studies in Biblical Theology, New Series, No. 9. London: SCM Press, 1968.

The Latter Prophets
Ronald E. Clements. *Prophecy and Covenant*. Studies in Biblical Theology, New Series, No. 43. London: SCM Press, 1965.

Ronald E. Clements. *Prophecy and Tradition*. Atlanta: John Knox Press, 1975.

Norman K. Gottwald. *All the Kingdoms of the Earth*. New York: Harper & Row, 1965.

Abraham J. Heschel. *The Prophets*. New York: Harper & Row. 1962.

Johannes Lindblom. *Prophecy in Ancient Israel*. Philadelphia: Fortress Press, 1963. A classic work.

Harry Mowvley. *Reading the Old Testament Prophets Today*. Atlanta: John Knox Press, 1979.

B. D. Napier. *Prophets in Perspective*. New York: Abingdon Press, 1963.

R. B. Y. Scott. *The Relevance of the Prophets*. Rev. ed. New York: The Macmillan Company, 1968.

G. von Rad. *The Message of the Prophets*. Translated by D. M. G. Stalker. London: SCM Press, 1968.

Claus Westermann. *Basic Forms of Prophetic Speech*. Translated by H. C. White. Philadelphia: Westminster Press, 1967.

Robert R. Wilson. *Prophecy and Society in Ancient Israel*. Philadelphia: Fortress Press, 1980.

Joshua

John Gray. *Joshua, Judges, and Ruth*. London: Thomas Nelson & Sons, 1967.

J. Maxwell Miller and Gene M. Tucker. *The Book of Joshua*. Cambridge: Cambridge University Press, 1974.

J. A. Soggin. *Joshua: A Commentary*. Translated by R. A. Wilson. Philadelphia: Westminster Press, 1972.

Judges

Robert G. Bolling. *Judges*. Garden City, N.Y.: Doubleday & Co., 1975.

James D. Martin. *The Book of Judges*. Cambridge: Cambridge University Press, 1975.

Samuel
Peter R. Ackroyd. *The First Book of Samuel*. Cambridge: Cambridge University Press, 1971.

_____. *The Second Book of Samuel*. Cambridge: Cambridge University Press, 1977.

H. Wilhelm Hertzberg. *1 and 2 Samuel: A Commentary*. Translated by J. S. Bowden. Philadelphia: Westminster Press, 1964.

John Mauchline. *1 and 2 Samuel*. London: Oliphants, 1971.

Kings
John Gray. *1 and 2 Kings: A Commentary*. 2nd rev. ed. Philadelphia: Westminster Press, 1970.

J. Robinson. *The First Book of Kings*. Cambridge: Cambridge University Press, 1972.

_____. *The Second Book of Kings*. Cambridge: Cambridge University Press, 1976.

Amos
James L. Mays. *Amos: A Commentary*. Philadelphia: Westminster Press, 1969.

Henry McKeating. *The Books of Amos, Hosea, and Micah*. Cambridge: Cambridge University Press, 1971.

James M. Ward. *Amos and Isaiah: Prophets of the Word of God*. Nashville: Abingdon Press, 1969.

Hans Walter Wolff. *Joel and Amos*. Translated by W. Janzen, S. D. McBride, Jr., and C. H. Muenchow. Philadelphia: Fortress Press, 1977.

Hosea
James L. Mays. *Hosea: A Commentary*. Philadelphia: Westminster Press, 1969.

James M. Ward. *Hosea: A Theological Commentary*. New York: Harper & Row, 1966.

Hans Walter Wolff. *Hosea*. Translated by Gary Stansell. Philadelphia: Fortress Press, 1974.

Isaiah 1—39
William L. Holladay. *Isaiah: Scroll of a Prophetic Heritage*. Grand Rapids, Michigan: Wm. B. Eerdman's Publishing Co., 1978.

Otto Kaiser. *Isaiah 1—12*. Translated by R. A. Wilson. Philadelphia: Westminster Press., 1972.

_____. *Isaiah 13—39*. Translated by R. A. Wilson. Philadelphia: Westminster Press, 1972.

William Whedbee. *Isaiah and Wisdom*. Nashville: Abingdon Press, 1971.

Jeremiah
John Bright. *Jeremiah*. Garden City, N.Y.: Doubleday & Co., 1965.

James M. Efird. *Jeremiah: Prophet Under Siege*. Valley Forge, Pa.: Judson Press, 1979.

William L. Holladay. *Jeremiah, Spokesman Out of Time*. Philadelphia: United Church Press, 1974.

E. W. Nicholson. *The Book of the Prophet Jeremiah: Chapters 1—25*. Cambridge: Cambridge University Press, 1973.

_____. *The Book of the Prophet Jeremiah: Chapters 26—52*. Cambridge: Cambridge University Press, 1975.

Ezekiel
Walther Eichrodt. *Ezekiel*. Translated by Cosslett Quin. Philadelphia: Westminster Press, 1970.

James L. Mays. *Ezekiel, Second Isaiah*. Philadelphia: Fortress Press, 1978.

J. W. Wevers. *Ezekiel*. London: Thomas Nelson & Sons, 1969.

Walther Zimmerli. *A Commentary on the Book of the Prophet Ezekiel, Chapters 1—24*. Translated by R. E. Clements. Philadelphia: Fortress Press, 1979.

Isaiah 40—55, 56—66

John L. McKenzie. *Second Isaiah*. Garden City, N.Y.: Doubleday & Co., 1968.

Christopher R. North. *Isaiah 40—55*. N.Y.: Macmillan Co., 1964.

————. *The Suffering Servant in Deutero-Isaiah*. N.Y.: Oxford University Press, 1956.

James D. Smart. *History and Theology in Second Isaiah: A Commentary on Isaiah 35, 40—66*. Philadelphia: Westminster Press, 1965.

Claus Westermann. *Isaiah 40—66*. Translated by D. M. G. Stalker. Philadelphia: Westminster Press, 1969.

R. N. Whybray. *Isaiah 40—66*. London: Oliphants, 1975.

Books on the Remaining "Twelve Prophets"

T. E. Fretheim. *The Message of Jonah*. Minneapolis, Minn.: Augsburg Press, 1976.

Donald E. Gowan. *The Triumph of Faith in Habakkuk*. Atlanta: John Knox Press, 1976.

Rex Mason. *The Books of Haggai, Zechariah, and Malachi*. Cambridge: Cambridge University Press, 1977.

James L. Mays. *Micah: A Commentary*. Philadelphia: Westminster Press, 1976.

George Adam Smith. *The Book of the Twelve Prophets*. Second edition. Garden City, N.Y.: Doubleday, Doran, & Co., 1929.

John D. W. Watts. *The Books of Joel, Obadiah, Jonah, Nahum, Habakkuk, and Zephaniah*. Cambridge: Cambridge University Press, 1975.

CHAPTER IV

Kethubim

Historical Survey

As already noted in the discussion of post-exilic prophecy, the return from exile in 538 B.C. and subsequent years and the rebuilding of the Temple in 520–515 B.C. did not transform the Judean people into a mighty nation immediately. The times were harsh; reality usually is! Those who returned settled down and did their best to survive. Suspicious of the peoples around them, especially those in the area of Samaria, the people of Judah rejected any offers of assistance. Even so there seems to have been considerable intermingling with some of the people in the area, especially at the point of marriage.

Very little is known about the history of this period in the land of Judah. After the rebuilding of the Temple in 520–515 B.C., almost nothing is known until ca. 444–398 B.C., the times of Ezra and Nehemiah. They were important figures in the development of the Jewish community. According to the work of the person(s) who compiled the books of Chronicles and Ezra-Nehemiah, these two figures were contemporaries in their work among the people of Judah. Whether that is correct has been a matter of debate for some time among the historians of the period, for there are several problems to be resolved if one argues for the same dates for the work of both men. Several theories have been suggested to explain the discrepancies and to make sense of the historical data (such as it is). Some suggest that both Nehemiah and Ezra served during the period of Artaxerxes' reign over Persia (which the text says); but they believe Nehemiah appeared in the period of Artaxerxes I (ca. 444 B.C.) and Ezra during that of Artaxerxes II (ca. 398 B.C.). Some argue that the careers of these two persons overlapped but only at the conclusion of Nehemiah's career (ca. 428 B.C.). Others are convinced that they served together. Whatever the final disposition of that chronological problem, it is clear that Nehemiah's work was primarily directed toward the political sphere and Ezra's toward the religious sphere.

Nehemiah held a position in the court of the Persian king. Having heard of the troubles of the people in Judah, Nehemiah asked the king for permission to go there to help them strengthen their society. Permission was granted, and Nehemiah was even granted the title of "governor" for a period of time. This caused some animosity toward him from the other officials in the area, namely Sanballat (governor of Samaria) and Tobiah (governor in Ammon). Both of these men were worshipers of Yahweh, but they were not found "acceptable" to the religious purists in Judah. When Nehemiah came and began to strengthen the community, these two attempted to cause him serious problems. In spite of these problems, however, the community was to some extent reorganized and the walls of Jerusalem rebuilt.

Before the walls were restored through the leadership of Nehemiah, Jerusalem had been sparsely settled. After the building of the walls, Nehemiah repopulated the city, partly with volunteers, partly by assignment of persons to the city by lot. Stability and some order were finally becoming a part of the lives of the people. Nehemiah's term of office then expired, and he returned to Persia. Shortly thereafter, however, it appears that he persuaded the king to allow him to go back a second time (somewhere ca. 432 B.C.). Upon his return he found that many problems still remained. In fact his old enemy, Tobiah, was living in the Temple! Nehemiah had Tobiah thrown out and took some drastic steps to insure that the religious precepts were strictly observed. He also learned that the grandson of the high priest had married the daughter of Sanballat. Nehemiah had this man deported from the country!

Even though some real progress had been made in stabilizing the community in Judah, there were many serious problems still facing the people. Something was needed to give them a focus for their society. With the arrival of Ezra such a focus came. Ezra was commissioned to give order to the religious dimensions of the community's life. To do this he brought with him a "book of the law" which he read to the people.

Exactly what this book was has been debated. Some have argued that it was the Torah essentially as it is now known; others have argued that it consisted of a Priestly type document much shorter than the Torah. Whatever it was, this "law" served as the basis for Ezra's reform for the people in Judah. It is interesting that one of the more pressing problems which needed reform lay in the area of mixed marriages. Ezra obviously believed that such marriages were detrimental to the purity and progress of the community. The solution which was imposed on the people for this problem was a resolution that all mixed marriages be dissolved! Spouses and children not of "pure" Hebrew heritage (if indeed there ever had been such a "pure" heritage) were to be sent away from the community of God's people.

One of the interesting sidelights to the entire matter of Ezra's reading of the law to the people consists in the fact that the people of Judah no longer were able to understand Hebrew. As a result of the exile, the people had adopted the Aramaic language as their common tongue. Aramaic had become the *lingua franca* of that area of the world at that time. Therefore when the law was read, it had to be translated into Aramaic, the language of the people, in order for the sacred writing to be understood.

After the time of Nehemiah and Ezra, there is very little known about the community in Judah. The focus of the community appears to have been centered in the religious law and in the person of the high priest who presided over the Temple and its apparatus in Jerusalem. The work of Nehemiah and Ezra had been quite significant, but it was the growing realization that this people was primarily a religious community which began to give it its distinctive nature. The shift from political to religious emphasis was a natural result of the historical reality! After all, this adherence to their religious ideals and laws had been sanctioned by the Persian government, allowing the people of Judah to remain a distinct religious entity without being a separate political nation. It was the adherence to these religious precepts which kept the Judean people from becoming only another segment of the people of Palestine. Faithfulness to the Torah, law, became then in theory the distinguishing factor in determining who was to be considered a member of this community. The influence of Ezra is clearly evident at this point, and he has rightly been called by some, the "Father of Judaism."

About the only thing that is certain in terms of the development of the Jewish community in Judah was that relations with the people in Samaria were growing worse. Sometime during the fourth or the third centuries B.C. there came a definite and specific break between the two groups. The people in Samaria constructed a rival temple of their own on Mt. Gerizim and also claimed the authority of the Torah for their own lives. Exactly how or when this happened is not known, but it certainly did. The enmity between these two groups had become quite intense.

Because the situation in Palestine was so politically uncertain and economically harsh, many Jewish people began during the post-exilic period to settle in various parts of the Graeco-Roman world, usually in flourishing cities. Sometimes these migrations of groups were done voluntarily, but there were occasions when political states which had authority over certain areas would forcibly move groups of Jewish people from Palestine to other areas. These groups are known in most circles as the *Diaspora* or the Jews of the Dispersion. One of these groups had remained in Babylon at the time of the return. Others were scattered throughout the Persian Empire, and later there came to be a very influential community at Alexandria in Egypt. In such situations these people gathered themselves together, not always necessarily because they were forced to do so, but in an attempt to preserve their identity and traditions as a people.

This sociological situation caused several innovations to be made in Jewish religious matters. Since the language of the early post-exilic period was Aramaic in Palestine, and the language of the Graeco-Roman world was Greek in the later post-exilic period, the Hebrew Scriptures (the books which at that moment were considered authoritative) had to be translated into other languages. The first encounter with this has already been observed when Ezra read the law to the people of Judah, necessitating the translation of the Hebrew text into Aramaic. These Aramaic translations are called Targums. Further, sometime during the third century B.C., at Alexandria in Egypt, the Torah was translated into Greek. This was the beginning of the translation of all the Hebrew Scriptures into Greek which is known as the Septuagint (frequently abbreviated as LXX). Supposedly translated by seventy (or seventy-two) scholars from Jerusalem, all of whom according to the tradition

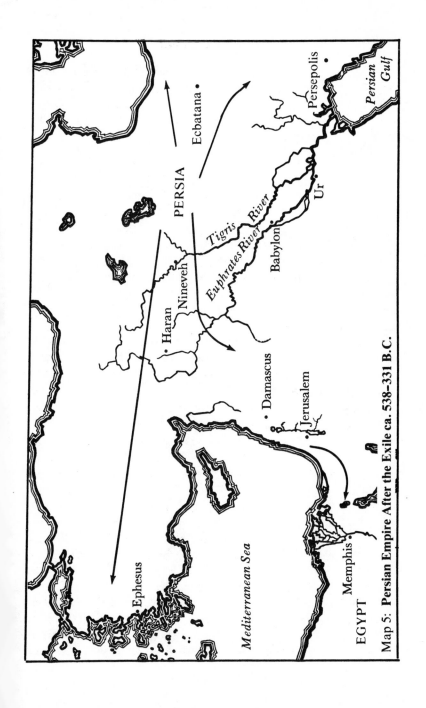

Map 5: Persian Empire After the Exile ca. 538–331 B.C.

came up with identical translations, the Septuagint version of the Old Testament writings was quite influential among the Jews of the Dispersion.

A second innovation which occurred was the development of the synagogue and the synagogue style of worship. All true worship for a Jew, however, was still centered in the Temple in Jerusalem, and each Jew was obligated to send a certain "tax" to Jerusalem each year for the support of the Temple and its apparatus. In addition each Jew was expected to come at least once each year to the Temple (if at all possible), but many could not attend. Therefore, some sort of substitute needed to be found to give expression to the religious faith of these religious communities in strange lands. Such a place needed also to be equipped to give instruction not only to the adults but especially to the young. Such an institution was developed and emerged as the synagogue. Exactly when and where this institution originally began is not agreed, some arguing that it began in Babylon during the exile, others arguing for a later date in some other place.

The synagogue, however, became the focal point for local Jewish communities. Services were held there on the Sabbath, naturally, and these services usually consisted of prayers, the reading of the Scriptures, and an exposition of the Scriptures in terms of explanation and exhortation. There were also mid-week services. Quite commonly there was a "school" attached to the synagogue, the purpose of which was to instruct the young particularly in the ways of the faith of the community. From these "schools" evolved the emphasis upon the interpretation of the Torah which became so prevalent around the turn of the eras and into the current era. The purpose of these "schools" was to understand and to interpret properly the Torah. The bulk of this studious investigation and the arguments and ideas which were generated were later incorporated into the *Mishnah* (oral traditions relating to the interpretation of the Torah) and the *Gemara* (oral traditions relating to the interpretation of the Mishnah) which together form the great "learning" of the Jewish people called the *Talmud*. That development is far ahead of our study here. The primary emphasis here must continue to be upon the community in Judah. Overall one can see that the post-exilic period was in many ways discouraging, frustrating, and difficult for the Jewish people, especially those in Judah, but in many other ways it was a time of growth and exciting new developments, some of which are still integral to the Jewish faith.

Subject to the Persians, initially, but allowed to keep their traditions and worship as they wished, the Jews in Judah continued to exist and obviously to grow in number. The times were harsh, and the community was subject to harassment from neighboring peoples. Some changes were needed to assist the people of Judah to be relieved from the situation. Such a change came when the face of the entire world was altered in 332 B.C. Having looked east for centuries in terms of world powers, the nations of this area now had to look west, first to Greece and then to Rome.

In 332 B.C. Alexander the Great began his amazing campaign through Asia Minor, Palestine, Egypt, Persia, and on to India. In a great battle in 331 B.C. he broke the power of the great Persian Empire, and his troops and armies spread throughout the entire area. Though a small and relatively insignificant part of the vast whole, the people of Judah were affected rather deeply by all this.

As most people know, Alexander dreamed of a world empire ruled by himself, with a common culture to bind all the different peoples together. This culture was to be basically Greek, but it was to be blended with the native cultures already in an area. Wherever Alexander went, he established Greek cities, encouraged the intermarriage of Greeks and native peoples, and introduced Greek culture. This process was called *hellenization*.

At the very peak of his power, however, Alexander died (323 B.C.). Almost immediately his generals began to fight among themselves for the empire. These wars are called the Wars of the Diadochi (or Successors), and they continued until ca. 301 B.C. At that point the empire had been basically divided into four smaller units. The two which most specifically affected Judah were the Ptolemaic Kingdom in Egypt and the Seleucid Kingdom centering in old Persia and extending into northern Palestine. The general, Ptolemy, had won control of Egypt and southern Palestine (which included Judah), and the general, Seleucus, had won control of the east and northern Palestine. As one could readily guess, they fought quite frequently over southern Palestine!

At first, however, the Egyptians controlled that area. Their policy was one of allowing native peoples their own ways and customs as long as they did not cause trouble and paid their taxes. In short, they were not zealous to enforce the policy of hellenization. During this period of time it appears that the Jewish people in Judah were basically organized around their religious traditions. In this society the high priest exercised a great amount of authority, mainly religious but to some degree political and civil as well (though this latter type was subject to many restrictions). And it is likely that he was "assisted" by a small group of leaders called "elders."

In 198 B.C. the situation dramatically changed. At the battle of Banias (Panium) the Seleucids won control over southern Palestine from the Ptolemies. At first the Jews were quite elated about the change, for the Seleucids allowed them a respite from taxation for three years, and they were allowed a great degree of religious autonomy, much as they had had after the days of their return from Persia. The problem inevitably came, however, at the point of hellenization. While the Ptolemies cared little about such matters, the Seleucids were quite keen on pushing the hellenization policy. To many Jews such action threatened the very life and existence of the community of God's people.

A major problem arose between the Jews and the Seleucids. It began in 175 B.C. when Antiochus IV, king of the Seleucid empire, was in need of some additional financial assistance. There were divisions among the Jewish people over the matter of hellenization. Some found nothing really wrong in it, while others fought vigorously in opposition. The high priest at the time was Onias III, a rather strong opponent of the process. His brother, Joshua, wanted to become high priest, however, so he offered Antiochus a bribe to be appointed to the position. In addition Joshua promised to push Antiochus' hellenization process in Judah. Not one to allow a fine opportunity to pass, Antiochus appointed Joshua to the position. This, naturally, outraged many of the Jews, but the situation was relieved somewhat because Joshua was a member of the high priestly family.

Joshua kept his word to Antiochus. He changed his own name to Jason (the Greek equivalent), encouraged Greek dress and customs, and erected a gymnasium in Jerusalem. Since the Greek games were performed in the nude, many Jewish lads submitted to painful operations to hide the mark of their circumcision. Such changes were not accepted by all with tranquility, however.

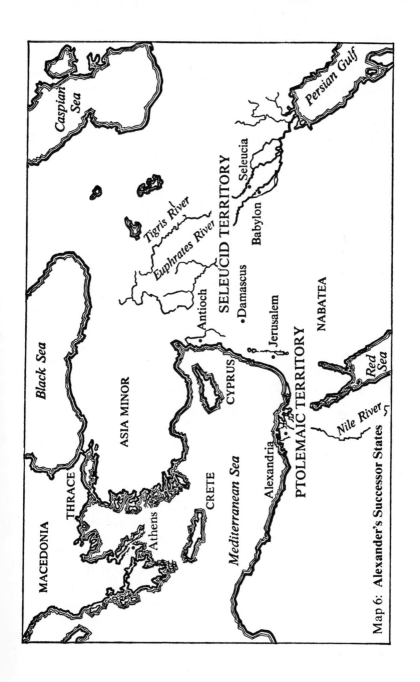

Map 6: Alexander's Successor States

And the problem continued to grow worse. In 171 B.C. another person, Menelaus (or Menahem), decided that he wanted to be high priest and outbid Jason for the office. It had been horrifying enough to the Jewish people when Onias was deposed for Joshua, but Joshua was a member of the priestly family. Menelaus was not! The policy of hellenization was then pursued with even more rigor. In 169 B.C. when a false rumor of Antiochus' death was circulated, Joshua attempted to regain the office. Antiochus, however, appeared and set matters in order. Menelaus then allowed Antiochus to plunder the Temple, even stripping the gold off its facade. The pot was boiling very rapidly.

Puzzled by all this opposition from these people, Antiochus attempted to determine exactly what was causing the antagonism between the people in Judah and himself. His very astute answer—their religion. If their religion was the cause of the problem, he felt, there was a simple solution—abolish the religion. Therefore in 168/7 B.C. Antiochus proscribed Judaism, i.e., he made it illegal for anyone to practice the Jewish religion. It became a capital offense to have a copy of the Torah, to circumcise the male children on the eighth day, to keep the dietary food laws, or to sacrifice to Yahweh, God of the Hebrew people. The Temple in Jerusalem was dedicated to Zeus; a statute of Zeus was erected there; and to add insult to injury, a pig was sacrificed on the altar of Yahweh! The explosion was very near.

The triggering event came very soon at a small village called Modein (or Modin) to the north of Jerusalem. A Syrian officer (the Seleucids were called Syrians by the Judeans) was enforcing the sacrifice to Zeus when a young Jew stepped forward to make the sacrifice. This infuriated an old priest of Yahweh named Mattathias who killed the Jew and the Syrian officer and with his five sons fled to begin a guerrilla war against the Syrians. Some people readily joined or supported this effort, but others were reluctant to do so. One rather influential group which did not immediately join the battle was known as the *Ḥasidim* (the "Pious ones"). These people were primarily interested in religious matters and tried to stay out of political affairs as much as possible. When on a Sabbath a segment of the Syrian army found a large group of *Ḥasidim* hiding in a cave and slaughtered them, the *Ḥasidim* joined in the rebellion.

Old Mattathias had died shortly after the conflict had broken out, but the fight was continued by his sons under the leadership of one of them, Judas known as the Maccabee (i.e., "Hammer"). It is his nickname which gave rise to the naming of the entire period. Numerous battles were fought, and the war continued. Finally, in 165/4 B.C. Judas through a series of brilliant military maneuvers defeated the Syrian forces and marched into Jerusalem. The proscription againt Judaism was lifted, and the Temple was cleansed and rededicated in December, 165/4 B.C. The event is still celebrated today as Hanukkah or the Feast of Lights.

Because the political events did not really satisfy Judas, however, he and his forces continued to fight against the Seleucids. The *Hasidim* had withdrawn by this time because their objective, the lifting of the proscription, had been accomplished. Judas was ultimately killed (as were all the brothers) but this resistance continued. To make a long and involved story short, suffice it to say that the last brother, Simon, had himself installed as the High Priest in Jerusalem exercising both religious and political power. Thus began (ca. 141 B.C.) a dynasty of Priest-kings which basically ruled over the Jewish people in Judah and which lasted until the middle of the first century B.C. To a certain degree the hopes of the old prophets (and others) for a restoration of both the people and the nation had now been fulfilled.

Literature

Literarily speaking the post-exilic era of Jewish history was an extremely active period. This is true not simply because of the number of older traditions which were reworked, edited, and finalized (e.g., the Torah, the Prophets), but also because of the large number of new writings which continued to emerge in this period. Not only were there many new works, there were also new types of literary creations being utilized during this time to wrestle with and to present the developing faith of the Jewish people. It must be noted here that contrary to the earlier times when most sources and other writings disappeared, during this period those other writings and sources continued to exist, and many are still extant along with those documents which ultimately became part of the authoritative canon.

Considerable research has been done since the turn of this century on the literary forms and genres which are found so abundantly in this last collection of the Hebrew canon. Entire books have been written on each so there are considerable resources available for the student who wishes to become more conversant with detailed analysis of these areas. Many of the forms and types which originated and/or were used so brilliantly by some of the writers of the Kethubim in this post-exilic period continued to be used even into the Christian era. Exactly what were these types and genres and how does one's acquaintance with them assist in understanding the Old Testament writings?

First, one is reminded of the prophetic books already examined which do indeed come from the post-exilic period. The pre-exilic prophetic collection basically included poetic materials quite frequently passed along in the messenger formula or the form in which the basic element was the threat or announcement of judgment. While there were other types of traditions as well, such as the call experiences, the visionary motifs, certain prose accounts dealing with incidents in the lives of the prophets, and the like, overall the pre-exilic prophetic books basically are collections of poetic proclamations by the prophets to the people.

In the post-exilic period, however, many of the prophetic books no longer contain primarily poetic oracles but rather are prose accounts of various types interspersed at times with poetic utterances (cf. e.g., Haggai, Zechariah). What the post-exilic prophets were attempting to do was to keep the people from being overly distressed and to offer to them a hope that the new age would soon come. While they had to challenge and sometimes chastise the people at various points the overall stress was that of encouragement, especially in the face of grinding hardship. The historical circumstances thus had led to the need for a different message and partly because of that need to new or modified literary approaches in the announcement of that message.

Closely related to the change in the prophetic movement is that concerning how the new community understood and interpreted past history. Already during the exile the Deuteronomic History had been written and the editing process on the latter prophets as well had begun, and these works were edited so as to speak to the needs of the restored community. There was the need to reinterpret the past with special emphasis on the new circumstances of the people after the exile. What did the old history have to say to this new situation? To answer that question there appeared a person (or group of persons) known as the Chronicler who rewrote the entire Torah and Deuteronomic History in a manner which would make it speak to the people where they were. This person was responsible for the books of 1 and 2 Chronicles, and Ezra and Nehemiah which are only two books in the Hebrew (Chronicles and Ezra-Nehemiah and in the Hebrew text Chronicles follows Ezra-Nehemiah!). This work has many affinities with the style, content, and interests of the P source-strata of the earlier writings (cf. above, pp. 40f.), for the interests of this compiler centered in the situation of the post-exilic community especially as that community gathered for worship. There is an inordinate amount of emphasis in these books placed upon the Temple and the Temple liturgy. What one finds, therefore, in the work of the Chronicler is a writing or rewriting of the history of Israel up to his own time in which the emphases of the new community are made focal points for the account.

Another major movement which came to full flower in the post-exilic age was that usually designated as Wisdom. This type of thought complex and literary style was not exactly new in Israel, for it had been given an official status and place of importance under the kingship of Solomon, but it remained for the post-exilic period to provide the time and setting for the fuller development of the movement.

Actually the wisdom movement is common in every culture. In almost every culture the movement has begun basically as a secular movement. Wisdom is the attempt on the part of people as people to learn how to cope with the world. Human life is not easy and learning how to get along in the world involves understanding how the world operates and how to relate to the operation of the world so that one can have a good, prosperous, and successful life. It is interesting to note that most of the other nations of the ancient world had wisdom traditions very early, especially in Egypt and Mesopotamia, but this movement was very slow in developing within the culture of the Hebrews. There are instances where the methods and means of wisdom are reflected in early times (cf. Judges 9:7ff.), but as a unified movement the progress toward a full-fledged development did not really emerge until the post-exilic period.

In wisdom ideology, therefore, the movement develops in two basic directions. First, and perhaps the oldest, is that of practical wisdom such as the teaching of parents to children, of teachers to students, or the like. Usually these take the form of short proverbial sayings, very practical in tone and nature, e.g., "If you don't play with fire, you won't get burned!" One can immediately recognize the similarity in basic understanding of this type of teaching with the already existing Deuteronomic ideology in Hebrew thought. Therefore the practical proverbial type of wisdom found a ready home among the Hebrew people; but as with all such ideologies which they utilized, the religious factor permeated the basic teachings. They believed that even practical wisdom was under the ultimate and overarching scrutiny of God. Since the world had been made by God, understanding how it operated would give one a greater understanding of God.

The second branch of wisdom ideology was concerned with attempting to explain what had happened when the "normal" order of life had broken down. It is one thing to argue that observing certain patterns of life leads to good life and success, and not observing those patterns leads to destruction and ruin. What about the times, and there are many, when a person who is good and upright and who obeys all the rules suffers all kinds of undeserved calamity? What about the persons who flaunt every rule and yet live a prosperous, happy, and successful life? How does one explain that set of circumstances? In response to such questioning there developed this second type of wisdom genre usually referred to as speculative or "philosophical" wisdom. Since the old Deuteronomic theology "died hard" within Israelite thought, it was into the post-exilic period when this speculative kind of thought and literature developed fully among the Hebrew people.

The basic literary unit of the wisdom tradition was the *mashal*. This word refers to the basic unit of presentation in the wisdom tradition, and the central motif in the *mashal* was that of comparison. Some saying or story would be related which was intended to cause the hearer or reader to compare that thought or point with another situation or setting in life. The comparison could be presented by means of various literary units— short pithy sayings, proverbs, riddles, parables, allegories, numerical proverbs (e.g., three things . . . yea, four . . .), fables, and the like. The most readily recognizable unit for modern readers from this array is the parable. These literary elements all fall under the larger category of *mashal* in Hebrew thought, and they tell a story or make a point which contained some principle which could be used in life, either generally or specifically, to enable the person open to true wisdom to have a better life. The student of the Old Testament writings will not be surprised to learn that almost all of these literary units were poetic in nature if not in form.

Closely associated with the teaching by *mashal* in poetic form is another common characteristic of Semitic teaching methodology, namely the device of teaching by *hyperbole,* i.e., exaggeration. This kind of teaching device is quite common in wisdom literature, for in order to make points clearly there is the need frequently to express them in absolute terms and to paint an extreme picture to demonstrate the basic idea. One should not, therefore, be surprised or misled in encountering wisdom traditions to find stories and sayings depicting great extremes in order to illustrate certain points.

The discussion of wisdom leads directly to a closely related type of story found frequently in the post-exilic period, especially the later post-exilic period. This is the type of story which developed among the Jewish people and which exalted the Jewish community, its ways, and especially its religious beliefs and customs. These stories usually told of the triumph of people who kept the law and remained faithful even to the point of facing terrible consequences or even death. Most of these stories are delightful and inspiring even though they are basically *stories,* not historical accounts, and most of them were not received into the final canon of authoritative books, but this did not diminish their popularity among the general populace. These stories can be designated by the term, *haggadah,* and examples may be found among the apocryphal literature in the books of Tobit and Judith.

The term, *haggadah,* however, is usually confined to the literature which originated among the Jewish people in the early years of the Christian (or Current) Era. These stories basically were supplementary to and illustrative of the teachings found in the old Law or Torah, but they are the same type of literary story which developed earlier in the post-exilic period, and the similarity between the earlier and the later stories warrants the same terminology at least in an analogous sense. Thus this type of story will be called *haggadic* for the purposes of this present study in dealing with the post-exilic material. And it seems fairly certain that this type of story is a direct outgrowth of the wisdom tradition.

One can already begin to understand why the wisdom movement, especially the speculative aspects and the haggadic type stories, was such an integral dimension in the life of the post-exilic community. The people had suffered a devastating defeat and deportation to Babylonia, had remained there for almost two generations, and were promised by their prophetic leaders a time of rejoicing and restoration in the old land in a new age. The fact that the prophetic oracles were poetic did not seem to matter to the people who chose to understand most of these teachings quite literally. The grim realities of the situation soon caused the people to despair, and the older theologies began to be called into question. It was difficult to be obedient when things were going so poorly; in fact,the situation frequently became worse especially when armies trampled across Palestine and looked on these defenseless people as "easy marks" to harass and, at times, persecute. The situation, there-fore, caused some persons to begin to question the older ideas and to wrestle with larger problems and to propose some different under-standings of God's relationship with his people. Speculative wisdom and haggadic type stories served to help in those troubled times in looking beyond the moment and in encouraging the keeping of the faith even when absolute certainty could not be assured.

Troubled times led also to another significant development in the religious and literary areas during the post-exilic era, and this new movement became very important and influential especially toward the latter part of the period. It involved a movement called *apocalyptic*, the word taken from the Greek meaning to "reveal" or to "uncover." This particular thought pattern probably had several foundations, but the single most important element in the initial development of apocalyptic thought appears to have come from Persian thought.

Persian religious thought understood the universe to be the arena for the gigantic struggle between the forces of good and the forces of evil, both of which were viewed as eternal. This struggle was going on in all places at all times and would ultimately eventuate into a final great catastrophic event which would conclude history as we know it. The forces of good would indeed triumph. While the battle is going on at the cosmic level basically, nevertheless the struggle permeates all the created order. Therefore the battle is also being waged within the historical process, and when the forces of evil have the upper hand, the people who have allied themselves with good suffer.

It is certainly not difficult to understand how the social, political, and economic situation of the post-exilic Jews in Judah would lend itself to an affinity with this kind of thought pattern. Struggling to keep their religious faith and being battered about on every side, these people could identify with such thinking. But the Persian ideas could not be accepted completely. It was absolutely unthinkable that evil could be co-eternal with God, for example; therefore certain modifications were made (as was usually the case) when this thought pattern was utilized by the Jewish community.

The apocalyptic movement in Israel developed out of this historical circumstance and the Persian thought pattern. Basically there are two ideas which are crucial to Jewish apocalyptic thought. The concept of *dualism* was prominent, even though modified. The battle being waged on the cosmic level between the forces of good and the forces of evil was being felt in this world, particularly by God's people, but it was believed that the time would come (usually very soon) when the persecution of the people would be withdrawn. In this type of situation the idea of two ages became very prevalent, the present evil age, dominated by forces of evil persecuting the people of God, would increase in intensity until God intervened, destroyed the persecutor, and established a new age in which the persecutor had been eliminated. The present situation was believed to be so harsh that nothing short of God's intervention could remove the evil. These two elements then, dualism and the two age motif, became foundational for apocalyptic thought.

The question, however, became one of exactly what the new age was supposed to be and where it was supposed to occur. Some modern interpreters view all apocalyptic literature as looking forward to a cataclysmic end of the entire universe followed by a new creation made especially for the faithful. All human history was viewed as coming to an end. This is a very narrow interpretation, for in many of the apocalyptic works there is no end of the world at all but rather an end to the persecution which would bring in a new age for the people of God. This new age would be located, moreover, in this world and in this historical continuum. Therefore, the specific ideas could and did vary from one writer to another.

The technical term used in theological circles for the study of "end things" is *eschatology*. Unfortunately many persons when they hear that something is "eschatological" immediately infer that the discussion has to do with the end of the world. The term, eschatology, can be used in differing ways. It indeed may denote the end of all things, but it can also denote the end of a particular era or segment of one's life or a specific period such as a period of persecution. Exactly which meaning was intended must be determined by an examination of the literary piece under consideration.

In addition, the term, eschatology, may be used (and often is by biblical scholars and theologians) to refer to something of great and special significance, something which has *ultimate* significance. These types of ideas and experiences can also be termed *eschatological*, and if the beginning student is not aware of these distinctions misunderstandings can occur. The primary point to keep in mind concerning eschatology is that the "end" must be understood against the background of the individual writing and not automatically understood as the "end of the world."

The two primary characteristics then of apocalyptic literature appear to be a genuine belief in dualism (the presence of good and evil forces in the created order) and in eschatology, the belief that there will be a climactic confrontation between those forces of good and evil which will inaugurate a new age. These characteristics are supplemented by numerous other motifs usually designated "secondary" apocalyptic characteristics. Probably the most well-known of these is the tendency in the writings towards exaggerated symbolism and imagery to illustrate the points the writer was attempting to present.

These images take varied forms. There are unusual and weird beasts, usually repesentative of kingdoms or nations. There is the use of the "horn" as a symbol of power, or sometimes one who exercises power, i.e., a ruler or king. There is the use of numbers to symbolize certain ideas. Four, for example, stands for the created order; three for the spiritual realm; seven is the number of perfection or completeness; ten stands for totality; and in Jewish and Christian apocalyptic works twelve symbolizes the people of God. The apocalyptic writers also liked to manipulate these numbers in that they would use multiples of them to emphasize the idea symbolized. For example, one thousand represents totality carried on to the largest degree. One other number which is used in apocalyptic is the number three and one-half. This peculiar digit always represents the length of time that the powers and forces of evil were allowed to exercise authority over the people of God. Sometimes the term was suggested by the phrase, "a time, two times, and half a time," or by forty-two months, or by 1260 days. All of these have the same meaning, however; evil was allowed to run its course but would come to an end in the not too distant future.

Colors were also symbolic in apocalyptic. White is the most frequently found and designated victory; there may be a few places where it suggests purity but not often. Red was the symbol for war, and black was the symbol for lack, want, pestilence, and the like.

Another feature of the apocalyptic genre was that most of the apocalyptic writings were pseudonymous, i.e., written in the name of some other person, usually a famous personage of the past such as Abraham, Moses, Baruch, Ezra, or the like. This procedure was supposed to give to the writing a note of authority and sometimes greater mystery. Quite frequently moderns do not understand this tendency in the post-exilic era toward pseudonymous writing, thinking that this kind of action is illegal or immoral, but this is to judge the people of a different time and age by our standards, not by theirs. To write in someone else's name then was not considered a crime at all but a tribute to that person or simply the way one wrote certain types of literature, apocalyptic especially.

Two other characteristics of apocalyptic were the distinct tendencies towards pessimism and determinism. The idea in apocalyptic was that the present age in which one lived was so much controlled by the forces of evil that there could be no hope for it. Closely related to that idea was the concept that history was running a course, a course which would ultimately be completed with the persecution gone and the people of God free to worship and live as they were required by their religious faith, i.e., in a new age. Both of these elements were designed to produce hope in the people who were experiencing persecution. One of the distinctive ways the apocalyptic writers had to illustrate this hope was by the use of a historical survey, told in highly symbolic language with the use of beasts and the like to represent nations and the flow of history. The survey usually began in the distant past and told how history had developed and how it had arrived at the present state.

The apocalyptic writer then predicted the end of the persecution and a new glorious age in which the persecution would be gone. Such historical surveys assist quite frequently in the dating of the books since the events of the past (from the perspective of the writer) were always correct, but the events predicted did not always turn out exactly as outlined. The historical period where the correct description of events and the partially correct came together, then, can usually be understood to have been the time of the writer.

These symbolic representations were usually depicted in the apocalyptic work as having been given or seen in a "vision." There is some disagreement among interpreters at this point, some holding that the writer really did see a vision in some sort of ecstatic trance, and others holding that the use of the vision was no more than a literary device which was simply part of the apocalyptic genre. Certainty at this point cannot be achieved, but the meaning of the text remains the same no matter which view one accepts. Further, when the writer makes use of the vision motif, there is almost always someone (an angel usually) present in the story to interpret the vision for the one who has seen this weird and unusual scene (cf. for example Daniel 8).

This point leads to another popular idea which has long been assumed about apocalyptic literature, namely, that the use of such elaborate and unusual symbolism was necessary to hide the meaning of the story from the persecutors. Such a view is still quite popular, but the fact is that if one reads apocalyptic works one finds that many of the symbols are interpreted in the text very clearly. Since the persecutors could also read, it seems less than likely then that the reason for the symbolism was to hide the message. Rather the elaborate symbolism was simply part of the apocalyptic literary style. Since evil and persecution were so hideous and horrible, these entities were presented in grotesque and gigantic figures, and since they were to be destroyed by one even greater, that destruction and the identity of the destroyer had to be presented in terms even more gigantic. The reason then for the elaborate symbolism was simply a result of that particular literary style.

Above all, one must remember in dealing with apocalyptic that the writing was intended to give hope to a people who were experiencing serious persecution. All the elements in each book were designed to sustain faith and engender strength for the horrible days ahead. The promise was that the persecution would soon be over and that the worst that the persecutor could do was nothing compared to the grand things to come for those who endured.

One can readily understand from this simple overview of the post-exilic period that the situation religiously speaking was most complex. If there was any single entity around which the religious life of the Jewish people in Judah revolved, it had to be the Temple in Jerusalem. Since there was no real political power and since the region was incorporated into large administrative units of the Persian Empire and later of the Greek successor states, the high priest basically exercised both religious and political power (what little there was). This caused some disturbance at times among certain persons who aspired to the office of High Priest, but so little is known of the precise details of the history of the people in Judah that one can do little more than speculate about them. We know that the Temple was the center of the community, that the people were more and more dependent upon the written documents of their faith, and that times were hard, so hard that many Jews began to migrate to other places in the Graeco-Roman world, establishing in some cities rather large Jewish communities especially at Alexandria in Egypt for example. Such persons were expected to send to Jerusalem and to the Temple the Temple-tax, one-half shekel per year, and if at all possible to come to the Temple each year to participate in an official act of worship, preferably at the time of one of the great feasts.

It was in this type of historical setting that the post-exilic Jewish community reflected upon its past, struggled with its present, and contemplated its future. Many different ideas and motifs were being examined and wrestled with during these troubled times, and it was in and from these wrestlings that the remaining Old Testament writings found their origins.

The Kethubim: Books

The last collection of books found in the Hebrew Scriptures is called the *Kethubim,* the Writings. Here one finds all the books commonly known to be in the Old Testament canon but which were not included in the other two collections, the *Torah* and the *Nebi'im.* It has been mentioned already that this last collection was not finalized until about the end of the first century A.D., and that there are several arrangements which are known of the books included within the collection. One of the most famous of the smaller units contained within the collection known as the *Kethubim* is a group of five books called the *Megilloth,* or Five Rolls. What makes them significant is that these books had become attached to various feast days in Jewish tradition, and each one was read on the appropriate day. These five are the Song of Songs, Ruth, Lamentations, Ecclesiastes, and Esther. It is a matter of debate as to exactly how ancient the traditions are which link these books with the actual feasts. More discussion of these matters will be included as the individual books in this larger collection are examined.

The Chronicler

1 & 2 Chronicles, Ezra-Nehemiah

In the Hebrew canon the last two books are the book of Ezra and the book of Chronicles, and as with the works of Samuel and Kings later generations divided them into two books each, Ezra, Nehemiah, and 1 and 2 Chronicles. Upon close scrutiny, however, it becomes very obvious that these books originated together and are the work of a single person (or group) writing in the post-exilic community, usually known as the Chronicler. The purpose seems to have been to assist the people in the restored community in the organization and structure of their lives as they attempted to be the people of God.

Numerous sources seem to have been utilized in the writing of this major work, some of which were also used by the Deuteronomistic Historians and some of which were not. There is a decidedly Priestly emphasis in this composition, but it seems to be somewhat different from the Priestly tradition included in the Pentateuchal books. Here the emphasis is upon the cultic apparatus and traditions which centered in the Temple in Jerusalem. All other history and understandings were interpreted in the light of this focal point of the new community.

One may possibly be confused with the fact that in the Hebrew canon Ezra-Nehemiah is placed before Chronicles, especially since the former is the logical conclusion to the latter. The historical period covered in Chronicles already had a fuller parallel in the Torah and the Deuteronomistic History while Ezra-Nehemiah contained new material and added to the existing histories. Therefore the books of Ezra-Nehemiah were probably considered "canonical" before those of the Chronicles, resulting in the placement of Chronicles after them even though the books of Chronicles were originally part of the same work and were originally prior to Ezra-Nehemiah.

The purpose of the work of the Chronicler was obviously to demonstrate that the true people of God were those in and around Jerusalem, those who worshiped in the Jerusalem Temple. This is clearly demonstrated in that the Northern Kingdom is not mentioned at all after the division of the Kingdom. To this writer it seems that God's Israel consisted of the people of the south and their descendants. This is reflected also in the writing itself where the inhabitants of the area of the old Northern Kingdom volunteered to help in the rebuilding, but those offers were rejected. The people of the south were warned not to have any contact or relationships with those people. Not only were the old inhabitants of Israel apostate, the newer inhabitants were both apostate and unclean being a mixture of the older Israelites and the newer peoples brought in by the Assyrians after the fall in 721 B.C.

During this period there arose the very real and bitter hatred between the Jews and the Samaritans, as these people came to be known. The hostility was so great that finally the Samaritans established their own temple (on Mt. Gerizim) and followed as authoritative their own version of the Torah, called the Samaritan Pentateuch. Exactly when the final and decisive break between the two communities came is debated but most date this somewhere during or immediately after the campaigns of Alexander the Great. If that is true, and if the work of the Chronicler presuppposed that break (both "ifs" here are highly conjectural), then the date of the Chronicler's work probably would have been ca. 300 B.C. In all probability some date in the fourth century B.C. is quite likely for this composition.

As already indicated the chief focus of this "history" centers in the Temple and its cultic celebrations in Jerusalem. Along with this is an emphasis on the importance and centrality of David. He was idealized almost to the point of perfection (quite a feat when one recalls the Samuel accounts!), and the Temple was considered the direct consequence of David and his planning. In fact the only kings of the Southern Kingdom mentioned are those who had some positive relationship with the Temple (Solomon, Jehoshaphat, Hezekiah, and Josiah).

The major critical problem relating to the work of the Chronicler lies in the relationship and dating of the figures of Ezra and Nehemiah. According to the accounts as they now stand these two leaders of post-exilic Judaism were contemporaries. Upon close examination one finds several points of conflict with this understanding. For example when Nehemiah came he found the people scattered, the walls of Jerusalem in ruins, and there was no real order or organization to the lives of the people. When Ezra came, he found the walls already built, and people living with some degree of order. When Nehemiah was on the scene the high priest was a man called Eliashib, but when Ezra was operative the high priest was the grandson of Eliashib, Jehohanan.

Many scholars, therefore, believe that the Chronicler made some mistake in his historical reckoning, basically at the point of misunderstanding Artaxerxes I and Artaxerxes II (king of Persia) as the same person. If this is true, then Nehemiah would have been in Judah ca. 444 and 432 B.C. under Artaxerxes I, and Ezra would have been in Judah ca. 400 B.C. under Artaxerxes II. Another hypothesis has been proposed which would place Ezra late in the time of Artaxerxes I (ca. 430 B.C.) shortly after Nehemiah, but that does not do away with the problem that in the Chronicler's work as it stands Ezra is portrayed as having come to Judah *before* Nehemiah. The weight of argument seems to point to Nehemiah's having come to Judah ca. 444 and 432 B.C. with Ezra following ca. 400 B.C. The explanation for the confusion may lie in the misunderstanding of which Artaxerxes was meant, but it is also possible that an answer may lie in another consideration. Upon close examination of the text it is obvious that there were two separate sources which were inserted into the history basically in "block" form. One of these sources dealt with Nehemiah, the other with Ezra. It appears that the insertion of these materials was done with very little editorial attention to historical accuracy, thus causing later interpreters difficulty at that point. One is reminded that the purpose of the Chronicler was not to write history *per se* but to present the post-exilic community as the people of God centered in the Temple and in the Law. Not all interpreters agree with such a hypothesis, however, and it is safe to say that there is no consensus at this point presently.

Chronicles: Outline

   I. Genealogies (Adam to David) 1 Chron. 1—9
  II. The Career of David 1 Chron. 10—29
 III. The Career of Solomon 2 Chron. 1—9
 IV. From the Divided Kingdom to the Exile 2 Chron. 10—36

    As can be readily observed the books of Chronicles follow a simple outline. The first section takes the reader from Adam to David almost entirely through listing of genealogies, the last chapter of which lists those who returned from exile. David's career is then highlighted with special emphasis upon his preparations for the building of the Temple and the cultic approaches which would be part of that total worship experience.

    One of the interesting aspects in dealing with the accounts in Chronicles is the mention in 1 Chronicles 21 of the figure of Satan. This figure has already been encountered in the book of Zechariah where the entity was a being in the court of Yahweh whose duty it was to accuse the people. The point at issue in Chronicles involves the designation, "Satan," as a personal name which replaced the "anger of Yahweh" (cf 2 Samuel 24:1). The reason Satan had become the scapegoat here with regard to the taking of the census apparently had to do with shifting the blame which traditionally had been attributed to David to someone else so that David's pure reputation could be preserved.

    A large portion of Chronicles deals with the division of the people connected with the Temple into various groups with specified duties. The central focus is directed toward the post-exilic period where the new community was centered in proper worship at the Temple. After David's death, the Chronicler depicted Solomon's reign as centered in his building of the Temple. The kings who followed and who were especially sensitive toward the Temple were praised for their greatness.

The last verses of 2 Chronicles (36:22–23) are reproduced at the beginning of the book of Ezra. In all probability those verses were reproduced in Chronicles when the books of Chronicles were separated from those of Ezra-Nehemiah. Otherwise the books of Chronicles would have ended on a negative note and, since in some collections the books of Chronicles concluded this entire section of the canon, would have caused the entire segment to have concluded negatively.

Ezra-Nehemiah: Outline

I. Restoration in the Land and Rebuilding the Temple Ezra 1—6
II. The Reforms and Advances Under Ezra and Nehemiah Ezra 7—Nehemiah 13

The book of Ezra-Nehemiah begins with the Cyrus proclamation which allowed the Jewish people to return to Judah and commissioned the rebuilding of the Temple. This decree is followed by an account of the return and the attempt to rebuild the Temple which was opposed by the people in the area of the old Northern Kingdom.

The problems of chronology associated with the accounts of Ezra-Nehemiah have already been mentioned (cf. above, p. 236). It is the view here that Nehemiah preceded Ezra into the land and began the work of restructuring the community organizationally and rebuilding the walls of Jerusalem. The rebuilding of the walls was understood to have been viewed as a large threat to the people to the north, and significant pressure was obviously brought upon the community in Judah by these people to impede that activity, but it was accomplished (in 52 days!), and Nehemiah attempted to impose strict standards upon the people of Judah to ensure that they would be a purified community. Especially emphasized were Sabbath observance, payment of the tithe, and the prohibition of mixed marriages, i.e., marriages with women outside the community of Judah. This ban on mixed marriage was done supposedly to keep the faith pure from outside religious elements which would naturally have accompanied people from other cultures.

These works and reforms were accepted nominally and assisted the new community to some degree of stability, but later when Ezra came onto the scene some of the reforms of Nehemiah still had to be reinforced. During the career of Ezra the major item of interest was the covenant renewal ceremony during which a "book of the law" was read to the people. What this "book" was is a matter of debate. Some have argued that this must have been the Torah in essentially the form in which it now exists, while others feel that perhaps part of the Torah was read. Whatever the document was, it seems to have become a standard for life within the new community. Thus with Ezra the Jewish people were well on the way to establishing a "religion of the book."

There was a public confession of sin during this covenant ceremony, and Ezra even more than Nehemiah railed against mixed marriages. He insisted that foreign wives and even the children be put away (cf. Ezra 10:2–5)! It is very easy for modern interpreters to be alarmed at such exclusivism, but to those leaders of this fragile community the issue was one of life or death. The purity of the community had to be established and enforced. If it were not, how could the unique people of God survive and how could preparation for the new age be accomplished? Nehemiah and Ezra did what they felt was right in the midst of their situation, and to their credit (and others) Judaism survived.

Psalms

As it presently is constituted the book of Psalms is divided into five books: 1—41; 42—72; 73—89; 90—106; 107—150, each of which is concluded with a doxology. Upon close examination it appears that some of these collections have incorporated within them smaller collections so that it is very difficult to determine the exact origin and age of many of the individual psalms. Earlier scholarship dated most of the psalms in the post-exilic period since the collection was made and used primarily in that era, but some of the psalms may well be very old and some are definitely pre-exilic in origin.

A very strong tradition held that David was the first great psalm writer. A psalm was understood as a poetic song which was to be sung to the accompaniment of a stringed instrument. Many psalms, therefore, bear the superscription "To David." The preposition l^e in Hebrew can mean "by," "to" or "for." The earlier understanding was that this term indicated that David was the author of the psalm, but the most likely explanation of the meaning is that the psalm was written "to" or "for" David in the sense that it was dedicated to him as the great psalmist. Since David was the first great psalmist, all psalms were considered to have been related to David in some way. (One remembers Moses and the law at this point.) The simple truth is that the origin of many of the psalms and their authorship are unknown.

A significant breakthrough came in the study of the Psalms when Hermann Gunkel suggested that they should be studied by literary type. This proved to be a major critical breakthrough because this type of methodology opened up the psalms to investigation from the standpoint of their origin according to form and use in the life-setting of the religious community. There are numerous "forms" (technically called *Gattungen*) which can be distinguished among those poems collected in the Psalter. There are *hymns*, usually of praise for God as creator (cf. Psalm 19) and/or sustainer of the people (cf. Psalm 135). Under this category most scholars also list the *enthronement* psalms celebrating the New Year (for example, Psalms 47; 93). In addition there are psalms of *lament* both of a private, personal nature and of a public or corporate nature. There are psalms of personal or corporate affirmation of *trust* in Yahweh (cf. Psalms 23; 62; 131). Since the psalms were of great value and use in the Temple ceremonies, it is not surprising to find *liturgical psalms* (cf., for example, Psalms 15; 24; 121) and psalms of exaltation of and pilgrimage to *Zion* (cf. 24; 46; 48; 84; and 120—134). In addition there are psalms of *thanksgiving* (cf. 30; 73; 103), *wisdom* psalms (cf. 1; 37; 111; and 119, which is probably a wisdom type psalm in honor of the Law), and psalms which are directed toward exalting the king, usually designated *royal psalms* (cf. 2; 18; 45; 110). One can learn how these psalms were used by the people in their worship by such texts as 1 Chronicles 16:8ff., Ezra 3:10ff., and perhaps Jeremiah 33:11.

Psalms: Outline

   I. Book I Psalms 1—42
  II. Book II Psalms 43—72

III. Book III Psalms 73—89
IV. Book IV Psalms 90—106
 V. Book V Psalms 107—150

It is generally agreed that Psalm 1 which is a wisdom psalm was placed where it is as an introduction to this entire collection. It may be that Psalm 2 was placed at the beginning of the first major collection (Psalms 3—41) since that collection seems to be in some way related rather closely to the person of David. Some have even designated this collection as the "Davidic Psalter." Some have suggested that this group may have originally been intended for private use because so many of the psalms are of the lament genre, but that seems unlikely since "books" were not really common possessions in that society.

There is another group of psalms which is designated the *Elohistic Psalter* by scholars because the personal name, Yahweh, has been frequently replaced by the generic term "God." These are found as Psalms 42—89 which are composed of collections of smaller groups of psalms some of which may have originated among groups of Temple singers (i.e., the Korahite and the Asaph psalms).

Another group of psalms comprise what is known as the second *Davidic Psalter* which includes Psalms 51—72. And the last larger grouping of Psalms, 90—149, is composed of numerous smaller units. Psalm 150 is believed to be the concluding poem for the entire and finalized collection. The fact that the final arrangement is blocked into five sections may be an attempt to emulate for this collection the authority of the five books of Moses. It is interesting to note that the five "books" do not always coincide with the collections!

One must read sympathetically and diligently the individual psalms in order to begin to have a real appreciation for these separate and individual units. Here within this collection one finds the inner feelings of the community of the Judean people. Sometimes one is shocked at what is there. It is at least surprising to find that people were encouraged to laugh gleefully when the infant children of the enemy have their heads bashed against rocks (cf. Psalm 137). In fact the entire gamut of human emotions is reflected in these poetic creations. But who, upon reading these varied literary creations mirroring differing times, circumstances,

and moods, can honestly deny many of the same feelings presented so
forcefully in these poems, baring as they do the human soul?

Proverbs

With the book of Proverbs one encounters the first complete and
full-fledged wisdom book among the Old Testament writings. As already noted, the earliest form of wisdom was characterized by practical
teachings which were designed to assist the individual in understanding
and thereby coping with the world. The rules of the created order had
to be learned and heeded if one was to have a successful and happy life
in this world. Proverbial teaching, then, followed this practical approach
to dealing with the world.

Wisdom in Israelite history could not remain entirely practical or
secular. It was quickly connected directly to the faith in Yahweh, God
of Israel, and the wisdom method, especially the proverbial type, became a very popular mode of teaching in the Hebrew tradition. Obviously a huge amount of such material existed among the people of
Yahweh, and some of this material was collected together into the book
of Proverbs. This book did not take its final shape, however, until the
post-exilic period, and it appears that numerous collections (as with the
book of Psalms) were placed together to form the seven collections now
comprising the book of Proverbs.

Many of the proverbs are very old, some dating back to the time of
Solomon, but many are more highly developed in content and structure
and probably date from the post-exilic era. The final collection of the
book in its present form dates probably from ca. 300 B.C. The idea
that all these go back to Solomon again reflects the "Moses-Law" and
"David-Psalms" syndrome.

Proverbs: Outline

   I. The First Collection: Proverbs of Solomon 1—9
  II. The Second Collection: More Proverbs of Solomon 10:1—22:16
 III. The Third Collection: "Words of the Wise" 22:17—24:22

It is generally agreed among interpreters of Proverbs that the first collection, chapters 1—9, is probably the latest (i.e., the least old) of all the collections brought together in this book. The more developed form of the proverbs and the more thematic nature of the material along with certain linguistic data all point to a later period for the origin of these sayings. This collection emphasizes the blessings to be experienced in a life governed by wisdom and the folly of a life which does not follow wisdom; its teachings warn against association with evil people especially evil women, and people are encouraged and challenged to follow the "way of the wise."

One interesting problem has to do with the first verses of chapter 1 (1:1–7). There are some interpreters who understand these verses as the introduction for the entire book of Proverbs. Others disagree, arguing that this section is only the introduction for the first collection. Certainty is not available in this matter, but these verses do set the tone for the entire book. Another interesting point to be observed in the examination of these verses is that one is able to see clearly how the religious dimension had permeated the wisdom movement in Israel.

> The fear of the LORD is the beginning of knowledge;
> fools despise wisdom and instruction. (1:7)

This verse could well be understood as the thesis of the entire book of Proverbs!

The second collection (10:1—22:16) in all probability contains some of the oldest of all the proverbs in the book. Here the reader encounters a long listing of simple proverbs, most of which are isolated and "self-contained." It is interesting to note that these proverbs are attributed to Solomon and that there are 375 of them. In ancient times people counted by the alphabet (cf. Roman numerals), thus each person had a "number" as well as a name. The name Solomon in Hebrew letters adds up to the total number of 375! Whether this was coincidental or deliberate may be debated, but this type of "coincidence" was quite frequent among wisdom traditions. The message is quite simple: if one does what is right, life will be happy and successful; if not, calamity will surely come.

The third collection (22:17—24:22) is of interest because within this collection are contained some proverbial poems which are directly parallel to an old Egyptian work called the "Wisdom of Amen-em-ope." The fact that such material is found in Hebrew wisdom writing probably serves to illustrate the "universal" appeal and understanding of wisdom in the ancient world. It also serves to demonstrate how open communication was among such persons dedicated to this type of study. The proverbs in this grouping were designed to give instruction to persons who were in apprenticeship for careers in public life.

"The Sayings of the Wise" which compose the fourth collection, a very short one (24:23–34), deal basically with the perils of laziness.

The fifth collection (25—29) is reported to have been composed of "proverbs of Solomon which the men of Hezekiah copied," but this collection can itself be divided into two separate groups of sayings. The first, contained in chapters 25—27, includes some very old proverbs, this being seen in the fact that they are the most secular of all the proverbs in the entire book of Proverbs. These may well go back to Solomon or even possibly before. The second group, 28—29, are much more "religious" in nature and therefore probably came from a somewhat later time. The early chapters attempt to give advice on how to avoid trouble in this world, and while the same motif is found in the latter part, these later advices are primarily religiously based and oriented.

The unity of the sixth collection (chapter 30) is greatly debated but no unanimity of opinion seems to be available as to how to divide the sources included in these verses. Most of the sayings seem to advocate "moderation," keeping to the middle-of-the-road in one's life. This same theme is portrayed in the numerical proverbs which are found in the last portion of this section.

Again with the seventh collection (chapter 31) as with the sixth there is a problem concerning unity. Two sections are clearly set together here, 31:1–9, and 31:10–31, the former giving advice on how to be a good leader and the latter an acrostic poem in honor of a good wife who even in those male-dominated times was considered a person of high quality, worthy of great praise.

In these various collections of proverbial wisdom there are many topics examined and discussed by the ancient wise men. These topics deal with life in its fullest extent and primarily were designed to direct the young and the unlearned in such a way as to bring success and stability into their lives. That wisdom sayings were popular is an understatement. Their popularity may well have been the result of the fact that all people have to learn how to cope with life—exactly what these sayings attempted to teach. The practicality of the wisdom teacher gave people direction for their encounters with the workings of society and the world, and these sayings may well have been of more pragmatic value than all the Torah and Prophets.

Job

Whereas the book of Proverbs and the practical wisdom approach to life and religion espouse essentially the Deuteronomistic ideas (i.e., do good and be rewarded; do evil and be punished), and whereas it is true that doing right, working diligently, and the like quite often mean success and happiness, it is nonetheless true that life is not always so simple. When suffering comes upon a person who is, humanly speaking, genuinely good, how does one speak to that situation or explain why? The older answers were that the suffering was for a "secret" sin, or possibly for the purpose of strengthening one's faith, or as a period of testing so that greater blessings could later be given. In reflecting upon life as it really is, people became painfully aware that these answers did not do justice to the problem.

That problem, what to make of a truly righteous person who was suffering unjustly, had been a theme of several ancient wisdom movements. Both the Mesopotamian and Egyptian cultures had stories dealing with such a situation in their traditions, but such questioning was really out of place within the early Hebrew religious development since it was so thoroughly dominated by what has come to be called Deuteronomic theology. People basically suffered because of their sins, even if those sins were secret to all, including the person suffering! In the post-exilic era, however, the horrid plight of the people in the restored community after the long exile could not really be explained any longer by this type of religious dogma. The exile could be easily understood as the just punishment for fomer evil and idolatrous living. All that was past, and great care was being taken to remain pure, keep the law and thus insure that new age which had been so long hoped for, but the new age did not come; the people were suffering. Why? What answer could be given? Such thoughts were quite probably responsible for the appearance of the book of Job.

The book itself seems to be the product of several differing literary sources. There is a prose prologue and epilogue which could well stand alone as a single story, though the epilogue presupposes the remainder of the book. There is a large poetic section in which Job and his three "friends" carry on a dialogue, and there is also a long section in which God speaks. In addition there are several chapters which give interpreters some trouble and thus are usually relegated to the status of later interpolations. Chapter 28 which is a magnificent poem about wisdom and chapters 32—37 which contain a summary by a young man named Elihu are the sections usually cited in this category.

Nothing is known about the author of the book except that he obviously was a member of the wisdom tradition. The date of the book has been much debated, some arguing for a very early date in the pre-exilic period but most agreed that the post-exilic period is a much more suitable context. Dates range from 500–200 B.C., but the probability is more likely for a date of ca. 400–300 B.C. Another question revolves around what kind of writing was used to relay this story. Some have argued that the book of Job was written as a drama, and more recently one of the more reputable scholars has argued that the book is a dramatized lament. Since most of the book is in poetic form, some have suggested that it is an epic poem. Other conjectures have been made as well. The book of Job in a sense defies absolute categorization, however, but it comes from a wisdom thinker of the later more speculative type who delighted in presenting religious ideas and discussion in story form. Whatever one calls it, the book of Job is a magnificent and moving piece of literature.

The text of the book of Job is not in a state of preservation which inspires confidence in our ability always to understand its intent exactly and precisely. In the third cycle of speeches between Job and his friends, for example, it is clear that some parts are missing and the arrangement has been garbled (see below). In the speech of Yahweh in 38:1—41:34 many scholars feel that some minor rearrangement and displacement of the text has occurred. And there are some places in the text where the Hebrew is so uncertain as to make accurate translation impossible (cf., for example, 19:23–27).

Debate over the purpose of the writing has also been heated and varied. Some think that the basic purpose of the book was to answer the question of why the righteous suffer. Others argue that the purpose was to answer the question of theodicy, i.e., the justice and righteousness of God when compared with the real state of the world. Neither of these problems is resolved, however. What seems certain is that the book was written to speak to the community of God's people in a period of intense questioning as to why their fortunes were not better and why they had suffered for so long. What were they now to think or to do? The answer to that question lay at the heart of the book of Job.

Job: Outline

I. Prose Prologue 1—2
II. Dialogue Between Job and His Three Friends 3—31
III. The Elihu Speeches 32—37
IV. The Yahweh Speeches and Job's Response 38:1—42:6
V. The Prose Epilogue 42:7–17

The story of Job begins with a description of a man from Uz (Job interestingly enough is not a Jew though he worships Yahweh) who is truly a good man. The scene then shifts quickly to the heavenly council where Satan (the Accuser) was reporting to God about the people on earth. Whereupon God asked Satan if he had considered Job who was truly a religious man. But Satan argued that Job was good and religious because it was to his advantage to be good and religious. With that the game was on.

Many persons today are disturbed by this account, wondering what kind of God would subject a human being to such agony and capriciously destroy innocent human life without cause for a kind of "whim." If this were a historical account, the question would be relevant. When one recalls, however, that this account is in the form of a wisdom story told to illustrate certain religious points, such questions no longer pose a problem. The main concern is then to understand the meaning of this harsh but at times delightful story.

In the story the screws began to be tightened on Job who at first had remained faithful and calm in the midst of his losses and suffering. In the dialogue with the three friends which begins in chapter 3 the old myth about Job and his patience has blown away! Job cursed the day of his birth, and this is quite close to cursing God since God was considered to be the giver of life. From this point on in the poetic discourses there is the alternation between a speech by one of the three friends and Job's response. Eliphaz spoke; Job responded. Bildad spoke; Job responded. Zophar spoke; Job responded. There are three cycles of these speeches, or at least there were originally. The last cycle has suffered some textual damage, however, and there is no last speech by Zophar as the text now stands.

The problem here partially revolves around chapter 28. This chapter is a fine piece of poetry in praise of wisdom, but as the text now stands this poem is placed upon the lips of Job. If Job had believed what is the content in this poem, however, there would have been no reason for the discussion with the friends nor would there be any reason for the work to continue, for the poem reflects a very "orthodox" view with regard to the world and its ways. Many scholars, therefore, regard chapter 28 as a later insertion into the text. There is no real textual evidence for this, and most scholars agree that the style and language of this poem are identical to the other poetic parts of the book, therefore quite probably by the same author. It seems likely, in the light of these considerations, that the poem was part of the original larger work, but how did it fit into the overall scheme?

Since Job began the long section (3—31) with a summary statement and concluded with a summary statement, it appears possible that the three friends may have some sort of summary as well. This summary would naturally reflect the traditional theology of wisdom which the three friends had been defending. This is exactly what chapter 28 is. Since the Zophar speech is missing, it could very well be that chapter 28 was originally the final speech of Zophar which was intended to conclude the argument of the three friends. Because the poem was so beautiful and so "orthodox" in terms of wisdom theology, later editors not fully understanding the purpose of the original writer transferred these marvelous lines to the lips of the hero, Job. This is, of course, only a conjecture, but it has some merit since it answers more questions than it raises!

The full dialogue between Job and his three friends is interesting to study. It began politely enough with the friends pointing out to Job that the righteous do not suffer unless there is some good reason. Job was therefore urged to confess his sin. Job protested that he had done nothing to warrant such suffering. He honestly wished that he could find the cause and thus relieve his torment resulting from his not understanding why these things were happening to him. The more Job protested, however, the more intense the friends became in their criticism of him.

> Know then that God exacts of you
> less than your guilt deserves. (11:6b)

Some friends!

It must be pointed out that the author of the book of Job was still operating within the complex of ideas connected with Sheol. There was not as yet any thought of a life-after-death with rewards or punishment. One was still rewarded or punished in this life. Questioning about that concept is raised in the book of Job, but the answer was still that of the gloom of Sheol.

> For there is hope for a tree,
> if it be cut down, that it will sprout again . .
> But man dies, and is laid low;
> man breathes his last, and where is he? . . .
> If a man die, shall he live again? . . .(14:7–14)

The answer of the author of the book to that last question was no! This was why Job's suffering and the suffering of any innocent people was so unfair and difficult to accept. The question had been asked, and it was at the probing of the speculative wisdom thinkers and of the later apocalyptic writers that ideas about life-after-death began to be discussed in Jewish thought.

One additional passage should be considered in connection with this section. This is the section found in 19:23–29, especially verses 25–27.

They read:

> For I know that my Redeemer lives,
>   and at last he will stand upon the earth;
> and after my skin has been thus destroyed,
>   then from my flesh I shall see God,
> whom I shall see on my side . . .

This passage is quite well-known to many persons, even those who are not students of the Bible, but whether they are properly understood is another matter. The verses are set within one of Job's replies to his "comforters." Job had been protesting his innocence, and he was so certain of it that he made this well-known statement.

The problem is that the text here is in such a state of disrepair that it is almost impossible to translate it correctly in order to understand it properly. Another problem lies in the translation of the Hebrew word *Go'el*, which means Avenger or Vindicator. The familiar translation, "Redeemer," is misleading. The idea involved here is that of the old concept of an Avenger whose duty it was to make certain that the murderer or slanderer of a person no longer able to offer defense would be brought to proper judgment. The good name of the person wronged would be cleared by this Avenger. Job seems to be arguing here not for a resurrection as some interpret the passage (already any life-after-death has been ruled out), but for a vindication of his good name after he has died. He did not think that this vindication would come while he was still alive. The garbled text here makes it unclear who the vindicator might be, but there is strong evidence to point in the direction of God. Somehow after Job was dead, he believed, God would see to it that any doubt about Job's claim to be basically innocent would be removed. This passage certainly does not predict some figure from the future.

The last long speech of Job is found in chapters 29—31. Some interpreters of Job, however, have argued that this speech is not the conclusion of the dialogue with his friends but the beginning of a new section where Job speaks with God. No matter how one divides the book, these chapters do represent Job's summary of justification for his own life and his searching for answers as to why he is suffering so much. Finally, he challenged God directly, even dared God, to come down and speak with him.

At this point in the narrative the Elihu speeches have been included. Elihu is presented as a younger man who had been listening to this conversation and who now was attempting to summarize and criticize both Job and his friends, but Elihu basically comes out at the same point as the friends. Whether this section was intended by the author as a respite from the dialogue, a pause for dramatic effect, or a summary of all that had gone on before, or whether this section is a later insertion into the text of Job, as many interpreters think, cannot be precisely ascertained. The religious thought is not really developed further by these chapters in any case.

Beginning with chapter 38 Yahweh responds to the challenge of Job given in chapter 31. He spoke to Job out of the midst of the whirl-wind, and what was revealed was not the answer to Job's questions but rather the magnificent majesty of God as Creator of all things. When this speech was finished, Job was quite subdued and uttered words quite famous:

> I have heard of thee by the hearing of the ear,
>   but now my eye sees thee;
> therefore I despise myself,
>   and repent in dust and ashes. (42:5–6)

It is in these verses that the key to understanding the message of the book of Job is to be found. The question of why the righteous suffer is not answered. The question of theodicy, God's justice, is not answered. Job's questions are not answered. What Job did come to learn was that "knowing" God, i.e., having an intimate experience and relationship with God, is crucial to life in this world. The author of the book of Job seems to be arguing that one cannot rationally explain all the manifold mysteries one encounters in the world as it is, but one can "know" God, and this "knowledge," i.e., relationship with God, will sustain one through good or bad times.

The answer of the book of Job to these kinds of problems is a religious answer, not a theological one. It is interesting that in the epilogue, God is depicted as being angry at Job's three friends because they had not spoken "what is right" about God as Job had! But these were the defenders of theological orthodoxy, while Job had cast doubts upon God's integrity. How could Job have "spoken right"? The point seems to be that Job was open and honest in his relationship with God, not hiding behind neat theology or pat answers to complex problems.

At the conclusion to the book Job's fortunes were restored. As with the prologue some persons feel uneasy with this turn of events. Did not this restoration prove exactly what the three friends had been saying all along? And what Job originally thought? Various theories have been postulated to assist in solving this problem, but the simplest and most logical solution seems to be that Job's fortunes were restored because the trial was over. Even in a story, to have God leave Job in a position of pain and suffering and despair would have certainly given an erroneous portrait of God as a capricious and unfeeling Being. This could not be allowed; therefore, once the message was clear, the situation had to be reversed, so that things would be as they were at the beginning. The restoration of Job's fortunes at that point, however, was simply irrelevant.

Ecclesiastes

Another of the speculative wisdom books is that of Ecclesiastes. Commonly known as *Koheleth* (i.e., one who calls or speaks to an assembly) the identity of the author of this collection of speculative musings is quite unknown. He seems to have been a teacher in a wisdom school, but exactly where is highly debated. Suggestions range anywhere from Phoenicia to Alexandria in Egypt to Palestine to Jerusalem, but the most probable place is Jerusalem. And the time of writing is also debated. Most scholars, however, date the work from 300–200 B.C.

It is well-known that the book of Ecclesiastes had perhaps the most difficult time of all being admitted into the canon of the Old Testament. The skeptical nature of its contents and the sometimes depressing tone of the arguments give to the work an aura of "anti-orthodoxy." Had it not been attributed to Solomon and had it not been for the last few verses (12:9–14) added by Koheleth's students the book would not have been included among the authoritative writings. Many find in it only extreme pessimism and negativism, but upon close scrutiny there is more positive material than one may have thought at first glance.

Ecclesiastes: Outline

It is a standing comment among interpreters of Koheleth that the book defies outline and organization. There is little agreement either as to the central theme of the book. If there is one, most commentators believe, it has to be the overarching idea of despair, "Vanity of vanities! All is vanity." The simple fact is that the book is a loose collection of sayings from this wisdom teacher which are somehow connected with the meaning of life. The sage attempts to be realistic about the world and its nature. Is there meaning in life? If so, where? Can one be happy in the midst of a world like this? If so, how? He attempts to make sense from the nonsense of life!

The first few verses (1:2–11) set the stage for the remainder of his reflections. Koheleth argues that there is in the world a certain regularity which demonstrates little except the futility of change. These ideas are then followed by what seems to be an attempt to find purpose and meaning in life. Such meaning can be sought in wisdom, work, pleasure, power, and wealth, but none of these separately nor all together can give final fulfillment and purpose of life. All of these pursuits are useful but ultimately break apart on the harsh reality of the world as it really is.

The things which should assist one in having a good life are "out of synch." One seeks for justice in the courts, but it is not there. One seeks for fairness for all people, but it is not there. One seeks to accumulate certain things to pass along, but all this labor can be for nought if the next generation does not appreciate the effort and the gift. Not even theological and cultic "orthodoxy" can give a true sense of purpose, because they are too neat while the facts of the world are not.

In spite of all Koheleth's pessimism, however, which most interpreters emphasize, there are also elements of hope in his teaching. He believed that making the best of one's work would bring some sense of direction and purpose even if that is not immediately evident. He saw in the cyclical nature of certain aspects of life, not only a monotonous humdrum, but some glimmer of hope. There are, for example, some things one can count on in this world, whether they are good or bad. That gives at least some degree of stability to life and something to plan around. Perhaps his most interesting expression and one giving a challenge to those who live in the world is found in 9:4b: ". . . for a living dog is better than a dead lion." The principle here is that where there is life, there is hope.

This emphasis upon the struggle of the individual against the world permeates Koheleth's sayings but is frequently overlooked by many interpreters. To find such a thread of hope recurring throughout the different teachings is somewhat surprising since Koheleth was still operating with the old concept of Sheol in terms of life and death. There would be no possibility, therefore, for injustices and unfairness to be made right in the future. The person has to accept the world as it is now, work as diligently as one can, enjoy life as much as possible (though Koheleth is not a hedonist by any stretch of the imagination); such an approach will give that individual some direction and purpose for living and make life as meaningful as it can possibly be.

The last major section of these collected sayings deals with a challenge to young people to enjoy their youth (11:9—12:8). He cautioned them, however, to remember that what they do presently would have to be "paid for" later! It is interesting to note that the section concludes with a symbolic description of a person in old age (12:1ff.). The proper translation of 12:1 should probably be, "Remember your *grave* in the days of your youth." That emphasis fits the theme of Koheleth—enjoy life where it is and when it is.

It is quite obvious that the last verses (12:9–14) are an editorial comment appended to the collection of the great sage's work, probably by some devoted students or disciples. There is a kind of apology here for the harsh, sharp, and sometimes depressing tone which the teachings reflect. Nevertheless, the readers were challenged to accept these searching analyses as "goads" to aspire them to greater heights of action and understanding. There is also a warning that such meditations as these are not for just anyone to pursue. It takes a special person to wrestle with such problems and not be overcome with despair and depression. Such speculation as Koheleth has presented, then, is better left to those who by nature and training are suited to that task.

The final two verses seem to summarize the entire teaching of the book. "Fear God, keep his commandments." This is the positive message which can be found in the meanderings of Koheleth, though many interpreters of this book never find it. The old sage's students obviously understood his teachings better than many subsequent interpreters!

Koheleth was honest enough to admit that he could not make all the pieces of life "fit" together and to admit that he could not make sense out of everything that goes on in the world. He understood that the foundation for real meaning in life must be located outside human nature and history and outside the world order—at least the world order known to humankind. Koheleth ultimately rested his hope upon the God to whom he had committed his mind and his life.

The Song of Songs

The Songs of Songs or the "most beautiful Song" has been a source of great embarrassment to prudish religious people for many centuries. This embarrassment results from the fact that this book is a collection of love poems which are in some instances fairly explicit in their description of physical lovemaking. To avoid that fact this collection of love songs has been interpreted as an allegory for many centuries.

Others have attempted to find in this book an exaltation of marriage, and one of the more recent theories explains these poems as a collection of songs and poems from ancient marriage festivals which frequently lasted for a week or more. In such ceremonies the bride and bridegroom were referred to as the Queen and King, and special poetry was sung or recited to them.

Another possibility which has been suggested is that these poems originated in the ancient world against the background of fertility deities such as Ishtar and Tammuz. They were then "secularized" when brought into contact with the Israelite culture and milieu and were subsequently used in wedding ceremonies.

The unity of the book presents a problem. Some interpreters find in the book a single theme (usually marriage) which is developed from the beginning (courtship) to the conclusion (marriage). Others, however, find little or no evidence of any unity or developmental sequence in the book, viewing the poems as simply a collection which revolve around the theme of human love.

The age of the poetic material included in this collection causes some debate also. Dates ranging from pre-exilic to post-exilic are supported. There is evidence that parts of the material may have originated at different times, but the date for the completed work in its present form seems to have been somewhere in the post-exilic period. The place of origin is not known, but perhaps a good guess would be Jerusalem. The work is attributed to Solomon probably because he was known to have composed over one thousand songs (and perhaps because he had seven hundred wives and three hundred concubines?!), but it is almost universally agreed that Solomon was not the author of this book as it presently exists.

Many scholars classify the Song of Songs as belonging to the wisdom tradition, noting that the attribution of the work to Solomon is evidence for that understanding. It is also argued by some interpreters that to investigate human love would have been a part of the task of the wisdom schools.

The embarrassment caused to some interpreters in their attempts to explain the purpose and aim of this collection of poems exalting the joys of sexual love is quite obvious when one examines the various approaches to the material. Some have argued that these poems must be an allegory symbolizing God's love for his people. Others insist that these songs must be understood within the context of the marriage covenant. One of the problems with that approach becomes evident in the study of the text itself where there appear to be three people involved, not just two!

It would be helpful for the modern reader to keep two points in mind in attempting to understand these poems. It is clear from a study of the cultural milieu of ancient times that the rigid restraints later placed on sexual activity were not always present. One recalls the patriarchs with numerous wives and concubines, and one is naturally aware that women were not considered equals in that society. Even so, a strong movement emerged and evolved in the history of Israelite thought which attempted to regulate sexual activity and to lift that great God-given gift to higher levels of understanding and practice. The Old Testament writers never isolate the "secular" from the religious activities of life, and this type of thinking naturally had implications for sexual relationships. Nevertheless this collection of love poems basically exalts the sheer joy and pleasure of human sexuality.

Song of Songs: Outline

I. The Celebration/Joys of Human Sexuality

It is difficult at points to determine just how to understand the separate portions of this collection, for it is uncertain as to how many persons are involved in the scenario. Some have argued for just two. Others have seen two males, a king and a shepherd, and one female. Others have seen two females and either one or two males. Some find a man and a woman and a chorus (similar to the Greek chorus in Greek drama). Some have argued that the work is a unity; others cannot find any formal structure at all. The latter are probably correct.

Just what is the place of such a collection of erotic love poetry which sometimes leaves nothing to the imagination in an anthology of religious literature? That these poems are basically meant to be understood as erotic poetry is reflected in the fact that in the second century A.D. they were sung in taverns amidst popular celebrations! The Hebrew people did not view sexual intercourse as inherently evil or dirty as some of the Greeks later did. The sexual engagement between a man and a woman was considered a gift of God, something to be enjoyed. The fact that sexual activity is often the object of abuse and degradation does not thereby decrease its value as a gift of God to be enjoyed within the proper framework. These poems exhibit the sheer delight of such a gift!

Yet there does seem to be even here in such a collection strong implications for setting sexual relationships within the proper context. One reads near the conclusion of the book:

> Set me as a seal upon your heart,
>   as a seal upon your arm;
> for love is strong as death . . .
> Many waters cannot quench love,
>   neither can floods drown it.
> If a man offered for love
>   all the wealth of his house,
>   it would be utterly scorned. (8:6–7)

Lamentations

This book is a collection of five poems all of which reflect the suffering and despair connected with the destruction of Jerusalem by the Babylonians. Included among these poetic pieces are dirges, communal laments, and individual laments. These literary compositions were quite probably composed very close to the time of the actual fall of Jerusalem in 586 B.C. The question of exactly where and when for each poem, however, has not yet been agreed upon.

Some scholars argue that all five of these poems originated in Judah, making this book unique in that this is the only Old Testament writing which originated primarily from among those persons not carried away to Babylonia. Others, however, argue that some or all of the poems originated in Babylonia. As for the date, most scholars believe that the poems were written very near to the time of the actual fall. But some others have argued for a much later date for certain chapters (1, 3, 4, 5), while still others have argued that perhaps a few chapters were composed after the first exile (597 B.C.) but before the final destruction (586 B.C.). Unanimity of opinion is not easy to find on the dating of the individual chapters, but the collection is generally thought to have come into being sometime shortly after the return of the exiles, i.e., somewhere ca. 525-475 B.C.

Traditionally the poems have been attributed to Jeremiah, though the text itself makes no such claim. This identification of Jeremiah with the literature probably came about because of Jeremiah's own teachings, his proximity to the events, and a reference in 2 Chronicles 35:25 to a "lament" of Jeremiah about the death of Josiah. Most scholars do not find enough similarity in style and language between the laments of Lamentations and the Jeremianic material, however, to warrant the conclusion that Jeremiah was the author of these five poems. Most believe that a fairly cultured person or persons composed the poems (perhaps a priest left behind in 586 B.C.?), for they are well-ordered and structured. In fact most of them (1, 2, 3, 4) are "acrostic" (i.e., alphabetic) with each line or thought beginning with the succeeding letter of the Hebrew alphabet. Some think that because of this phenomenon, these poems were originally written rather than orally proclaimed, but such a theory is only speculative.

Lamentations: Outline

I. Lament over the Causes of the Destruction of Jerusalem 1
II. Lament over the Horrors of the Siege 2
III. Personal Lament and Expression of Trust 3
IV. Description of the Horrors of the Capture of Jerusalem 4
V. Plea for Restoration 5

While each of these poems is essentially self-contained, a careful reading of the book depicts a kind of theme which may permeate the arrangement. In the first poem there is a lament about the destruction of the great city Jerusalem, but there is included a definite confession of sin which would have been quite appropriate for the initial section of such a collection. The idea here was not simply that the city had been destroyed, but that it really had deserved to be destroyed. Not only did the nation as a whole become corrupt and sinful (1:8, 9, 14, 17, 18), but the leaders of the nation were deceitful and selfish (1:19) thereby hardening the people in their sin.

Chapter 2 contains a pathetic depiction of what happens in times of war. Murder, rape, pillage on the part of the conqueror but also drastic measures on the part of the conquered in order to survive: "Should women eat their offspring? . . ." (2:20b). There follows then a long acrostic poem (chapter 3) which begins as a personal lament and passes along into a community lament. But in the process there is a searching for some hope which could possibly endure beyond the horror (3:25–33).

There is then the description of the horrors of the capture of Jerusalem and the aftermath in terms of human suffering (chapter 4). From this chapter one learns that some of the surrounding nations, notably Edom, either participated in the siege and destruction or took advantage of the survivors who had been left defenseless in the land. The final poem (chapter 5) contains another community lament which concludes with an earnest petition for the restoration of the people (cf. Psalms 74; 79; 80).

The book of Lamentations as a composite work appears to have been intended as a confession of guilt and an acknowledgement of a just punishment on the people in the matter of the destruction of the land. The description of the horrors of the times appears to have served a twofold purpose: to demonstrate that full payment had been exacted for the sin of the people and as a warning for later generations so that this horror could be avoided in the future. These purposes seem to be served when one is reminded that the book was read each year on the ninth day of Ab (August) at a commemorative festival which reminded the Jewish people of the disaster that overtook them because of their unfaithfulness to God in "former" times.

Ruth

The story preserved in the book of Ruth probably originated sometime in the pre-exilic period, perhaps very early, and was passed along until the post-exilic age at which time it was written down in its present form. Most interpreters consider that this story began as a saga type literary piece and evolved finally into a short story or *novella* type tale similar to the Joseph story of Genesis 37—50. The fact that the setting for the story is that of the period of the Judges explains why the Septuagint translators placed the book after the book of Judges in their rearrangement of the Old Testament writings.

Where the story originated is a matter of some debate, some scholars arguing that it began from some historical incident which occurred long ago, some arguing that it resulted from a myth connected with a fertility cult centered at Bethlehem, and still others that the story was simply a tale composed during the post-exilic period with symbolic meanings (especially with regard to the names of the characters). It is possible that more than one explanation may be necessary to fully explain the origin and final form of the material, but most of these conjectures remain simply conjectures! The fact is that this story in its present form is quite similar to the haggadah type stories which flourished in the later post-exilic period and probably should be interpreted as such.

As for the date of the book as it now stands, the majority of interpreters believe that a post-exilic setting fits more of the circumstances and evidence than any other period. There are those, nevertheless, who argue for a pre-exilic dating, some even suggesting a date as far back as the time of Solomon. The linguistic characteristics of the writing itself suggest a post-exilic date, however, since there are a number of Aramaisms in the book, usually a sure sign of the post-exilic era.

The question of authorship is not really a matter of discussion since no author is named in the book, and the traditions concerning authorship are not very strong or reliable. The primary critical question, however, concerns the purpose which the book was intended to serve. Some interpreters view the story simply as one emphasizing the providence of Yahweh and urging faithfulness to the customs and laws on the part of the people. There are others, however, who interpret the book of Ruth as one of the reactions of protest against the exclusivism of the post-exilic community, especially certain aspects of the reforms of Nehemiah and Ezra. These interpreters see in the non-Israelite woman, Ruth, a symbol of the non-Israelite wives of the post-exilic period who were being cast out of the community along with the children of the marriages. Since Ruth became a true worshiper of Yahweh and kept the laws of Yahweh, she became one of the ancestors of the great king David! The intention of the writing, then, would be to serve as a caution to the extremely harsh treatment of the non-Israelite wives in Judah.

There are others who do not believe that the reforms of Nehemiah and Ezra had as yet been enacted when the book of Ruth was written. Rather, these interpreters believe that the book was intended as a means of strength and support for the returning exiles and the hard times they were encountering. The term "return" is used quite frequently in the book, and the appeal to keep the law in spite of harsh circumstances, it is argued, fits the early post-exilic period. Certainty on this matter is not possible though it seems that either of the explanations which relate the book to the post-exilic times may be correct. It is not beyond the realm of possibility that certain aspects of each may be appropriately understood as the background and purpose of the book as it was intended by the final author.

There is one further problem, critically speaking, which has not been resolved. This relates to the passage at the conclusion of the book which identifies Ruth with the lineage of David. Most scholars feel that this section (4:17ff.) does not belong to the original story but was appended later when the book was redacted in its present form. Some others feel, however, that the genealogical comment incorporated into these verses was part of the original tradition and perhaps the primary reason for the story's having been preserved. Again here is a point which cannot be demonstrated with certainty. Whatever the resolution of that problem, however, the major concern still remains as to why the author went to such lengths to make such a large point of this seemingly inconsequential bit of information. The reason must have had something to do with the purpose of the book in its historical situation in the post-exilic age.

Ruth: Outline

I. Background for the Story 1:1–5
II. Struggle of the Two Women Upon Returning to Judah 1:6—2:23
III. Naomi Advises Ruth How to Keep the Law 3:1—4:12
IV. Happy Ending for All 4:13–22

Set in the period of the judges the book of Ruth portrays the struggle of two women against the hard realities of the world of that time. A family of Hebrew people had moved to Moab because of a famine in Judah. The two sons then married Moabite women, but shortly after they had settled down the husband of Naomi and the two sons died. In a strange land, separated from any family, Naomi decided to make the treacherous journey back to Judah alone. One of her daughters-in-law took Naomi's advice and returned to her family, but Ruth insisted on remaining with Naomi, uttering these famous words so often quoted by starry-eyed lovers: ". . . where you go I will go, and where you lodge I will lodge; your people shall be my people, and your God my God" (1:16–17). The two of them returned to Judah, but times were still hard there.

Naomi sent Ruth into the fields of a kinsman, Boaz, to glean. It was a requirement of the law (which was supposed to assist the destitute) that the reapers in the fields were to leave something behind for the poor (cf. Deuteronomy 24:19ff.; Lev. 19:9ff.; and 23:22ff.). When Boaz found out who this woman was, i.e., Naomi's daughter-in-law, he gave strict orders for his workers not to harm her (a hint perhaps of the manner in which women, especially poor women, were treated?). When Ruth reported all this to Naomi, the older woman was delighted. She obviously knew the levirate law and explained it to Ruth and gave her instructions as to what to do.

The younger woman did exactly what the older woman instructed. For Ruth to produce a child which would insure the continuation of the family according to the beliefs of that day would be a great boon. It could also lead to some measure of security in other ways as well, such as a permanent relationship in marriage (which it did). The episode of Ruth with Boaz at the threshing floor has caused some interesting debate, some finding in the story the remnants of an ancient fertility cult in Bethlehem. This seems very unlikely, however, because the basic thrust of the story lies in the details dealing with levirate marriage. Ruth asked Boaz to be the *Go'el* or Vindicator for her in this situation. Since there was another kinsman closer than he, Boaz indicated that this matter must first be cleared with that person. It is interesting to note that Boaz asked Ruth to spend the night with him, whether out of concern for Ruth's safety in returning to Naomi at night or personal pleasure or both is not known.

True to his word Boaz contacted the next of kin about the situation. There was a certain ritual which obviously had to be completed which would clearly indicate that the other kinsman had refused to perform the requirement. It is interesting to note the account of the action (4:7ff.) which differs somewhat from the specifications given in Deuteronomy (25:5–10). Some interpreters think that the differences mean that this story is therefore older than the law in Deuteronomy, while others believe that this shows the story of Ruth to be later than Deuteronomy!

Ruth and Boaz were subsequently married; a son was born who became the grandfather of David; true devotion to Yahweh and his laws had been richly rewarded. It is difficult not to see in this story, and especially the conclusion, a message directed to the post-exilic Jewish community in Judah which would challenge these people to trust and commitment to God and the law, and perhaps a less negative attitude toward the people of the area who were not Jews. The story raised the possibility, at least, that some Gentiles might become true worshipers of God if given the opportunity.

Esther

Set in the time of the Persian Empire among the Jews of the "Eastern Dispersion," the book of Esther tells the delightful story of how the Jewish people were able to overcome persecution and turn the persecution onto the persecutors. The story is variously called a tale, a novella, a historical romance or a wisdom composition. It is in reality a haggadic type story which probably has some of all these elements within it.

As many persons are aware the book of Esther had a difficult time finding a place within the canon of the Old Testament writings. One of the chief reasons was that God is never directly mentioned in the book, and there is only one place (4:14) where the Deity may even be alluded to and that is not a certainty. Later on, "additions" were written and added to the book to make it appear more "religious." In truth the reason for its having been written was probably to serve as the aetiological explanation for the origin of the feast of Purim. This feast was a late addition to the Jewish calendar of feasts, being mentioned first only in 2 Maccabees (15:36–37), a book probably to be dated ca. 50 B.C.

The exact origins of this feast are not known, but it appears to have originated somewhere in Persia and developed through the years, finally being accepted as a Jewish festival among all Jewry. Some have conjectured that the feast of Purim had its origin and roots in the Persian New Year's celebration, while other scholars have maintained that the story of Esther and thus the roots of the festival derive from an ancient myth which depicted battles between two sets of deities. In this theory Mordecai and Esther represented the Babylonian deities, Marduk and Ishtar, while Haman and Vashti represent the Elamite gods, Uman and Mashti. That interpretation, while ingenious, seems to be a bit strained.

Some interpreters have argued for a specific historical event relating to a persecution of the Jewish people which would have given rise to the story in its present and elaborated form. The question, however, is whether any historical basis for the story can be found. So little is known of the specific history of the Jews during this period that any guess remains a guess. Since so little is known, some interpreters have conjectured that the origins of the feast must lie in the Maccabean era where we know of a specific persecution under Antiochus. There are several indications which could support such a theory, but the story itself seems to be so tightly connected with a Persian setting that separating the feast from that origin seems arbitrary.

The most plausible explanation might be that there was an attempt, which was somehow thwarted, to persecute Jews somewhere in the

Persian Empire. From this historical event the story of Esther grew, and this account became the story which explained the origin of a popular feast, probably of secular Persian origin, called Purim. The word Purim comes from the word for "lot," *pur*, because the day arranged for the Jews to be persecuted was chosen by "lot." Even though the name Purim was finally the designation for this feast, at first the celebration seems to have been referred to as "Mordecai's day."

As for a date which can be given to the book, several have been suggested ranging from the period of the Babylonian captivity to the Maccabean era. Since the matter of a date has to be a guess, one could suggest some general period of time somewhere during the third to the second centuries B.C. (i.e., 300–150 B.C.). An additional matter of discussion concerns the background for the actual literary development of the story. There are those who see in the tale a blending together of several other stories, a story about Vashti, a story about Esther and her becoming a queen, a story about Haman and Mordecai which reflects the persecution motif. All these elements were then blended together in order to form the book of Esther in its present form. It is difficult to obtain certainty about these critical problems with regard to this book.

The feast of Purim was a most popular time among the Jews, for this occasion was a time of celebrating the victory and survival of the Jewish people in spite of all the difficulties they had experienced. On the feast of Purim the participants were allowed to consume wine until they could not distinguish the difference between "Blessed be Mordecai" and "Cursed be Haman"! It was a time of joy, of giving of gifts, of remembering the poor. It was a time to remember that there are good times and there are bad times in the history of a people. But Purim serves as a reminder that if the people are dedicated enough to their survival, they will continue to live.

Esther: Outline

I. Esther Becomes Queen 1—2
II. The Plot to Destroy the Jews 3
III. Mordecai and Esther Counter the Plot 4—8
IV. The Tables Are Turned and Purim Is Begun 9—10

The author of the story of Esther has woven together a fine tale which glides quite easily from one event to another. The story is set within the time of the Persian king, Ahasuerus (Xerxes I, 485–464 B.C.), and the initial chapters tell how Esther became queen. She was greatly assisted in this effort by Mordecai who instructed her not to tell the king that she was a Jewess. Because of her great beauty Esther was chosen as the queen, but the king was not aware that she belonged to the group of people known as Jews.

Mordecai then learned of a plot to kill Ahasuerus, told Esther, who told the king. At this point in the narrative the figure of Haman is introduced. Haman disliked Mordecai (who refused to bow down before Haman) because Mordecai was a Jew. This infuriated Haman who concocted a plan which would exterminate all Jews, and he persuaded the king to agree to the plan. The date was then set for the slaughter of the Jews, eleven months hence!

But when Mordecai learned of this plot, he immediately began to talk with Esther about how this horrible verdict might be rescinded. Risking her life, Esther went to the king to propose a banquet for the king and Haman. (It is interesting to note just how many banquets are involved in this short story.) The ironies of the situation are quite well depicted by the author. Haman was exposed as the evil conspirator he was; when he accidentally fell on the queen's couch, just as the king was returning to the room, Haman's fate was sealed. He was to be hanged on the very gallows which he had prepared for Mordecai; interestingly enough these gallows were about seventy-five feet high.

Esther pleaded with the king on behalf of the Jewish people since the decree had not yet been rescinded. The king heard Esther's plea, and another decree was sent out to counter the previous one. This decree allowed the Jews to take vengence on their enemies! According to the story seventy-five thousand enemies of the Jews were slain at that time. The comment in the text that plunder was not taken was quite likely intended to emphasize that the killing of enemies was to be done for survival only and not for personal gain. There is a peculiar explanation of why two different days were mentioned in the tradition for the celebration of this event (cf. 9:17–19).

The short epilogue (chapter 10) concluded the story with Mordecai reigning as second only to the king (cf. the Joseph story). Esther was no longer in the picture. The book referred to in 10:2 which was supposed to have included the exploits of Mordecai is not otherwise known.

Exactly what can one make of this story? Obviously it is the source for the origin of the feast of Purim among the Jewish people, but the tone of the book and the outcome are somewhat disturbing to many modern readers. What one must first remember is that this is a story, not an account of a historical occurrence. It has already been argued, however, that there might be some historical kernel lying behind the tale, but the story as it stands is a story which had a message for the people of its own time.

One of the major points sometimes overlooked by interpreters of this book is the strong emphasis on Jewish relationships with Gentiles. As one can determine from the story these relationships could be either good or bad, depending partly upon how the Jewish people themselves reacted to certain situations. One of the presuppositions of the story, then, is that not all Gentiles are bad and relationships with Gentiles can be positive. It is also possible that the story was meant to encourage Jews of the dispersion to become involved in civil governmental causes as a way of assisting the Jewish people as a whole.

This writing offers encouragement to the Jewish people in the face of periodic persecution and/or harassment by people who are threatened by what they do not understand, or who attempt to use such groups as convenient scapegoats for their own guilt or hostility. While modern thinkers do not sanction the idea of slaughtering one's enemies simply because one can, this teaching of the book of Esther was intended to give hope to a people who in this post-exilic period were quite poor, down-trodden, and harassed.

Daniel

As one approaches the book of Daniel, the last of the Old Testament writings to be composed, one is struck with the new literary genre exhibited by the last six chapters of the book. These chapters constitute the longest and most consistent example of the literary type known as *apocalyptic* in the Old Testament (cf. above, pp. 228ff.). There have been several other portions of books which reflected the "ancestry" of this type in that they were characterized by wild visions with weird imagery. One recalls Ezekiel 1, the visions of Zechariah, perhaps part of Joel, and a portion of Isaiah 24—27 which is generally thought to be a later post-exilic section which found its final place in the Isaiah collection. There had not been as yet a full-fledged apocalyptic work.

The book of Daniel, as it presently stands, is not entirely an apocalyptic work even yet, though the religious thought patterns of the whole are quite apocalyptic. The first six chapters are composed of a collection of haggadah type wisdom stories set within the period of the Babylonian exile. These are delightful tales about four young Jewish men who remained loyal to their religious beliefs under the most trying of circumstances. One immediately is reminded of the post-exilic period as an appropriate historical setting for the origin of these stories.

The final six chapters of the book are composed of four genuinely apocalyptic visions which attempt to depict the flow of history from the Babylonian captivity to the time of the people being addressed. The history of these times has already been outlined (cf. above, pp. 219ff.). Under the hellenization policy of the Seleucids many Jews in Palestine were very dissatisfied and restive until the situation became so bad that Antiochus IV decided to proscribe Judaism. It became a capital crime to keep the regulations of the Torah, to possess a copy of the Torah, or to worship Yahweh, God of the Jews. Antiochus established the worship of Zeus in the Temple in Jerusalem by erecting there a statue of the god and enforced the worship of Zeus in the surrounding provinces.

The inevitable explosion came in 167 B.C. with the revolt of old Mattathias and his sons who led the fight against the Syrians (as the Seleucids were sometimes called). In such a setting persecution was the order of the day as far as the experiences of the Jewish people were concerned. Horrible atrocities were committed against them (cf. 2 Maccabees), and they were torn between keeping their religious traditions and becoming apostate. The classic conditions which prompted an author to present an apocalyptic work were surely present.

The book of Daniel, written during this period of persecution, was the response to this harsh and evil time. In typical apocalyptic fashion the book, as a literary creation, was set within the period of the Babylonian exile. Apocalyptic writers typically used pseudonyms. The tendency of apocalyptic to set the stories and visions in a time long ago was at least partially the result of the writers' style; an elaborate set of visions including wild symbols and images could be used to depict the flow of history from the past to the time of the people hearing these stories. No deceit or fraud was intended by such devices; these were simply accepted literary strategies connected with this particular literary genre. The author, therefore, simply remains unknown.

Dating any apocalyptic work is a tricky business, but this can sometimes be done by carefully examining the historical surveys given in such highly symbolic terms within almost every one of this type of writing. Daniel is no exception. What the reader does is to follow the survey along to the point where the history ceases to be exactly accurate and begins to "miss the specifics." Such a place can be found in Daniel (11:40ff.) when the author predicts the death and place of death of Antiochus IV but is incorrect in his prognostication. The author was correct in predicting that Antiochus would die shortly, but Antiochus did not die in the place nor in the manner expected. This bit of information, then, allows the historian to date the book of Daniel ca. 165 B.C., after the proscription of Judaism by Antiochus but shortly before his actual death in 164/3 B.C.

Another interesting, and as yet unsolved, problem related to any study of the book of Daniel concerns that of the language of the book. While most of the Old Testament documents were written in Hebrew, the book of Daniel was written in Hebrew and Aramaic. The book begins in Hebrew, 1:1—2:4a, switches to Aramaic, 2:4b—7:28, and then switches back to Hebrew again. The curious point is that the language switches do not appear at the natural breaks in the material. Chapters 1—6 form one unit, and chapters 7—12 form another. One can see that there is, therefore, an overlap between the two languages in terms of internal content. The solution to this problem has not been found, but there is one conjecture which may point in the proper direction. This theory suggests that chapters 1—6 originally existed in Aramaic, while chapters 7—12 were originally written in Hebrew. When the final author or editor placed these two sections together, he translated the first portion of each section into the language of the other so as to form an interlocking appearance of unity for the completed work. No general consensus, however, for the solution of this problem now exists.

It is exceedingly important for the reader of Daniel to remember that this book was written to a people undergoing extreme and intense persecution for the purpose of bolstering their faith and their commitment to that faith in the face of such suffering. The author is urging these people to keep the faith, for the persecution would *soon* be over. These chapters are not, and were not intended to be, timetables for the end of the world, as many have come to understand them. This book was intended as a call to faithful devotion in harsh times with the promise that God would ultimately take away the persecution and reward those who remained faithful, even to death.

Daniel: Outline

I. Stories About Daniel and His Friends 1—6
II. Apocalyptic Visions of Daniel 7—12

As already noted the first six chapters of Daniel are a collection of six haggadah type stories with the typical features of unfounded antagonism by certain groups toward the Jews and their customs, the hardships encountered by the Jews especially where they were attempting to keep their religious customs and laws, and the ultimate victory of the people of God when they were faithful in keeping their customs and laws. There are also stories about kings and nations which highly exalted themselves but were brought back to their proper station by the God of Israel. All of these themes are included in Daniel 1—6.

The setting for the stories in the book of Daniel is the Babylonian exile basically, but it is interesting to note that some of the stories are set later in the Persian period. Not all of the stories include the figure of Daniel; one concerns only Daniel's three friends. In each of the stories the interpreter can discern the purpose of the author or editor in that each of these episodes would remind the hearers in the Maccabean era of some aspect of their own situation under Antiochus IV.

The first story appears to set the stage for the entire book. Daniel and his three friends were languishing in Babylonian exile. They had been given Babylonian names, but interestingly enough Daniel was usually called by his Hebrew name whereas the three friends were known by their Babylonian names. In this first story the Hebrew youths were faced with the problem of how they could keep the Jewish dietary laws; working with the Babylonian official they made an agreement to test their food against that of the "king's table." Naturally they won the bet!

The second chapter has to do with a dream which Nebuchadnezzar had had, an image composed of various types of metals. This image and its meaning is quite similar to that of chapter 7 which is an apocalyptic vision (and which will be discussed shortly). Chapter 3 is the famous story of the huge image which people were required to worship or be thrown into the "burning, fiery furnace." The three Hebrew children (as they are sometimes known) refused to do this. (Where Daniel was, we are not told.) This story would immediately cause the hearer of that particular historical moment to think of the statue of Zeus which the Jews were being forced to worship. Shadrach, Meshach, and Abednego refused to worship the image, arguing that their God could deliver them from the burning ordeal, but further stating, "But if not, be it known to you, O king, that we will not serve your gods or worship the golden image which you have set up" (3:18). Herein lay the challenge to the people of that time. Even if they were not delivered from persecution by Antiochus, they were still not to worship another god.

Chapter 4 contains the story of Nebuchadnezzar who exalted himself as a god but was struck with a form of insanity (called today *zoan-thropia*) to convince him that he was simply mortal. The hearer from that time would immediately think of Antiochus who had called himself, "God manifest." Interestingly enough there is no historical evidence that Nebuchadnezzar ever suffered from such a malady, but there is some evidence that Nabonidus, a later king, had some mental problems. Again there may be a historical kernel in the origin of this story, but as it stands it is a story told to illustrate a religious point.

The purpose of chapter 5 was to demonstrate what ultimately happens to rulers and nations who deal cavalierly with God's people and take lightly the power of Yahweh when his honor is ridiculed. Here God's honor was being mocked by these people who were desecrating the vessels taken from the Temple. The judgment inevitably came upon these enemies of God. Again the people of that time would remember that Antiochus had plundered the Temple, even stripping gold off its facade. Chapter 6, containing the well-known episode of Daniel and the lions, demonstrates the unwarranted hatred and jealousy some people have for Jewish people and the lengths to which they will go to do harm to them. Daniel, keeping his faith in God and adhering to the customs of his religion, ultimately triumphed over them, and his enemies were the ones finally destroyed.

As already indicated, beginning with chapter 7 there is a definite change in the literary genre in the book of Daniel. One finds in chapters 7—12 a full-fledged apocalyptic work in contrast to the haggadah type stories of 1—6. In this passage (chapter 7) there is a strange and mysterious vision with four beasts, out of the last of which came a "little horn" with a big mouth. There is a scene of judgment depicted here with God (the Ancient of Days) doing away with the "little horn" and giving the kingdom to a figure called the "son of man." This weird scene was then explained to Daniel. The four beasts represented four kingdoms (Babylonia, Media, Persia, and the Greek states). Out of the fourth came the "little horn" with the big mouth; this represented Antiochus IV who was persecuting the people of God (cf. 7:24–25). But God would judge Antiochus, take away the persecution, and allow his people to live as they were supposed to live, keeping God's laws and worshiping only God. The "son of man" in this vision represents, therefore, the people of God to whom the Kingdom is entrusted. One should keep in mind that the nations of the world were not all destroyed in this scene; the persecutor was but not all the nations (cf. 7:11–12). These images are symbolic, to be interpreted somewhat as one would interpret poetry. The point is, therefore, that there is no teaching here about the end of the world, but only about the end of the period of persecution. In typical apocalyptic fashion the time is divided into two periods, the present age under the dominion of evil and the new age where the persecution will be eliminated and God's people will be God's people "normally" again.

There seems to be in the series of visions in chapters 7—12 a progression from a more general to a more specific recapitulation of history. Chapter 7 was very general, though the point was clear. Chapter 8 is a bit more specific with the vision of the ram with two horns and the he-goat from the west with one. That large horn was broken on the he-goat; four smaller horns came up in its place, and from one of those there appeared again the "little horn" with the big mouth! The fact that this vision was understood as simply apocalyptic imagery and was not really an attempt to deceive anyone can be seen quite clearly when the figures are explained very specifically in 8:20–26.

The visions found in chapters 9 and 10—11 are simply more specific in that they attempt to relate the general history of those times in a much more definite manner to the events which the Jewish people were experiencing. The teaching here is that all of these judgment events would culminate not in the end of time as some have attempted to interpret the text, but rather the "time of the end." The "end" of what? In this context it seems clear that the "end" is the end of the persecution. Antiochus was going to die, and when that occurred the persecution would be lifted. The persecution was soon lifted and Antiochus died shortly, but Antiochus did not die where or how the author of Daniel had specifically thought (cf. 11:40–45). That was of small concern, however, and was not the primary point. Once the persecution had ended the people of God could again worship as they pleased and serve God as they knew they should. To them that indeed was a new age or era.

At this point there is an interesting and new development in Old Testament thought. One recalls that the basic concept of death in the Old Testament writings centers in the idea of Sheol. Even the authors of Job and Ecclesiastes, speculative wisdom thinkers that they were, still understood the "end" in that manner. They had raised the question about the fairness of life with regard to the concepts of death related to Sheol. With the apocalyptic movement even more pressure was brought to bear at this point, for people who were being loyal to God and God's commandments were being horribly persecuted and killed. What about their sacrifice? Was it to be all in vain? The answer to that had to be a resounding no! Therefore, under the pressure of this kind of historical circumstance and new questions raised by these kinds of experiences, there gradually came to be developed an interesting array of ideas connected with life-after-death in Hebrew thought.

One of the earliest of these can be found in the book of Daniel. The question in almost every apocalyptic work which had to be answered was that of what kind of positive consequence would come from remaining true to the religious traditions, and suffering the consequences of that loyalty, which sometimes was death. Different apocalyptic works depicted different scenarios with differing views as to what form the positive results would take. Daniel 12 depicts a scene which introduces the reader for the first time to an Old Testament doctrine of the resurrection of individuals. The idea of resurrection had been present before, but it had been basically tied to the restoration of a group, namely the nation in Judah. Now, however, it had come to be interpreted individualistically, at least in that historical moment.

The passage in Daniel 12:1–4 should be studied very carefully, since many people have found ideas present in the text which are not really there. First, one notes that the resurrection depicted is not a general resurrection of all people. Only "some" are raised. The second point which must be carefully examined is the meaning of the term usually translated "everlasting." Standing in the twentieth century culture with its roots deeply influenced by Greek thought patterns, the modern reader tends to identify "everlasting" with eternity. The Hebrew mind-set, however, did not really have the same concept of everlasting which moderns do. The term in the Hebrew is the idea of "age," i.e., a long period of time. Job, one recalls, did not want to live "forever." The meaning, of course, was that Job did not want (at that moment) to live out his alloted time span since his suffering was so great. The word and idea used in Job seems to be the same as the word used here in Daniel.

What is being said, then, by the author of Daniel is that there will be some people raised to life, in a new "age," and some people raised for shame in a new "age." Against the background of the times one can ascertain fairly quickly that the some who are raised to "life" are those who had experienced martyrdom and persecution at the hands of Antiochus. They would be raised to be rewarded for their steadfastness and loyalty to God. Those who were raised to "shame and contempt" were those who had done the persecuting and who had horribly wronged God's people. Was it the intent that these people live "forever"? The text does not say explicitly but the clear implication seems to be that these people who were to be raised would live in this historical order, the martyrs receiving good life for their loyalty, the persecutors receiving punishment for their evil. When the "age" or alloted life span was completed, these people would then die and return to Sheol. It is interesting to note just how difficult it was for the people to break away from the Deuteronomic theology and their ancient traditions!

The author of Daniel was convinced that there would be a new age for God's people, an age in which the persecution was gone. There appears to be little evidence for the thought that Daniel expected the end of the world or a final cataclysmic destruction of the universe. There is in this book the simple but strong belief that those who remained faithful to God would ultimately be victorious because God remains in control of the world order even when the forces of evil temporarily seem to have grasped great power. The concept of resurrection presented here is the reflection of the confidence and trust that the author had in his God who, he believed, would ultimately destroy evil and establish good. The person then who remained loyal to the faith and did not apostasize in the face of persecution was allied with something, or rather someone, who could make certain that the suffering and the pain would not have been in vain, that God's will ultimately would triumph, that what these faithful people had given their lives to was more important than anything else in all the world.

Suggestions for Further Study

History

Peter R. Ackroyd. *Exile and Restoration: A Study of Hebrew Thought in the Sixth Century B.C.E.* Philadelphia: Westminster Press, 1968.

_____. *Israel Under Babylon and Persia.* London: Oxford University Press, 1970.

Elias Bickerman. *From Ezra to the Last of the Maccabees.* New York: Schocken Books, 1962.

F. F. Bruce. *Israel and the Nations: From the Exodus to the Fall of the Second Temple.* Grand Rapids, Michigan: Wm. B. Eerdmans Publishing Co., 1963.

Werner Foerster. *From the Exile to Christ: A Historical Introduction to Palestinian Judaism.* Translated by Gordon E. Harris. Philadelphia: Fortress Press, 1964.

James D. Newsome, Jr. *By the Waters of Babylon: An Introduction to the History and Theology of the Exile.* Atlanta: John Knox Press, 1979.

Robert H. Pfeiffer. *History of New Testament Times: With an Introduction to the Apocrypha.* New York: Harper & Bros., 1949.

B. Reicke. *The New Testament Era: The World of the Bible from 400 B.C. to 100 A.D.* Translated by David E. Green. Philadelphia: Fortress Press, 1968.

D. S. Russell. *Between the Testaments.* London: SCM Press, 1960.

_____. *The Jews from Alexander to Herod.* Oxford: Oxford University Press, 1967.

Wisdom
Walter Brueggemann. *In Man We Trust: The Neglected Side of Biblical Faith.* Richmond: John Knox Press, 1972.

James L. Crenshaw. *Old Testament Wisdom: An Introduction.* Atlanta: John Knox Press, 1981.

Gerhard von Rad. *Wisdom in Israel.* Translated by James D. Martin. Nashville: Abingdon Press, 1972.

R. B. Y Scott. *The Way of Wisdom in the Old Testament.* New York: The Macmillan Co., 1971.

James Wood. *Wisdom Literature: An Introduction.* London: Gerald Duckworth & Co., Ltd., 1967.

Apocalyptic
Paul D. Hanson. *The Dawn of Apocalyptic: The Historical and Sociological Roots of Jewish Apocalyptic Eschatology.* Philadelphia: Fortress Press, 1975.

Leon Morris. *Apocalyptic.* Grand Rapids, Michigan: Wm. B. Eerdmans Publishing Co., 1977.

H. H. Rowley. *The Relevance of Apocalyptic.* 3rd edition. New York: Association Press, 1964.

D. S. Russell. *The Method and Message of Jewish Apocalyptic.* Philadelphia: Westminster Press, 1964.

Walther Schmithals. *The Apocalyptic Movement: Introduction and Interpretation.* Translated by John E. Steely. Nashville: Abingdon Press, 1975.

Extra-Canonical Writings

R. H. Charles. *Apocrypha and Pseudepigrapha of the Old Testament.* 2 vols. New York: Oxford University Press, 1913.

Bruce Metzger. *An Introduction to the Apocrypha.* New York: Oxford University Press, 1957.

Leonhard Rost. *Judaism Outside the Hebrew Canon: An Introduction to the Documents.* Translated by David E. Green. Nashville: Abingdon Press, 1976.

Dead Sea Scrolls

F. M. Cross. *The Ancient Library of Qumran and Modern Biblical Studies.* Rev. ed. Garden City, New York: Doubleday & Co., 1961.

G. R. Driver. *The Judean Scrolls.* Oxford: Basil Blackwell, 1965.

Helmer Ringgren. *The Faith of Qumran.* Philadelphia: Fortress Press, 1961.

Roland de Vaux. *Archaeology and the Dead Sea Scrolls.* London: Oxford University Press, 1973.

Geza Vermes. *The Dead Sea Scrolls in English.* Baltimore: Penguin Books, 1962.

1—2 Chronicles, Ezra-Nehemiah

Peter R. Ackroyd. *1 and 2 Chronicles, Ezra, Nehemiah: Introduction and Commentary.* London: SCM Press, 1973.

R. J. Coggins. *The Books of Ezra and Nehemiah.* Cambridge: Cambridge University Press, 1976.

————. *The First and Second Books of the Chronicles.* Cambridge: Cambridge University Press, 1976.

Jacob M. Myers. *1 Chronicles.* Garden City, New York: Doubleday & Co., 1965.

_____. *2 Chronicles*. Garden City, New York: Doubleday & Co., 1965.

_____. *Ezra. Nehemiah*. Garden City, New York: Doubleday & Co., 1965.

Psalms
Hermann Gunkel. *The Psalms: A Form-Critical Introduction*. Translated by Thomas M. Horner. Philadelphia: Fortress Press, 1967.

John H. Hayes. *Understanding the Psalms*. Valley Forge, Pennsylvania: Judson Press, 1976.

Sigmund Mowinckel. *The Psalms in Israel's Worship*. Translated by D. R. Ap-Thomas. Nashville: Abingdon Press, 1962.

Roland E. Murphy. *The Psalms, Job*. Philadelphia: Fortress Press, 1977.

J. W. Rogerson and J. W. McKay. *Psalms*. Cambridge University Press, 1977.

Artur Weiser. *The Psalms: A Commentary*. Translated by Herbert Hartwell. Philadelphia: Westminster Press, 1962.

Claus Westermann. *Praise and Lament in the Psalms*. Translated by Keith R. Crim and Richard N. Soulen. Atlanta: John Knox Press, 1981.

Proverbs
William McKane. *Proverbs: A New Approach*. Philadelphia: Westminster Press, 1970.

R. B. Y. Scott. *Proverbs. Ecclesiastes*. Garden City, New York: Doubleday & Co., 1965.

R. N. Whybray. *The Book of Proverbs*. Cambridge: Cambridge University Press, 1972.

Job
Eduard P. Dhorme. *A Commentary on the Book of Job*. Translated by Harold Knight. London: Thomas Nelson & Sons, 1967. Originally published in 1926.

Robert Gordis. *The Book of God and Man. A Study of Job*. Chicago: University of Chicago Press, 1965.

Norman Habel. *The Book of Job*. Cambridge: Cambridge University Press, 1975.

Marvin H. Pope. *Job*. Garden City, New York: Doubleday & Co., 1973.

H. H. Rowley. *Job*. Rev. ed. London: Oliphants, 1976.

Samuel L. Terrien. *Introduction and Exegesis to Job* in The Interpreters Bible. Vol. 4, pp. 877–1198. Nashville: Abingdon Press, 1954.

Ecclesiastes
Wesley J. Fuerst. *The Books of Ruth, Esther, Ecclesiastes, the Song of Songs, Lamentations*. Cambridge: Cambridge University Press, 1975.

Robert Gordis. *Koheleth: The Man and His World*. New York: Jewish Theological Seminary of America Press, 1951.

R. B. Y. Scott. *Proverbs, Ecclesiastes*. Garden City, New York: Doubleday & Co., 1965.

Song of Songs
Wesley J. Fuerst, see above under Ecclesiastes.

Marvin H. Pope. *Song of Songs*. Garden City, New York: Doubleday & Co., 1977.

Lamentations
Robert Gordis. *The Song of Songs and Lamentations*. Revised and augmented edition. New York: KTAV Publishing House, 1974.

Delbert R. Hillers. *Lamentations*. Garden City, New York: Doubleday & Co., 1972.

Ruth
Edward F. Campbell. *Ruth*. Garden City, New York: Doubleday & Co., 1975.

John Gray. *Joshua, Judges, Ruth*. London: Oliphants, 1967.

Esther
Wesley J. Fuerst, see under Ecclesiastes.

Carey A. Moore. *Esther*. Garden City, New York: Doubleday & Co., 1971.

Daniel

James M. Efird. *Daniel and Revelation: A Study of Two Extraordinary Visions*. Valley Forge, Pennsylvania: Judson Press, 1978.

Raymond Hammer. *The Book of Daniel*. Cambridge: Cambridge University Press, 1976.

Louis F. Hartman and A. A. DiLella. *The Book of Daniel*. Garden City, New York: Doubleday & Co., 1978.

Andrew Lacocque. *The Book of Daniel*. Translated by David Pellaver. Atlanta: John Knox Press, 1979.

Norman W. Porteous. *Daniel: A Commentary*. Philadelphia: Westminster Press, 1965.

Conclusion

The basic purpose of this study has been to attempt to acquaint the uninitiated student with the history of the Old Testament period, with the methodologies involved in attempting to examine carefully the Old Testament documents themselves and the traditions lying behind them, and, most importantly, with the religious teachings of these marvelous books. To cover, even superficially, all of these areas could not be an easy task simply because of the long period of history involved (ca. 2000–164 B.C.), and not all scholars agree on how to reconstruct the known history. But other complications are also present. The ancient traditions, from which many of the Old Testament books were made, had been passed along for many centuries before they crystallized into the documents as they presently exist. That these traditions had been used and reused, quite frequently being altered in the long process of transmission, seems to be obvious, and this fact makes it very difficult to be as definitive as one would like when dealing with this material.

The sheer number of all the theories, ideas, and speculations relating to the study of the Old Testament writings have made it impossible to mention more than a few. The fact is that the study of the Old Testament and its times involves one in many different disciplines and methodologies; the field is almost limitless. What the beginning student must remember, therefore, is that there are many more interesting and fascinating things to learn about this marvelous collection of books.

Most persons are not aware that there is in addition to the Old Testament writings themselves a tremendous amount of literature, still extant, which can assist in furthering one's study of the religious development begun in the Old Testament. There are many Jewish writings which came from the late post-exilic period and the early Christian years which did not find their way into the sacred canon. These included haggadah type stories like Tobit and Judith, apocalyptic works like

1 Enoch and 4 Ezra, historical writings like 1 and 2 Maccabees, collections of wisdom like the wisdom of Ben Sirach or Ecclesiasticus, and collections of poetry or psalms like the Psalms of Solomon. There are many more such writings found in two collections usually called the Apocrypha and Pseudepigrapha of the Old Testament (cf. above, pp. 21ff.). More recently another group of writings has been discovered which originated in an Essene (ascetic-type) community along the Dead Sea at a place called Qumran. These writings are popularly known as the Dead Sea Scrolls and reflect another dimension of Judaism current at the end of the Old Testament period and yet another interpretation of the ancient documents and traditions.

Within what later came to be understood as "main-line" Judaism another development was taking place with regard to the interpretation of the sacred texts. There was being passed along a large number of oral traditions (which supposedly were understood as going back to Moses) which were supposed to clarify the demands of the Torah. After all, what does it mean specifically to keep the Sabbath? Such teachings were passed along and came to be known as the Mishnah. They were finally codified ca. A.D. 200. If the Torah needed some interpretation, however, so did the Mishnah. Therefore there arose and developed a set of oral teachings which were interpretations of the Mishnah. This collection was called the *Gemara*. When the Mishnah and the Gemara were finally written down together, they formed the great collection of Jewish "learning" popularly known as the *Talmud*. Studying this material can assist one in understanding the kind of interpretive procedures and methods which were used during the late years of the old era and the first years of the new era (i.e., late B.C. and early A.D.) within the Jewish faith.

But the Jewish community was not the only group which claimed the Old Testament as the roots of its faith. The Christian community argued that it was the fulfillment of the hopes and promises of these ancient writings, and it then produced a sacred literature of its own called the New Testament, many books of which used the Old Testament extensively. The Old Testament, then, served as a sacred book for two of the greatest religious traditions of the Western world, namely Judaism and Christianity. Incidentally, these writings are also considered authoritative for the faith of Islam. It is of some importance then to understand something about these ancient books.

One of the most difficult problems which interpreters of the Old Testament writings encounter is that of finding one major theme or idea which can be understood as *the* unifying theme for all these different books. Many valiant attempts have been made and various theologies of the Old Testament have been written to support one or another theory, but success or consensus of opinion in this matter has not been achieved.

The concept of covenant has often been suggested as *the* theme or idea which binds all the Old Testament writings together, but the simple fact is that various books do not reflect the idea of covenant at all. Other scholars have argued that the basic unifying motif consists in certain creedal cultic confessions and that ideas associated with such confessional statements serve as the key to the unity and understanding of the Old Testament writings. Still others have isolated certain differing units of tradition within the ancient documents and found the development of Old Testament thought centered in the struggle between those traditions within the history of the Hebrew people. One of the more interesting of these proposals argues that the key to the development of Hebrew thought and history lies in the struggle between the Moses-Sinai traditions and its advocates and the David-Zion with its supporters. Further, there are those who like to emphasize the importance of the significant historical events which Israel experienced, especially as these were interpreted in a theological manner; this approach is commonly referred to as *Heilsgeschichte*, "salvation history." It is argued that in certain special historical events and the religious interpretation of them, one can detect the very element, God's actions in the historical process, which gives all the books meaning and makes the entire Old Testament intelligible.

Once in the history of Old Testament study it was quite popular to understand the religious ideas of these writings as evolutionary in nature. Scholars argued that the religion of the Old Testament began as a primitive, animistic type and evolved into a more spiritual, sophisticated type. One popular understanding in this type of approach was that the earlier form of Hebrew religion centered in the group but that such an understanding evolved into the more sophisticated ideas centering in the individual. One can see that such theories were more likely to produce evidence for the preconceived ideas of the interpreter than to search out the real teaching of the documents themselves.

Each of these approaches and theories, however, has something very positive to commend itself to the student of the Old Testament writings. It is not really surprising to find such varied ideas; the writings of the Old Testament even in their present form were written over a period of at least three hundred years, and the traditions and sources used by the writers and editors of the books extend back over at least another one thousand years. During this lengthy period of time the people of Israel developed from a nomadic or semi-nomadic group of separate tribes—each with its own traditions, history, experiences, and religious under-standings—into a loosely-knit confederation; then into a nation—first unified, and then divided—that experienced a destruction from which the larger nation never recovered. The Hebrews then went into exile in a strange land, returned, experienced difficult times, and finally estab-lished a new political entity in the late second century B.C. Through all of that history, the culture around the Hebrew people was developing and changing, nations were rising and falling, and the simple but steady process of maturation in religious thinking in the light of all these developments was taking place.

Whatever one decides about the question of the development of the religious thinking within the Old Testament books and the changes which inevitably were taking place over such a lengthy period, it is also true that certain elements seem to have remained basically the same throughout all the levels of tradition and the various cultural and social changes. Yahweh, for example, was understood from the very begin-ning as a God who is *personal,* and this understanding continued throughout the various types of literature and the various levels of tradition. This God wished to enter into relationship with the world and more specifically the people in the world. In fact creation was depicted as having been done (at least partially) for that reason, that God could have fellowship with the human race.

This understanding led to another closely related idea which viewed Yahweh as a covenant-making God from the very beginning. God was willing to enter into agreements with human beings and to commit himself to a specific relationship. That agreement was always made, however, on Yahweh's terms and for Yahweh's purposes. The covenant relationship with the Hebrew people, which was viewed as a *special* relationship, was created by God for the purpose of making God's "name" (i.e., his being or personality) known in all the world. This selection of a special people for a special purpose is known as election.

Further, Yahweh has an essential nature understood by almost all the Old Testament writers either implicitly or explicitly. This nature, generally speaking, can be characterized by the designation *righteous*. There is in this characterization both a moral and a non-moral dimension. The non-moral relates to the idea of Yahweh as a "holy" God, i.e., a God who is "other than" and "separated" from the human race and the created order. Yahweh's being was such that certain actions and attitudes *naturally* flowed from his person—and these actions and attitudes were usually quite different from what the world expected or considered valuable. Yahweh was *righteous* because by nature he did what was right. The moral dimension grew out of this understanding of God, for to do right was to act in accordance with Yahweh's nature and essence; to do wrong was to act against that nature and essence as it was in the process of being revealed to the people.

What one finds from the Law to the Prophets and through the Writings is, therefore, the revelation of a God who has certain basic qualities and an essential being, but who was constantly a surprise to the people. This God was not one who could be manipulated by the rituals, words, or actions of a person or persons; this God was not one who required the sacrifice of children or other such activities; this God did not accept substitutes such as ritual sacrifices for the essential requirements of his law or covenant obligations. This was a God whose presence with the people was supposed to make them different from the ordinary understandings of human requirements and to empower them to do tasks which seemingly were impossible. This was a God who understood their problems and forgave their sins but who was not deceived by their lack of commitment and hypocrisy.

The revelation of Yahweh as God of Israel, his relationships and presence with the people over long centuries, and the continuous reinterpretation of Yahweh's commands in the light of new situations and experiences form the basis for the books of the Old Testament which relate all these things to and for God's people. Perhaps several verses

from various places in the Old Testament will serve to illustrate something of the greatness of the faith of Israel.

> I am Yahweh your God, who brought you out of
> the land of Egypt, out of the house of bondage. (Exodus 20:2,
>   paraphrase)

> Hear, O Israel: Yahweh is our God, Yahweh alone;
> and you shall love Yahweh your God with all your heart,
> and with all your life, and with all your might. (Deuteronomy
>   6:4–5, paraphrase)

> O Yahweh, God of hosts,
> Who is a God like unto you . . . (Psalm 89:8, paraphase)

> I am the first and I am the last;
> besides me there is no god. (Isaiah 44:6b)

For faithfulness and belief in this God many have suffered and died,
even "till this day."

Bibliography

As an aid to studying the Old Testament in depth, certain resources are listed below for further investigation. Note that these are to be consulted in addition to the works cited at the conclusion of each chapter. This listing should not be considered as complete, but only as a guide for further study.

Bible Atlases

Oxford Bible Atlas. H. G. May, editor. New York: Oxford University Press, 1962.

Shorter Atlas of the Bible. L. H. Grollenberg. Translated by Mary F. Hedlund. Edinburgh: Thomas Nelson & Sons, 1959.

The Westminster Historical Atlas to the Bible. Revised edition. G. E. Wright and F. V. Filson, editors. Philadelphia: Westminster Press, 1966.

Bible Dictionaries

Dictionary of the Bible. James Hastings, editor. Revised edition by F. C. Grant and H. H. Rowley. New York: Charles Scribner's Sons, 1963.

Interpreter's Dictionary of the Bible. G. A. Buttrick et al., editors. 4 volumes. New York: Abingdon Press, 1962. *Supplementary Volume,* 1976.

One-volume Bible Commentaries

Interpreter's One Volume Commentary on the Bible. Charles M. Laymon, editor. Nashville: Abingdon Press, 1971.

The Jerome Biblical Commentary. R. E. Brown, J. A. Fitzmyer, and R. E. Murphy, editors. Englewood Cliffs, New Jersey: Prentice-Hall, Inc., 1968.

Peake's Commentary on the Bible. Revised edition. M. Black and H. H. Rowley, editors. New York: Thomas Nelson & Sons, 1962.

Books on Archaeology

W. F. Albright. *Archaeology and the Bible*. Memorial edition. Cambridge, Massachusetts: American Schools of Oriental Research, 1974.

John Gray. *Archaeology and the Old Testament World*. London: Thomas Nelson & Sons, 1962.

H. T. Frank. *Bible, Archaeology, and Faith*. Nashville: Abingdon Press, 1971.

Kathleen M. Kenyon. *Archaeology in the Holy Land*. 3rd edition. New York: Praeger, 1970.

D. Winton Thomas, editor. *Archaeology and Old Testament Study*. London: Clarendon Press, 1967.

G. E. Wright. *Biblical Archaeology*. New revised edition. Philadelphia: Westminster Press, 1962.

Histories

John Bright. *A History of Israel*. Third edition. Philadelphia: Westminster Press, 1981.

E. L. Ehrlich. *A Concise History of Israel*. Translated by James Barr. New York: Harper & Row, 1962.

Jack Finegan. *Handbook of Biblical Chronology: Principles of Time Reckoning in the Ancient World and Problems of Chronology in the Bible*. Princeton, New Jersey: Princeton University Press, 1964.

John H. Hayes and J. Maxwell Miller, editors. *Israelite and Judaean History*. Philadelphia: Westminster Press, 1977.

Siegfried Herrmann. *A History of Israel in Old Testament Times*. Translated by John Bowden. Philadelphia: Fortress Press, 1975.

Martin Noth. *The History of Israel*. Translated by Stanley Godman. New York: Harper & Brothers, 1960.

George W. Ramsey. *The Quest for the Historical Israel*. Atlanta: John Knox Press, 1981.

Roland de Vaux. *The Early History of Israel: To the Period of the Judges*. Translated by David Smith. Philadelphia: Westminster Press, 1978.

Geography and Background

Yohanan Aharoni. *The Land of the Bible: A Historical Geography*. Translated by A. F. Rainey. Philadelphia: Westminster Press, 1967.

Denis Baly. *The Geography of the Bible*. Revised edition. New York: Harper & Row, 1974.

Everyday Life in Bible Times. Revised edition. Washington: National Geographic Society, 1976.

Martin Noth. *The Old Testament World*. Translated by Victor I. Gruhn. Philadelphia: Fortress Press, 1966.

Johannes Pedersen. *Israel: Its Life and Culture*. New York: Oxford University Press, I–II (1926), III–IV (1940).

Roland de Vaux. *Ancient Israel: Its Life and Institutions*. Translated by John McHugh. New York: McGraw-Hill, 1961.

Methodologies

Ronald E. Clements. *One Hundred Years of Old Testament Interpretation*. Philadelphia: Westminster Press, 1976.

Norman Habel. *Literary Criticism of the Old Testament*. Philadelphia: Fortress Press, 1971.

John H. Hayes, editor. *Old Testament Form Criticism*. San Antonio, Texas: Trinity University Press, 1974.

J. Maxwell Miller. *The Old Testament and the Historian*. Philadelphia: Fortress Press, 1976.

Walter E. Rast. *Tradition, History, and the Old Testament*. Philadelphia: Fortress Press, 1972.

Gene M. Tucker. *Form Criticism of the Old Testament*. Philadelphia: Fortress Press, 1971.

Introductions to the Old Testament

B. W. Anderson. *Understanding the Old Testament*. Third edition. Englewood Cliffs, New Jersey: Prentice-Hall, Inc., 1975.

Brevard S. Childs. *Introduction to the Old Testament as Scripture*. Philadelphia: Fortress Press, 1979.

Otto Eissfeldt. *The Old Testament: An Introduction*. Translated by Peter R. Ackroyd. New York: Harper & Row, 1965. A standard classic.

Georg Fohrer. *Introduction to the Old Testament*. Translated by David E. Green. Nashville: Abingdon Press, 1968. Revision of an older work by Ernst Sellin.

John Hayes. *An Introduction to Old Testament Study*. Nashville: Abingdon Press, 1979.

Norman Gottwald. *A Light to the Nations: An Introduction to the Old Testament.* New York: Harper & Brothers, 1959.

W. Lee Humphreys. *Crisis and Story: Introduction to the Old Testament.* Palo Alto, California: Mayfield Publishing Co., 1979.

Otto Kaiser. *Introduction to the Old Testament: A Presentation of Its Results and Problems.* Translated by John Sturdy. Minneapolis, Minnesota: Augsburg Publishing House, 1975.

J. Alberto Soggin. *Introduction to the Old Testament.* Translated by John Bowden. Philadelphia: Westminster Press, 1976.

Artur Weiser. *The Old Testament: Its Formation and Development.* Translated by Dorothea M. Barton. New York: Association Press, 1961.

Old Testament Religion and Theology

Ronald E. Clements. *Old Testament Theology: A Fresh Approach.* Atlanta: John Knox Press, 1979.

Brevard S. Childs. *Biblical Theology in Crisis.* Philadelphia: Westminster Press, 1970.

Robert C. Denton. *Preface to Old Testament Theology.* Revised edition. New York: Seabury Press, 1963.

Walther Eichrodt. *Theology of the Old Testament.* 2 Vols. Translated by J. A. Baker. Philadelphia: Westminster Press, 1961, 1967.

Georg Fohrer. *History of Israelite Religion.* Translated by David E. Green. Nashville: Abingdon Press, 1972.

Gerhard Hasel. *Old Testament Theology: Basic Issues in the Current Debate.* Grand Rapids, Michigan: Wm. B. Eerdmans Publishing Co., 1972.

Edmund Jacob. *The Theology of the Old Testament.* Translated by A. W. Heathcote and P. J. Allcock. New York: Harper & Brothers, 1958.

Yehezkel Kaufmann. *The Religion of Israel: From Its Beginnings to the Babylonian Exile.* Translated by Moshe Greenberg. Chicago: University of Chicago Press, 1960.

John L. McKenzie. *A Theology of the Old Testament.* Garden City, New York: Doubleday & Co., 1974.

Helmer Ringgren. *Israelite Religion.* Translated by David E. Green. Philadelphia: Fortress Press, 1966.

Gerhard von Rad. *Old Testament Theology*. 2 Vols. Translated by D. M. G. Stalker. New York: Harper & Brothers, 1962, 1965.

H. H. Rowley. *Worship in Ancient Israel: Its Form and Meaning*. Philadelphia: Fortress Press, 1967.

James A. Sanders. *Torah and Canon*. Philadelphia: Fortress Press, 1972.

Samuel Terrien. *The Elusive Presence: Toward a New Biblical Theology*. San Francisco: Harper & Row, 1978.

Walther Zimmerli, *Old Testament Theology in Outline*. Translated by David E. Green. Atlanta: John Knox Press, 1978.

Glossary

AETIOLOGY (sometimes etiology). A narrative story whose purpose is to explain the origin of certain natural phenomena, customs, names, etc. Quite frequently in the Old Testament writings aetiological explanations have been incorporated into larger narratives which were not originally aetiological.

AMPHICTYONY. Term used to describe a loosely knit coalition of cities or tribes joined together under a common commitment to a god, centering in a central shrine. Such a coalition was primarily structured for purposes of protection.

APOCALYPTIC. A type of literary genre with certain religious understandings which flourished ca. 200 B.C. – A.D. 100. This literature appeared in times of persecution to rally the persecuted faithful to remain loyal in the face of strong opposition. The basic ideas connected with this literature revolve around a dualistic view of the created order, i.e., a struggle between the forces of good and the forces of evil, and the conviction that the present age of persecution would soon come to an end with God's intervention and the destruction of the persecuting forces. The writings were also characterized by elaborate symbolism and imagery.

APOCRYPHA. Literally, "hidden" books. The term is a technical one which refers to those books which were included in the Greek translations of the Old Testament but which were not accepted as canonical by the persons who finally selected the last portion of the Hebrew canon.

B.C.E.–C.E. Terms presently in use in many quarters which replace the older designations B.C. and A.D. The designations mean Before the Common (or Current) Era and the Common (or Current) Era.

CANON. Literally, a "reed," thus a standard of measure. This term refers to the body of literature accepted as authoritative for a group of believers.

ESCHATOLOGY. This term refers to a "study of the end." It is loosely defined and used by many biblical scholars, some interpreting eschatology as referring to the end of present history as we know it, or to the end of an era or age in the history of the people of God with an emphasis on the glories of the new age, while others give a much broader understanding of the word as indicating something of ultimate significance.

FORM-CRITICISM. A methodological discipline used by biblical scholars which concentrates on the oral preservation and transmission of the traditions connected with a group. Typical of this type of investigation is a search for recurring structures and patterns in the materials and a search for appropriate settings for these traditions in the life of a people.

GATTUNG. The German term used to describe the genre or type of a literary unit.

HEXATEUCH. A term frequently used in Old Testament studies designating the six books, Genesis through Joshua.

HISTORICAL CRITICISM. A term used to denote a certain type of approach to a biblical book or passage where the interpreter attempts to study the text from the the historical standpoint of the original author (editor) and readers. The emphasis is on attempting to discover the who, what, where, when, why, and to whom of the original document or passage.

KETHUBIM. Hebrew for "Writings." It is the technical term for the third and last segment of the Jewish canon.

MESSIAH. A title which evolved from the Hebrew term meaning "anointed." Anointing in the early Old Testament writings usually designated the setting apart of an individual for a particular task or office. The term had political implications, since the king was the one most frequently "anointed."

NEBIIM. Hebrew for "Prophets." It is the technical term for the second segment of the Jewish canon. This collection is divided into two parts: the Former Prophets (Joshua, Judges, Samuel, and Kings) and the Latter Prophets (Isaiah, Jeremiah, Ezekiel, and the Book of the Twelve).

PARALLELISM. One of the basic characteristics of Hebrew poetry. There are usually three types recognized by most scholars: synonymous (where the second line restates the meaning of the first line); antithetical (where the second line states the opposite or an antithetical view from the first line); and synthetic (where the second line builds upon and expands the meaning of the first line).

PENTATEUCH. Literally the "five scrolls." This is another term for the first five books of the Old Testament, Genesis through Deuteronomy

PSEUDEPIGRAPHA. This is a designation for those books which were known by and popular within the Jewish community toward the close of the Old Testament era and the beginning of the Christian era but which were not included in the Hebrew canon and in the Apocrypha. Many of these works are apocalyptic in nature.

REDACTION CRITICISM. A methodological approach to the books of the Old Testament which concentrates on the final form of the various books as wholistic entities. The basic idea is that the author or final redactor of the finished document had certain emphases, motifs, and points to make which caused him to write, structure, and edit the book in such a way as to present his interpretation through the form of the completed work.

SAGA. A term which designates a literary type of narrative or story centering on characters, incidents, and significant events from the past (usually a distant past). Such stories were told for the significant meaning contained therein rather than historical accuracy. Some scholars separate those specific stories which deal with "heroes" into another category designated as *legend*. For the purposes of this book the term *saga* was used in a broad way so as to include the category of the legend.

SEPTUAGINT. The Greek translation of the Hebrew Old Testament. This project began in the third to second centuries B.C. in order to make the Hebrew Scriptures available to Jewish people scattered throughout the world of that time who no longer spoke or understood Hebrew. The symbol commonly used to designate this work is LXX, since seventy (or seventy-two) persons were supposed to have been involved in the project.

SITZ-IM-LEBEN. A erm basically related to the form-critical method which means "setting-in-life."It usually refers to the specific social context in which certain forms functioned for particular purposes, preserved the literary types, and helped to pass along the literary unit.

SOURCE-CRITICISM. A type of methodological approach to the biblical texts in which scholars seek to determine what sources may have been used in the composition of the book as it now exists. Most attention in this area has been focused on the sources of the Pentateuch, i.e., J, E, P, D, etc.

TETRAGRAMMATON. Literally the "four letters." This term is used for the sacred name of God found in the ancient Hebrew traditions, namely, Yahweh. Since the Hebrew text was written without vowels, the name for God was YHWH. This name came to be considered so sacred and taboo that the Hebrew people would not pronounce the name, substituting instead the word for "my lord" (*Adonai*). See also "Yahweh."

TORAH. The Hebrew term for instruction, law, teaching. It came to designate the first and most important segmen of the Hebrew canon, usually called the "Law."

TRADITION-CRITICISM. This is a methodological approach to the biblical materials which attempts to study certain themes or motifs which can appear in various parts of the larger texts. Most frequently, however, this discipline is limited to a study of how the traditions centering around a certain theme or motif were passed along in the early and oral stages of its development.

YAHWEH. The personal name of God used by the Hebrew people, especially in the earlier Old Testament period. Later the word was not pronounced (cf. under *Tetragrammaton*), and the general term for God, *Elohim*, was used more frequently.